The Indian Heritage
of New Hampshire
and Northern
New England

The Indian Heritage of New Hampshire and Northern New England

Edited by THADDEUS PIOTROWSKI

McFarland & Company, Inc., Publishers
Jefferson, North Carolina, and London

The present work is a reprint of the library bound edition of
The Indian Heritage of New Hampshire and Northern
New England, *first published in 2002 by McFarland.*

LIBRARY OF CONGRESS CATALOGUING-IN-PUBLICATION DATA

The Indian heritage of New Hampshire and northern New England /
edited by Thaddeus Piotrowski.
p.   cm.
Includes bibliographical references and index.

ISBN 978-0-7864-4252-2
softcover : 50# alkaline paper ∞

1. Indians of North America—New Hampshire.   2. Indians of North
America—New England.   I. Piotrowski, Thaddeus M.
E78.N54 I53   2008   974.004'97—dc21   2001007508

British Library cataloguing data are available

Cover illustration: Chief Passaconaway and a map of New England

Manufactured in the United States of America

*McFarland & Company, Inc., Publishers
Box 611, Jefferson, North Carolina 28640
www.mcfarlandpub.com*

Contents

PART III: COLLECTIONS, SITES, TRAILS, NAMES

Preface

Readers acquainted with my earlier books will perhaps wonder why I have switched from documenting the tragic history of Europe, and in particular the horrendous history of Poland during World War II and the Holocaust, to regional Native American history. The transition was not difficult to make: the European story I wanted to tell has now been told; it is time to look for parallels in American history.

Like Poland in 1939, in the seventeenth century this part of North America was divided between two powerful occupation forces, the French and the British, each seeking territorial dominion and each willing to exploit the indigenous population to further its own cause. The French got a New France; the English, a New England. The only losers in this imperialist battle were the Indians, who, no matter what they did or whose side they took, eventually lost everything. It sounds so familiar: Poland, Nazi Germany, the Soviet Union.

This work begins with "prehistory," a word that is not at all to the liking of the Indians (and who can blame them? Was there no Western history before Herodotus, whom Cicero called *pater historiae*?), and it ends with settlement. The first part of the story is told by contemporary archaeologists; the second is recounted by seventeenth-century missionaries and explorers, eighteenth- and nineteenth-century historians, and present-day scholars.

My friend Donald M. Reynolds has penned a motto for the New York Monuments Conservancy, which he directs: "The wise man preserves that which he values and celebrates that which he preserves." I offer this work in celebration of what little has been preserved of the life, times, and culture of the great Indian nations that inhabited this part of planet Earth and that now have all but vanished.

To the University of New Hampshire for its continued support of my scholarly endeavors—this time in the form of the Carpenter Professorship Award—I am indeed grateful. A special thank you to the UNH-Manchester library staff, especially Carolyn White, for their assistance. For permission to use the many articles from the *New Hampshire Archeologist*, my thanks to the New Hampshire Archeological Society. To Ruth Marshall Chalmers and Louise Marshall Clark, a warm thank you for their permission to include their father Harlan A. Marshall's manuscript in this work. For his expert cartography, I again thank Michael Curran. To David Stewart-Smith, part Pennacook himself, for his steadfast support of this project, for his permission to quote extensively from his Ph.D. dissertation, and for reading the manuscript, *w'li bankani*.

And to Terri, my wife, and to Renia, Ala, and Andrzej, my children, all my love.

Thaddeus Piotrowski
Manchester, New Hampshire
Fall 2001

Indulge, our native land, indulge the tear,
That steals impassioned o'er a nation's doom;
To us each twig from Adam's stock is dear,
And tears of sorrow deck an Indian's tomb.

John Farmer and Jacob B. Moore
Gazetteer of the State of
New-Hampshire, 1823

Introduction: The Northeast

Thaddeus Piotrowski

For those of us who have witnessed the magnificent comings and goings of the seasons in fair New England, who have traversed its boundless forests teeming with life unseen, who have drunk from and bathed in its many crystalline lakes, ponds, and streams, it is difficult to imagine that this part of Earth once lay in the path of glaciers and thus was repeatedly, and for thousands of years each time, covered by enormous sheets of ice that in their wake left yawning gorges and towering mountains, vast mounds of glacial till, massive lakes, and tons upon tons of sediment before retreating northward.

The Pleistocene Epoch of geologic time both in Europe and North America was marked by at least four such glacial advances and retreats. No doubt major shifts in Earth's weather patterns were responsible for these phenomena, but the reasons for the shifts themselves are still unknown. Earth's last major ice age, known as the Wisconsin, began about 60,000 years ago.

Judging by its terminal moraine system (a mass of rocks, gravel, sand, clay, and other debris carried and deposited by a glacier at its lower end), the last glaciation, which began in the Arctic Circle, extended from the Atlantic coast near Martha's Vineyard in Massachusetts westward through Long Island, Staten Island, New Jersey, Pennsylvania, and New York state to the midwestern states. Eastward from the Mississippi Valley, this ice sheet overlapped the terminal moraines of two previous ice ages, the Kansan and Illinoisan, and in some places even utterly obliterated traces of their existence. The Wisconsin's terminal moraine is still clearly visible in the state whose name it bears today. Contemporary archaeologists hold that the history of human occupation of North America is intimately linked with the final phases of this glaciation.

The Wisconsin ice age actually contained a whole series of lesser advances and retreats. These oscillations culminated in the final retreat of the ice sheet in northern New England about 14,000 years ago. The melting ice left large bodies of water such as the Great Lakes and the Finger Lakes of New York; these have remained, but others—such as the one at the Hudson Valley river basin—have long since vanished. A number of glacial lakes also formed all over New England. The lake in the Manchester, New Hampshire, area was one such, and the Pleistocene sediments it left behind buried all remnants of the solid bedrock beneath the city. As that lake drained, the Merrimack River (formed in east-central New Hampshire by the junction of the Pemigewasset and Winnipesaukee`rivers) began to cut a channel in the soft glacial sediment. The series of falls and rapids along the river are places where its downcutting uncovered long-buried bedrock sills. The fifty-foot drop at Amoskeag in Manchester is the largest of these and marks the northernmost limit of the Merrimack lowland, the only territory in New Hampshire—besides the coastal region—that is so close to sea level.

Eventually the great lakes of the Pleistocene gave way to broad tundras. Trees were sparse then, and the vegetation was similar to that of northern Canada: predominantly herbaceous, consisting of lichens, mosses, and sedges, with clumps of dwarf birches, willows, and other trees sprouting here and there. The climatic conditions of that time must have been like those of the present-day Barren Grounds in Canada: temperature extremes with deep permafrost.

Studies of the Northeast indicate that the withdrawal of the ice was usually followed by a landscape consisting of the flora mentioned above, then by conifers (mainly spruce, fir, and pine), which eventually quilted the tundra. In time, a deciduous forest complemented the coniferous one and, in the South, replaced it entirely. In New England, the appearance of the tundra is dated between 13,500 and 12,500 B.P.,* the spruce maximum is placed at about 10,500 B.P., the pine maximum at about 8,500 B.P., and the deciduous forest climax at about 7,000 B.P.

The spreading forest offered a fair haven to black bears, mountain lions, lynx, wolves, beavers, otters, quail, partridge, and the plentiful Virginia deer—to name but a few of the more recent woodland inhabitants. Farther south, horses and camels roamed the emerging prairies, and giant sloths nibbled at the trees.

The earliest human inhabitants of the Northeast did not gather; they were primarily big-game hunters. Their prey consisted predominantly of such now-extinct animals as giant mammoths and mastodons, dire wolves, saber-toothed tigers, and giant beavers, as well as the contemporary musk ox, caribou, elk, and moose that roamed the tundras and the emerging coniferous woodland. By 10,000 years ago, however, most of the great beasts of the late Pleistocene had become extinct throughout all of North America and only the wild fauna that we wonder at and enjoy today remained. (Were the great beasts hunted to extinction? These people's mastery of the atlatl, or spear thrower, makes this a real possibility.)

SMYTH-NEVILLE COMPLEX

The area around Amoskeag Falls in Manchester, New Hampshire, has been yielding its buried archaeological treasure for the past 200 years. This artifact-rich territory represents, in and of itself, an excellent case study of New England prehistory. Of the many Indian sites that existed along the Merrimack River, especially in and around Manchester, none has proved more helpful in determining the character of the life and times of our ancient predecessors than those at Amoskeag: the Smyth site and the archaeologically older Neville site.

The entire complex, consisting of

*B.P. stands for Before Present—the "present," by convention, being 1950. When used in conjunction with Carbon-14 dates, B.P. refers to radiocarbon years, which are not the same as calendar years. For example, after calibration, or adjustment, the radiocarbon-dated time period extending from 11,000 to 10,000 B.P. converts to 13,000 to 11,000 calendar years ago.

many individual sites, originally served as temporary or semipermanent quarters for countless ancient bands of hunters, gatherers, and fishers. Before the power dams blocked the river in the middle of the nineteenth century, fishing at Amoskeag was among the best in the area, if not the entire state. Atlantic salmon, shad, sturgeon, alewives, lampreys, and other species of fish ran the falls each spring, and it was their great abundance which prompted the Indians to name the falls "Amoskeag," or "the place of the fish" (see "Indian Names in New Hampshire" for other renditions of this name).

The residents at Amoskeag also took advantage of the Merrimack River to travel downstream to the Atlantic Ocean and upstream to the White Mountains (by way of the Pemigewasset River) as well as to the Lake Winnipesaukee region (by way of the Winnipesaukee River) where useful fine-grained rocks with good flaking characteristics were available.

The Smyth site, named after the former governor on whose estate it was located, lies on the east bank of the Merrimack River on a high sandy bluff immediately to the north of Amoskeag Falls. At the time of the excavation the property was owned by the New Hampshire Insurance Company. Today, the employee parking lot of the New Hampshire Tower paves the site.

Directly west of the Smyth site and about forty feet lower lies the Neville site, also named after the family in whose yard the dig took place. On old city maps the site is located on the Merrimack River terrace at the northwest corner of the now-relocated West Salmon Street and River Road. To the south of the Neville site stood the famed little red Stark house built in 1736 by Archibald Stark, the father of Major General John Stark, the revolutionary hero who bequeathed to New Hampshire its famous motto: "Live Free

or Die" (paraphrased by locals as "Live, Freeze, and Die"). The Stark house was moved to its present location on Elm Street in 1968 to avoid demolition.

It is significant that most of the known northeastern archaeological sites are located on well-defined knolls, terraces, or ridges. Clearly good drainage (a dry "living room" floor), access to water and the fish therein, and a reliable supply of lithic materials, or waterways leading to good sources of raw materials for weapons and tools, were the principal motives for such choice of residences. But just as clearly, these prime real estate sites betray the presence of a keen aesthetic sense in our forefathers. The area in the vicinity of Amoskeag Falls is one such place.

The archaeological digs at Amoskeag were carried out in 1967–68, when it became known that the New Hampshire Department of Public Works and Highways intended to rebuild and expand the old Amoskeag bridge and to relocate West Salmon Street, and that the massive New Hampshire Insurance building was to be constructed on the site of the old Smyth mansion. Thus, an investigation that should have occupied professional archaeologists for decades (perhaps *previous* decades) was carried out in a relatively short span of time, in the absence of supportive funding, and on schedules set by the state and big business.

Smyth site. The Smyth site was situated on a large sand wave constructed by the prevailing southwesterly winds, which transported the sand, gravel, and debris left by the glaciers onto the river bank to form the bluff. As the first people and their successors settled on the bluff some 7,000 years ago, the discarded implements of their technology gradually accumulated and were covered over by the continuous deposition of materials from the exposed lake beds of the valley floor and walls.

From these "tool kits" we are able to reconstruct a cultural sequence of the peoples involved (see "Ancient Lifeways at the Smyth Site").

The most unique contribution of the Smyth site to our understanding of our predecessors lies in physical anthropology. In 1968 the remains of eight human skeletons were excavated from the Smyth site. These, some other skeletons found in the Manchester-Auburn area (see "Indian Sites in the Manchester-Auburn, New Hampshire, Area"), and a few others found throughout the state comprise the total collection of prehistoric skeletons from New Hampshire. The Smyth series consists of four males, two females, an infant, and one fragment. (The gender of the last two could not be determined.) Aside from the infant, the fragment, and the young woman, who was about 19 years old, the range of ages of the remaining persons at the time of death was from 25 to 35. Only one reliable estimate of stature could be obtained: one male was five feet, nine inches tall.

The excavated remains indicate the presence of a remarkably robust civilization in New Hampshire. Both males and females had powerful arm, leg, and neck muscles, judging by the size of the areas of the bones to which they were attached. They had narrow skulls and large protruding noses with big nostrils and small nasal depressions in their high and wide bridges. Their molars were large and revealed areas of marked muscular attachment. Their lower jaws were large and deep. The teeth varied in size and were relatively free of dental caries, although alveolar abscesses were common. There was no sign of bone injury; one individual's left hip joint had been dislocated for some time before death, but whether this was due to a birth defect or an accident remains a mystery. They were also free of any signs of arthritis, a prevalent and debilitating malady in most ancient cultures. If these findings can be generalized, it would seem then that our predecessors in northern New England belonged to a race of tall, robust, healthy people. Unfortunately the precise age of the skeletons has not been determined.

Neville site. The Neville site was located at the northern end of a postglacial terrace that was cut by the Merrimack River at about 200 feet above sea level, some 60 feet below the highest lake beds. After some time, the river swung away in a westerly direction and then returned again to the weathered terrace, removing the accumulated topsoil and depositing a few inches of fluvial sand. The river then left the terrace for the second time and has since remained in its current meandering channel, occasionally cutting down to bedrock to form falls along its entire length.

The first people occupied the terrace about 8,000 years ago, and their hearth debris, broken tools, and organic and lithic wastes were eventually buried by the wind-blown sand as the surface of the terrace and that of the bluff above it continued to rise. The cultural sequence revealed by artifacts discovered at the Neville site is truly remarkable inasmuch as it clearly demonstrates the presence of archaic cultures in the eighth millennium B.P. in northern New England (see "The Neville Site: 8,000 Years at Amoskeag").

CULTURAL SEQUENCE

Paleo-Indian period. Although researchers (including the authors in this volume) vary in assigning dates to all the periods and to their subdivisions, in northern New England the Paleo-Indian period is generally placed between 11,000 and 9,000 B.P. The nomadic big-game hunters, called Paleo-Indians, who arrived in this area between 11,000 and 10,000 B.P. were, no doubt, the descendants of the Asians who crossed the Bering Strait in several migratory waves between 18,000 and 15,000 years ago (or perhaps even earlier), when the oceans lay some 300–400 feet below their present levels and exposed a massive land bridge extending over 1,000 miles from north to south and just as wide, called Beringia, between Asia and North America. At that time the Merrimack River ran at a higher level in a much broader and shallower valley. There were probably fish in the river and streams, but perhaps they were fewer in number and of a different variety than those of later years. The same is true of the local flora and fauna. The climate and water temperature were both much cooler then due to the presence of the retreating glaciers and snowfields in the White Mountains. The falls at Amoskeag had not yet formed.

The Paleo-Indians probably moved about in search of game in extended family units called *bands*. Due to local conditions, their diet must have been based largely on meat, though some floral resources may have already been available. We know of their presence here from the discovery (two at the Smyth site and one at the Neville site) of Clovis points, the typical fluted spearheads of the Paleo-Indians named after the site where they were first unearthed: Clovis, New Mexico. Although the average length of these razor-sharp spearheads is three to five inches, some as large as nine to twelve inches have been found out west, crafted perhaps as monuments in tribute to some great hunters, leaders, or spirits. Since one of these local artifacts is older than the river terrace on which it was found, archaeologists speculate that these projectile points must have belonged to another people, place, and time and that they were

brought to Amoskeag by later inhabitants. (The three major sources of paleolithic materials in northern New England were Mt. Jasper located near Berlin, New Hampshire, for rhyolite [igneous or volcanic rock]; the Hathaway Formation in northern Vermont for chert [sedimentary rock]; and the Munsungan Lake area in northern Maine, also for chert.)

Clearly the ancient hunters who made these finely crafted spear points must have passed this way or perhaps lived in the Amoskeag area for a time. (The Whipple site in New Hampshire, with radiocarbon dates of 10,680 B.P., is more illustrative of the Paleo-Indian period than the Smyth-Neville complex, which is predominantly Archaic.) The traces of their passing extend to the very tip of South America and, beginning in Siberia, all that distance had to be traversed by foot.

As the great beasts of the late Pleistocene Epoch became extinct, the people who remained in this area turned to the hunting of other species, to gathering, to fishing, and, much later, even to rudimentary agriculture, the typical economy and occupations of later settlers as well.

Archaic period. The Archaic period of time in northern New England extends from 9,000 to 3,000 B.P. It is subdivided as follows: Early Archaic from 9,000 to 8,000 B.P.; Middle Archaic from 8,000 to 6,000 B.P.; and Late Archaic from 6,000 to 3,000 B.P. During this time, as the climate became warmer and drier and as the glaciers retreated northward, new land with new flora and fauna emerged. Certainly the people of the Archaic period still hunted and fished, but just as certainly their subsistence now included all of the indigenous resources of their more bountiful environment.

Although a few of the artifacts recovered from the Neville site (for example, the previously mentioned Clovis points as well as four flake tools) date to the Late Paleo-Indian/Early Archaic periods, most come from the Middle Archaic period and resemble those of the people living along the coast in Massachusetts, Rhode Island, and Connecticut. Among the recovered artifacts are spearheads, flake scrapers, flake knives, perforators, hard and soft hammers, an ax, and heavy choppers coming from at least three different cultural traditions classified as Neville, Stark, and Merrimack on the basis of types of projectile points. These findings indicate wood- and bone-working activities, tool production, and—judging by the high concentration of mercury in the soil—a great deal of fishing. We can therefore conclude that the economy of these early occupants was based on hunting, cutting, and scraping activities.

The Neville site, it seems, was initially just one more fishing camp established by nomadic people during their spring and summer travels. In the fall they would generally move to areas where nuts, berries, and other wild edible plants were abundant. They probably spent the winter months in their forest camps where firewood and game were plentiful. The subsequent large concentration of heavy tools at the Neville site, however, suggests that it may have been an important base camp. Judging from the variety of different projectile points, the site must have been occupied often and by many different groups of people.

The localized nomadic existence came to an end sometime before 6,000 B.P., when permanent year-round campsites emerged on the terrace. Then, for reasons still unknown, the terrace was abandoned for long stretches of time between 6,000 and 5,000 B.P. The strata of earth representing this period are almost devoid of artifacts, and those that have been unearthed represent a new cul-

tural tradition belonging perhaps to some passing hunters from the west.

The reoccupation of the Neville site after the fifth millennium occurred from the west and north. It was during this time that the bluff to the east (the Smyth site) underwent an exceptionally heavy occupation. Eventually, the Smyth site became a base camp, and the Neville terrace was reserved for a more narrow range of fishing-related activities.

Woodland period. The Woodland period in northern New England began about 3,000 B.P. and ended around 400 B.P. (i.e., in our seventeenth century) with the arrival of the Europeans. Like the Archaic, it too is subdivided into early, middle, and late: Early Woodland 3,000 to 2,000 B.P.; Middle Woodland 2,000 to 1,000 B.P.; and Late Woodland 1,000 to 400 B.P.

The last 3,000 years at the Neville site have not lent themselves readily to interpretation due to a compression and jumbling in the lower plow zone and site disturbances. Fortunately, since the Woodland sequence for southern New England is known, almost all of the Neville artifacts from this period have been adequately accounted for by comparison to types with known temporal ranges. (The Smyth site is more illustrative of the Woodland period. See "Ancient Lifeways at the Smyth Site.")

Some 3,000 years ago the postglacial period of warmer climate, which began about 7,800 years ago, gave way to cooler temperatures. Judging by adaptive patterns elsewhere, life at the Neville site during the Woodland period also reflected these atmospheric changes. The most distinctive features of the Woodland period are the development of the horticultural techniques introduced in the Late Archaic period and the extensive use of ceramics. Clay from nearby lake and river banks provided the raw material; stones, crushed shells, and plant fibers provided the strength to withstand drying, firing, and everyday use. In time, dyes and artistic designs were added.

At the end of the Woodland period, due to an increase in population (thanks to horticulture) and the consequent need for communication networks as well as economic interdependence, important developments were taking place in the social and political life of the people living in northern New England. And then the big ships arrived, and the indigenous people became "Indians."

CONTACT ERA

All of the Indians of New England are now classified as Algonquian, a large family consisting of over 20 languages spoken by the Indians of North America. The designation "Abenaki" has been applied to the members of the Algonquian Confederacy in northern New England: Eastern Abenaki are those, roughly speaking, in the Maine area, and Western Abenaki are those in New Hampshire and Vermont. Recently David Stewart-Smith has proposed the term "central Abenaki" to further differentiate the peoples in the vast area occupied by confederated groups between the Kennebec and Connecticut, rivers, which would include all of New Hampshire (Stewart-Smith, "Pennacook Indians and the New England Frontier," chap. 1). At the time of their discovery, the northern New England Algonquians had three words to designate their homeland: *W'banakik* ("Dawnland," or the land where the sun first rises), *Norumbega* (the Algonquian word for New England), and *Ndakinna* ("Our Land," a land whose vast resources could be shared by all). Canada (*Kanata*), their "village," whose border at the time lay somewhere beyond New

Hampshire's Lake Winnipesaukee, eventually became their ultimate refuge.

For better or worse—and there is a great deal of chaff among this winnowed wheat—the primary sources of our information regarding the Indians in the Northeast at the time of contact are the journals, letters, and other writings of white explorers and missionaries, who came to the New World in what appeared to the natives as floating islands with trees (masts) that caught the clouds (sails) and moved upon the water.

Sebastian Cabot surveyed the eastern seaboard in 1508 or 1509. Giovanni da Verrazano, a Florentine adventurer, was commissioned in 1524 by Francois I, king of France, to explore America. Bartholomew Gosnold (probably the first white man to touch New Hampshire soil) landed here in 1602. In that year, John Brereton wound up in Massachusetts. Captain Martin Pring sailed up the Piscataqua River in 1603. Samuel de Champlain made a landing in Rye, New Hampshire, in 1605 and then sailed into the mouth of the Merrimack River, which he promptly named Riviere du Gas. In the same year, Captain George Weymouth visited the Maine coast and kidnapped five Indians. (Two other explorers did the same, thus arousing the first native distrust of the whites.) In 1614 Captain John Smith, using Monheagan Island as a base, explored the New England coast in several small boats and made observations of the locations, characteristics, and strengths of the various Indian nations. Thomas Morton arrived in 1619 and was forcibly deported from New England in 1628. Sir Ferdinando Gorges, in 1622, procured a grant with Captain John Mason, governor of Portsmouth, for a territory they called Laconia, which included parts of New Hampshire and Maine. Mason began a settlement at the Piscataqua River in 1623. Christopher Levett explored the coast of Maine in

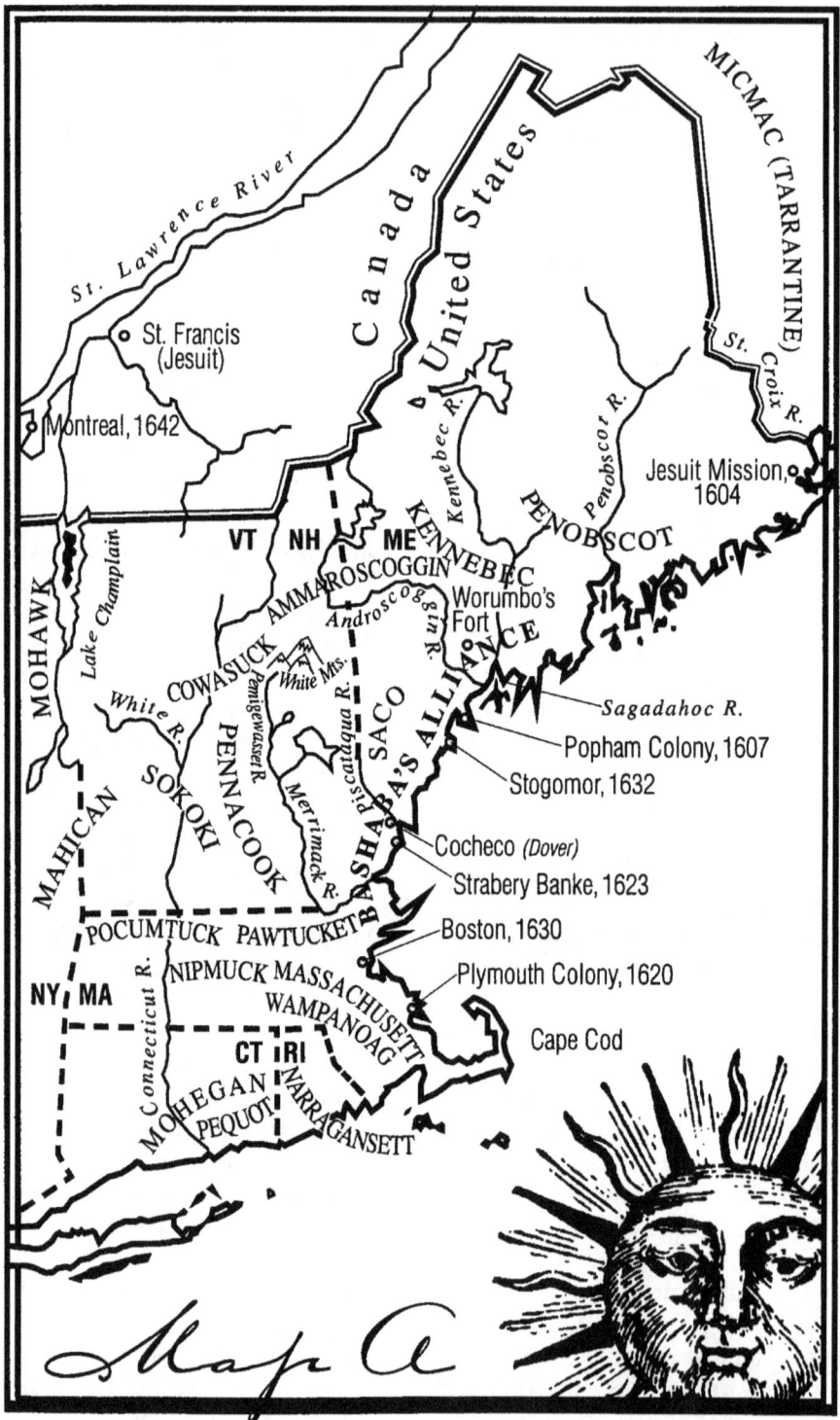

Distribution of Indian tribes in seventeenth-century New England.

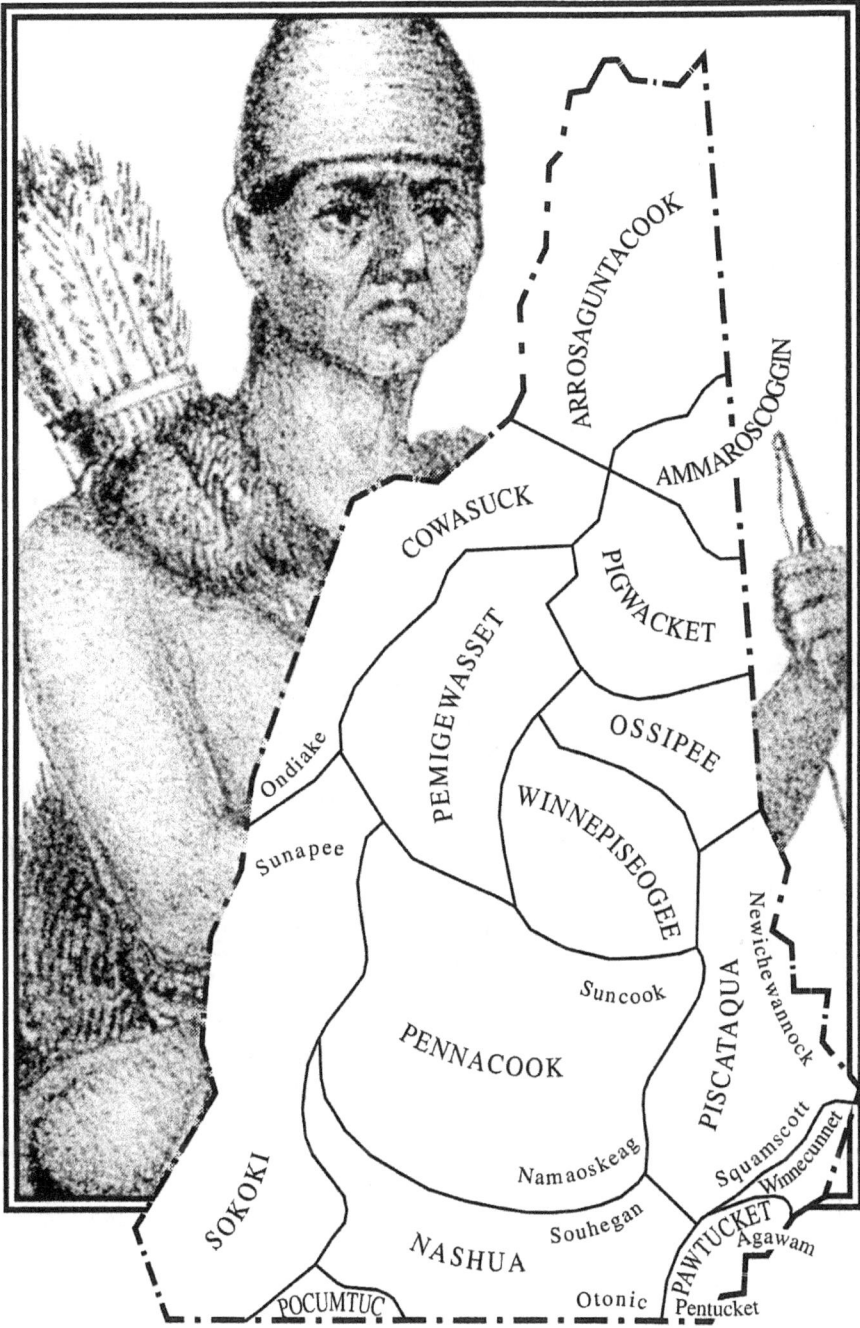

ARROSAGUNTACOOK

AMMAROSCOGGIN

COWASUCK

PIGWACKET

PEMIGEWASSET

OSSIPEE

Ondiake

WINNEPISEOGEE

Sunapee

Newichewannock

Suncook

PISCATAQUA

PENNACOOK

Squamscott

Winnecunnet

Namaoskeag

SOKOKI

PAWTUCKET

Souhegan

Agawam

NASHUA

POCUMTUC

Otonic

Pentucket

Map B

Distribution of Indian tribes in New Hampshire, ca. 1630.

1623–24. Edward Winslow arrived in Plymouth in 1624. There were William Wood (1629), Governor John Winthrop (1630), Roger Williams (1631), John Eliot, who also arrived in Boston in 1631 and later became the "Apostle of the Indians," John Josselyn (1638), Daniel Gookin (1644), and others as well. (For some of their accounts, see "The Manners, Customs, and Some Historical Facts About the Indians of Northern New England.")

At the time of their discovery by European explorers and missionaries, the principal Indian tribes (in boldface type below) and bands (in regular type) and their relative geographical distribution in the New Hampshire area were as follows (see map B):

Ammaroscoggin (Amariscoggin, Amerascoggin, Androscoggin)—below Lake Umbagog along the Androscoggin River in the northeastern parts of New Hampshire, but mostly in Maine

Arrosaguntacook (Arosaguntacook)—in the Lake Umbagog region and northeastern parts of New Hampshire and in Maine

Agawam—within the Pawtucket territory along the coast on both sides of the New Hampshire–Massachusetts border to the east

Cowasuck (Coos, Coosuc)—along both banks of the upper Connecticut River, the boundary between New Hampshire and Vermont

Namaoskeag (Amoskeag)—within the Pennacook territory at Amoskeag Falls in Manchester

Nashua—in southern New Hampshire and extending beyond its border into Massachusetts

Newichewannock—within the Piscataqua territory between the Piscataqua and Cocheco rivers on the upper part of the Piscataqua River, the boundary between New Hampshire and Maine.

The Newichewannock united with the Piscataqua and the Winnecunnet toward the end of the seventeenth century to form the Cocheco.

Ondiake—within the Cowasuck territory along the New Hampshire–Vermont border above the Sunapee in the vicinity of Lyme, New Hampshire

Ossipee—in the area of the lake and river by that name

Otonic—at the southern border of New Hampshire with territory extending into Massachusetts

Pawtucket—centering in Lowell, Massachusetts, at Pawtucket Falls, their territory included several bands located in the Massachusetts and southeastern New Hampshire areas

Pemigewasset—in the western region of the White Mountains

Pennacook—in southern New Hampshire, northeastern Massachusetts, and the southern part of Maine. In New Hampshire, they occupied the intervales at Penacook (Concord), but also had summer residences at Amoskeag in Manchester and at Pawtucket Falls in Massachusetts. Their sphere of influence, however, was very wide.

Pentucket—within the Pawtucket territory on both sides of the New Hampshire–Massachusetts border to the east (in the vicinity of Haverhill, Mass.), inland west of the Agawam band

Pigwacket (Pequaket, Pequawket)—in the upper valley of the Saco River

Piscataqua (Piscataquauke)—on the east bank of the Piscataqua River. See Newichewannock.

Pocumtuc—along the Connecticut River valley in north-central Massachusetts and partly in southwestern New Hampshire

Sokoki—on the Connecticut River in the central Connecticut Valley at the southern end of the border between New Hampshire and Vermont

Sunapee—at the lake by that name at the northern end of the Sokoki territory in New Hampshire

Suncook—in the northeastern corner of the Pennacook territory

Souhegan—within the Nashua territory along the Souhegan River; their principal village was near Amherst, New Hampshire

Squamscott—along the lower end of the Piscataqua territory in the region of the Exeter River in Exeter and in Stratham

Winnecunnet (Winnecowett)—along the New Hampshire coastline in the vicinity of the Hamptons. See Newichewannock.

Winnepiseogee (Winnipesaukee)—in the area of the lake by the same name

Pennacook Confederacy. Prior to the arrival of the Europeans an alliance of Indian tribes began developing in New Hampshire under the able leadership of Passaconaway, the famed sagamore of the powerful Pennacook. By the early seventeenth century the Pennacook Confederacy, as it was known, was functioning rather well, and representatives from some dozen allied Indian tribes throughout New Hampshire, southern Maine, and northeastern Massachusetts often convened for councils, ceremonies, and celebrations at Penacook, Pawtucket, and Amoskeag.

The Pennacook Confederacy, whose main purpose was to secure peace through unity and council, was not unique. On the east, it was bounded by the Eastern Abenaki Alliance under the leadership of the Etchemin sagamore Bashaba; to the south lay the Massachusett Tribal Coalition; to the west was the Iroquois Confederacy or, more precisely, the fierce Mohawk nation of "men eaters"; and to the north were the unified Algonquians of the St. Lawrence Basin.

Social organization. The typical Indian village consisted of about a hundred families. Each village was governed by a local sagamore, or leader. The title, usually a hereditary one, was passed on from father to son. If the sagamore had no male son, a daughter might be selected to replace him. But the widow of a sagamore could also assume a leadership role as a squaw sachem; such was the case, for example, at Naumkeag (Salem, Mass.) and Pawtucket (Lowell, Mass.). A grand sagamore would often preside at communal meetings involving several villages or even tribes. Indians considered wise and courageous would be chosen as advisors to the sagamore and would act as his or her bodyguards in times of war.

Although stable villages and even Indian towns existed throughout New England, the Indian way of life necessitated a great deal of travel: to fishing grounds in the spring, to the interior in the fall and winter, to sources of lithic materials, to social gatherings and ceremonies, to trading posts, to refuges when they were displaced or threatened, to designated meeting places in preparation for united warfare against the New England colonists or their Mohawk enemies, and finally to their places of exile in Canada.

Between 1600 and the end of the French and Indian Wars (1763), when their numbers were severely depleted by disease, aggression, and war, or when they were displaced by the colonists, the Indians would regroup, reconfigure their tribal alliances (for example, Pennacook, Ossipee, Pigwacket, Saco, and Ammaroscoggin grouped together), gather for war (for example, at Lake Winnipesaukee, where the modern tribes still gather around Father's Day), or simply seek refuge elsewhere (at various times, for example, Penacook [Concord] and Cocheco [Dover]) became refuges for the Narragansett and Wampanoag; Pigwacket became a refuge for the Pennacook, Accominta, and Saco Indians; and Cowass, Missisquoi, Canawake, and St. Francis became refuges for them all).

Tarrantine War and the "Indian fever." Not long before the founding of Plymouth Colony by the Puritan Pilgrims (1620), two major events—both of catastrophic proportions—occurred in the history of the New England Indians, which greatly facilitated the takeover of the Indian tribal lands by the white man.

When the European explorers began their voyages along the coast of New England at the beginning of the seventeenth century, the Etchemin (called Penobscot by some) residing to the east of the Kennebec River in Maine were the most powerful tribe in the area, and their northern neighbors, the Micmac ("Allies," also known as Tarrantine, or "Traders") were among the most feared. At that time the Bashaba Alliance, embracing many of the tribes along the southern coast of Maine and the interior, stretched all the way to Cape Ann in Massachusetts and included agricultural communities. The Tarrantine were predominantly traders who established trade with the French in the Gulf of St. Lawrence and the upper Gulf of Maine well before Champlain's voyage and who jealously guarded their privileged position. At the time they were allied with the eastern Etchemin, who lived beyond the St. Croix River. The arrival of Champlain opened new possibilities for French trade between the Gulf of Maine and Massachusetts Bay, and in order to become the exclusive middlemen of that lucrative venture, the Tarrantine not only strained their relationship with their eastern Etchemin allies but also sought to break the Bashaba Alliance.

Meanwhile, in 1607 an English settlement, the (George) Popham Colony, was founded at the mouth of the Kennebec River at Sagadahoc. It failed after about a year but others would follow. Although the subsequent competition between the French and the English for native trade did not create the tribal rivalries of the day, it certainly served to exacerbate them. Later, both sides would exploit the Indians to their own advantage and send "the devil to destroy the devil" as the saying went.

In the same year that the Popham Colony was founded, the Tarrantine attacked Saco. This attack was sparked no doubt by a blood debt: the murder of Champlain's Tarrantine Indian agent, Panonias, in reprisal for the previous murder of some Abenaki who were allied with the Saco. In the attack on Saco, French weapons were used, and the Tarrantine easily won the day. This event marked the beginning of the terrible Tarrantine War, called by Chandler Potter, the erstwhile historian of Manchester, "a war of extermination" (Potter 1856, 23). That war involved many of the New England tribes along the coastline and the interior from Maine to Massachusetts. It ended in 1615 with the murder by the Tarrantine of the Etchemin sagamore Bashaba, the leader of the Eastern Abenaki Alliance. The Tarrantine raids on their terrified southern neighbors, however, did not cease with the end of the war; they continued until the 1630s, that is, until these neighbors procured the protection of their own European allies: the English. Needless to say, the Tarrantine aggression had a disastrous effect on New England's Indian population.

The other tragic event, with even more disastrous consequences, was the outbreak in 1616 of the so-called Indian fever, which raged for several years and affected not only the coastal Indians of Maine, New Hampshire, and Massachusetts but also—although less severely—those of the interior. No doubt the Indians at Amoskeag also suffered from it since the Merrimack River provided a direct access route from and to the Atlantic coast. According to the observations of Captain John Smith, Captain Dermer, General Gookin, and others, the plague (which *only* affected the Indians) was so deadly that formerly thriving villages boasting 300 to 500 residents were sometimes completely wiped out in its wake. Commenting on the extent of this depopulation, Captain Smith observed: "[T]hey had three plagues in three years successively neere two hundred miles along the Sea coast, that in some places there scarce remained five of a hundred … but it is most certaine there was an exceeding great plague amongst them; for where I have seene two or three hundred, within three years after remained scarce thirty" (Potter 1856, 24).

The nature of this epidemic as well as its origin remain a mystery. In all probability this "pestilential putrid fever" was either chicken pox, hepatic fever, or smallpox, or some combination of two of these or of all three—all white man's diseases. General Gookin provides one description:

What the disease which so generally and mortally swept them away, I cannot learn. Doubtless it was a pestilential disease. I have discoursed with some old Indians, that were then youths, who say that the bodies, all over were exceedingly yellow (describing it by a yellow garment which they showed me) both before and after they died, and produced hemorrhaging from the nose [Colby 1975, 23; Hoornbeek 1976–77, 36].

Referring only to the Pawtucket, Gookin tells us that in pre-epidemic times that tribe consisted of 3,000 men, but that by 1674 (the date of his writing) they had been reduced to "not above 250 men, besides women and children" (Gookin,

12). According to the 1927 estimate of Harry L. Watson, in 1614, at the time of Captain Smith's observations, the Pennacook population of New Hampshire was anywhere from 6,000 to 8,000 strong. Due to pestilence and war, by 1630 the number had fallen to 2,500, and by 1674 to about 1,250.

More recent demographic studies tell us that there were over 150,000 Indians throughout New England before the epidemic. David Stewart-Smith estimates that from 15,000 to 22,000 of these were members of the Pennacook/Pawtucket group occupying the Merrimack Valley, the Piscataqua, the lakes region, and the Connecticut Valley. He estimates that by the end of that three-year plague, "the time of Great Dying," nearly 90 percent of the Indian population of coastal New England had perished (see "The Pennacook Lands and Relations: Family Homelands"). Dean Snow has estimated that the Western Abenaki population (which included the Indians of New Hampshire) was reduced by 98 percent from 10,000 to 250 individuals (Snow, 34).

In any case, due to war and disease, by the time the white settlers arrived in the Northeast the Indians were in no position to wage war against them in the defense of their territory. In *The Journal of the Pilgrims at Plymouth*, written in 1622 and published by George Cheever in 1848, we read:

Samoset of the Massasoits … spoke, among other things, of the pestilence. He told us that about four years ago, all the inhabitants died of a[n] extraordinary plague, and there is neither man, woman, nor child remaining, as indeed we have found none; so as there is none to hinder our possession, or to lay claim unto it [Marshall, "The Manners," 6].

Indeed, some white men took these disasters to be a sure sign of divine Providence at work in their behalf. "Thus," said

Thomas Morton in 1632, "God made way for his people by removing the heathen and planting them in the ground" (Colby 1975, 22). And Daniel Denton wrote in his journal: "[H]ow strangely they have decreased by the Hand of God.... and it hath generally been observed that where the English come to settle, a Divine Hand makes way for them" (see "An Investigation into the Cause or Causes of the Epidemic which Decimated the Indian Population of New England, 1616–1619"). Writing in 1670, Denton no doubt also had in mind the smallpox epidemic that had decimated the remaining Indian population in 1633, but why did he omit the obvious fact that that time the "Hand of God" did not spare the English communities either?

Indian-European relations. Through the efforts of men like John Eliot, Daniel Gookin, and Chief Passaconaway, the Indians of New England remained peaceful for a number of years with the many white settlers who followed closely upon the heels of the explorers and missionaries. European technology was often exchanged for Indian knowledge of survival in the wilderness. The Indians taught the settlers to place small fish in each hill of corn for fertilizer. They taught them to grow squash and pumpkins within hills of corn; to trap the wild animals of the forest by means of snares, log traps, and pits; to fish effectively in the rivers and streams; to make and store maple syrup and sugar; to make and use snowshoes; to preserve fresh meat; to catch ducks; to tan hides; to dye hair; to raise, prepare, and eat corn; to clear potential farmland by girdling trees; to safely use herbs, roots, and bark; and to prepare antidotes for snake bites. The Europeans even adopted some of their superstitions, which lingered on long after the Indians had disappeared. Most important, the natives were willing to

share their land and its bountiful resources with the newcomers.

But peace was difficult to maintain when ranging settlement cattle, swine, and dogs ravaged the Indian cornfields; when the Indians were forced to abandon their homes and their ancient hunting grounds by the ever-increasing numbers of white settlers who were constantly moving into the rich and resource-filled frontier of New England; when unscrupulous means were used to "purchase" Indian land; when white man's rum wreaked havoc among the Indians; when the signing of "submissions" and covenants was required of Indian leaders (Passaconaway and his eldest son, Nanamocomuck, signed their submissions in 1644 and again in 1645); when trade and peace agreements were broken as often as they were made; when powwowing was forbidden (1646) as worship of "falce gods" and the "devill"; when peaceful Indians were jailed for crimes they did not commit, hung in public, sold into slavery, and kidnapped to be sent overseas for show-and-tell spectacles; and when Indian scalps fetched a handsome bounty. Neither was peace easy to maintain when both the New England colonists and the French resorted to using "the devil to destroy the devil," or when white troops descended on Indian villages and campsites killing and maiming people and burning the crops which were to stave off the hunger of the long New England winters. There is ample evidence for all of the above—and much, much more.

Understandably, the Indians retaliated and began a bitter campaign against the settlers in the hope of stemming the tide that threatened to engulf them. But it was already too late. Four years after the "Articles of Peace" (dated September 8, 1685) between the English and the Indians inhabiting the provinces of New Hampshire and Maine were signed, one of the worst Indian attacks on record took place: the Cocheco (now Dover, N.H.) massacre of June 28, 1689, during which 23 whites were killed and 29 taken as captives. Attacks on the settlers of Oyster River, New Hampshire; Andover, Massachusetts; and many other places followed—reprisals also followed. The last Indian raid occurred in the Androscoggin Valley almost a century later, in 1774.

THREE GREAT SAGAMORES

Passaconaway. Passaconaway was one of the most noted Indian chiefs in all of New England. According to Chandler Potter, his name, *Papisseconewa*, means "Child of the Bear." Although Potter's translation has been contested, none has been offered thus far to replace it. From all accounts he was a tall individual, courageous in time of war, magnanimous in time of peace, and dearly loved and respected by the tribes of the Pennacook Confederacy over which he presided. He was also feared, for great supernatural powers were attributed to him by friends and foes alike.

Recognizing the superiority of the English and wishing to set up a buffer zone between his people and the Mohawk, his dreaded enemy to the west, Passaconaway followed a policy of conciliation with the white settlers to the point of deeding (in 1629) vast amounts of land to the Reverend John Wheelwright and his associates while reserving the right to hunt and fish thereon. The English repaid Passaconaway for his good will and generosity by subsequently conscripting the aid of the Mohawk to challenge and, in the 1666 battle of Fort Eddy (just north of Concord), to break the power of the Pennacook. After that incident the Pennacook never regained either their numerical strength or their former prestige in New

Hampshire. The Mohawk attacks did not subside until 1680, although in 1683–84 the New Englanders attempted to employ them once more against the eastern Indians.

In 1642 the English—ever suspicious of an Indian conspiracy to overthrow them—as a precautionary measure sent out men to arrest some of the principal Indian chiefs. Forty men came after Passaconaway but he escaped in the course of a storm. His son Wonalancet, however, was captured, paraded about ignominiously with a rope around his neck, and fired upon like a dog when he tried to escape. In spite of this provocation, Passaconaway kept the peace, even to the point of surrendering the few guns he had to the Massachusetts authorities.

In 1647, when John Eliot visited Pawtucket Falls, Passaconaway refused to hear him preach and, moreover, retired from the vicinity with his family because he was afraid the English would kill him. The following year, however, he welcomed Eliot and allowed him to evangelize (Potter 1856, 57–58). "This last spring," stated Eliot, "I did meet old Passaconaway who is a great Sagamore and hath been a great witch in all men's esteem, and a very politic, wise man. Last year he and his sons fled when I came pretending fear that we would kill them. But this year it pleased God to bow his heart to hear the Word" (Proctor, 22).

Eliot tells us that Passaconaway actually "did believe what I taught them to be true. And for his own part he was purposed in his heart from thenceforth to pray unto God, and that hee would persuade all his sonnes to doe the same, pointing to two of them who were there present, and naming such as were absent" (Potter 1856, 58). Some have interpreted these words to mean that Passaconaway actually converted to Christianity. Potter surmises that "the Old Sagamon was doubtless sincere in his change of religion, and continued in the christian belief till his death" (*ibid.*). The historical record neither confirms nor negates Potter's words.

But his "conversion" changed nothing. In the end, this great chief of the mighty Pennacook was reduced to begging from the Massachusetts General Court a portion of the land he had given them in the first place. The date of his petition was March 9, 1662; the petition was approved by the General Court on May 9, 1662; and the survey laying out the grant was dated March 27, 1663 (for the text of the petition and survey see "Cartagena Island"; Potter 1856, 61–63).

The Massachusetts land grant gave Passaconaway some acreage in what is now Manchester, Londonderry, Merrimack, and Bedford. Chandler Potter wonders at the "great liberality of the 'Great and General Court' of Massachusetts, in granting to Passaconnaway of his *own territory*, so good a fishing place, and at the suggestion of the Surveyors, that the 'two small islands' and the 'small patch of intervaile Land' be added to the grant" (Potter 1856, 63). And he was probably correct in stating that if "the extent and value of fisheries at this place" had been known, Passaconaway would have been denied his petition.

There is great pathos in Chief Passaconaway's 1660 so-called farewell speech to his dwindling nation, for it is not a speech counseling peace from a position of strength; rather, it is an admission of defeat and ignominy, a capitulation to a destiny that seemed to demand the extinction of what was once a proud and powerful nation:

Hearken to the words of your father. I am an old oak that has withstood the storms of more than an hundred winters. Leaves and branches have been stripped from me by the winds and frosts—my eyes are dim—my limbs totter—I must soon fall! But when young and sturdy, when my bow—no young man of the Pennacooks could bend it— when my arrows would pierce a deer at an hundred yards—and I could bury my hatchet in a sapling to the eye—no wigwam had so many furs—no pole so many scalp locks as Passaconnaway's. Then I delighted in war. The whoop of the Pennacooks was heard upon the Mohawk—and no voice so loud as Passaconnaway's. The scalps upon the pole of my wigwam told the story of Mohawk suffering.

The English came, they seized our lands; I sat me down at Pennacook. They followed upon my footsteps; I made war upon them, but they fought with fire and thunder; my young men were swept down before me, when no one was near them. I tried sorcery against them, but they still increased and prevailed over me and mine, and I gave place to them and retired to my beautiful island of Natticook. I that can make the dry leaf turn green and live again—I that can take the rattlesnake in my palm as I would a worm, without harm—I who have had communion with the Great Spirit dreaming and awake—I am powerless before the Pale Faces.

The oak will soon break before the whirlwind—it shivers and shakes even now; soon its trunk will be prostrate— the ant and the worm will sport upon it! Then think, my children, of what I say; I commune with the Great Spirit. He whispers [to] me now—"Tell your people, Peace, Peace, is the only hope of your race. I have given fire and thunder to the pale faces for weapons—I have made them plentier than the leaves of the forest, and still shall they *increase*! These meadows they shall turn with the plow—these forests shall fall by the axe—the pale faces shall live upon your hunting grounds and make their villages upon your fishing places!" The Great Spirit says this, and it must be so! We are few and powerless before them! We must bend before the storm! The wind blows hard! The old oak trembles! Its branches are gone! Its sap is frozen! It bends! It falls! Peace, Peace, with the white men—is the command of the Great Spirit—and the wish—the last wish—of Passaconnaway [Potter 1856, 60–61].

Peace did come, but it came at a great price.

No one knows where Potter got that well-written version of the "farewell speech." Perhaps, drawing on early accounts of Passaconaway's great prowess, he simply "improved" on the one recorded in 1677 by the Reverend William Hubbard (Hubbard 1990, vol. 1, 48–49), who, in turn, claimed that it had been conveyed to him by an unnamed "person of quality"—and *both* versions may have been written in keeping with the well-known classical historians' practice of putting memorable words into the mouths of their famous characters. The chief reason for questioning the authenticity of both versions of this speech is their reference to Passaconaway's initial warlike disposition toward the English settlers. The historical record indicates quite the contrary.

Passaconaway probably died on the land he received from the Massachusetts General Court—some say at the age of 120. But then, no one knows when he was born (only that it was after 1550) nor the date of his death (only that it was after 1665). Curiously, his death is not recorded in the annals of New England history. He probably died in 1666, the year the dreaded Mohawk declared war on his people at Penacook.

It would be most comforting to believe that the great chief ended his life near the river he loved so well in New Hampshire, the "Live Free or Die" state,

the "First in the Nation," the state that so many other "great chiefs" of this great country have visited and will continue to visit every four years around January. May the generous spirit and the peaceful legacy of Passaconaway show them the way!

Wonalancet. Wonalancet, Passaconaway's second son, was born around 1619. He married an Abenaki woman from the St. Francis River area and succeeded his father as the sagamore of the Pennacook in 1669. His name is translated as "Governor" by some and "Breathing Pleasantly" by others, which may be interpreted to mean that he did not snore. Like his father, Chief Wonalancet was of a peaceful and mild disposition "preferring the ease and comforts of peace, to the hardships and deprivations of war" (Potter 1856, 66).

From 1669 until the summer of 1675 Wonalancet and his people resided on an island in the Merrimack River above Lowell, Massachusetts, called Wickasauke. Here (as well as at Naticook and Penacook) they planted their crops, but during the spring fish run they moved to Amoskeag. Of the 275 Indians living in the Lowell area at the time, 75 were Christians—Wonalancet was one of them.

The Indian war against the English waged by Metacomen of Pokanoket, which was known as King Philip's War and which began in the summer of 1675 and involved most of the tribes in New England, left Wonalancet's people—who were determined to remain neutral—prey to both sides. Some were put to death by Philip, who considered them traitors; others were put to death by the colonists, who considered them Philip's accomplices and hated both hostile and "praying Indians" alike. When the war broke out, Wonalancet and his people withdrew to Penacook and awaited the end of the hostilities. But even there they were hassled. When

Captain Samuel Mosely arrived at Penacook in 1675 expecting to find them, they
withdrew into the forest. He, in turn,
destroyed their village and their food
supply.

By the summer of 1676 the warring
Indians had lost nearly 3,000 men,
women, and children, and hundreds more
had been sold into slavery. King Philip
was killed in August 1676. Many of the
survivors (the Wamesit, Cocheco, Piscataqua, and a few veterans of King
Philip's War, called "strange Indians" by
the colonists) joined the Pennacook and,
at the beginning of September of that
year, about 400 Indians went with Wonalancet to Cocheco at the invitation of
Major Waldron, who had promised them
amnesty. Unfortunately, unbeknownst to
the Pennacook, on September 6 came
orders from Boston to "seize all Indians."

In one version of the story, a military
display was proposed for the amusement
of the Indians in which they were invited
to participate. In the supposedly sham
fight that followed, an English cannon was
set off, killing and maiming many of the
betrayed Indians, and English troops surrounded and disarmed the rest. About half
of the 400 Indians, those known to be
friendly Pennacook, were released (Wonalancet among them), but the other half
were taken to Boston. There, seven or
eight were hanged, and the rest were sold
into slavery.

After this fiasco Wonalancet and
many Wamesit Indians (the Wamesit
were located in the Lowell-Chelmsford,
Mass., area and at this time consisted of
Pennacook, Pawtucket, Nashobah, and
Nipmuc families) returned to Wickasauke
only to discover that his land was occupied by the English. In the winter of 1677
he, his family, and eight Wamesit men
along with some women and children
went either to the Abenaki reservation
of St. Francis or to Canawake, both in

Quebec. The rest of Wonalancet's people,
an unknown number, chose to remain
behind.

Wonalancet returned to Penacook in
1685, and in that year and the next he sold
the central Pennacook homelands to
Jonathan Tyng and his partners. This
"million-acre" purchase involved lands
extending on both sides of the Merrimack
River for a breadth of six miles from
the Souhegan River just north of Nashua
to Lake Winnipesaukee. To the New
England settlers, often one sagamore's
name—any sagamore's name—affixed to a
deed was sufficient to establish their pro-
prietary rights forever. Later, the governor
general of New England, Edmund
Andros, would declare that such deeds
were "of no more worth than a scratch
with a bear's paw" (Stewart-Smith, "Pennacook Indians and the New England
Frontier," 215–16).

There is great significance in the fact
that in 1685 false rumors of an impending
Mohawk invasion were being fanned by
the English and that the Pennacook land
deal coincided with the treaty of 1685,
whose articles of peace guaranteed protection from the Mohawk. In reality no
such invasion was afoot and therefore no
protection was needed. Three years later,
Hope Hood, or Wahowah, an ally of Kancamagus (recognized as a Pennacook sagamore in 1685), declared: "[I]f ever it were
war again, it would not be as it was formerly, for the Indians and the Mohawks
were all agreed throughout the whole
country that they would not fight to kill
one another any more" (*ibid.*, 213).

Wonalancet returned to the Merrimack Valley again around 1692 and was
subsequently placed in the care of
Jonathan Tyng. He died destitute and was
buried by Tyng in June 1697 in Tyngsboro, Massachusetts. Tyng, who profited
so much at the expense of Wonalancet
while the Sagamore was still alive, was

reimbursed by the General Court of Massachusetts for expenses incurred while taking care of Wonalancet in his old age and for the burial.

Kancamagus. Kancamagus, also known as John Hodgkins or Hogkins, was the son of Nanamocomuck, Passaconaway's eldest son. It was probably when Wonalancet set out for Canada that his star rose. Under his chieftaincy the Pennacook—many of whom returned from their slavery in Massachusetts—became formidable foes to the English settlers. Kancamagus was the leader of the raid on Cocheco on the night of June 27, 1689, when Major Waldron was killed. That date marked the Pennacook entry into King William's War (1688–99). From that time on, Kancamagus had a price on his head. He subsequently joined forces with Worumbo, the chief of the Ammaroscoggin. In the fall of 1690 Captain Benjamin Church attacked Worumbo's Fort at Ammaroscoggin (Auburn, Maine). In the course of this attack Kancamagus's sister was killed, and his wife and two children were taken prisoner. It is said that the great chief died shortly after signing the truce of Sagadahoc on November 29, 1690. The treaty was signed, as Samuel Drake put it, "on the water in canoes, when the wind blew" (quoted in Bouton 1866, 438, n.), "a *fluctuating* and *unstable* sort of business," commented Cotton Mather in 1702 (quoted in Stewart-Smith, "Pennacook Indians and the New England Frontier," 233), as indeed it proved to be.

PART I

PREHISTORY

1

New Hampshire's Prehistoric Settlement and Chronology

Victoria Bunker

New Hampshire's full prehistoric settlement pattern system can never be known because only its remnants survive at archaeological sites. It is as if we are trying to complete a jigsaw puzzle with most of the pieces missing. With the completion of more archaeological surveys, we are discovering sites in locations archaeologists once believed were never occupied. Perceptions of where and how people lived in New Hampshire during the prehistoric past have evolved as new archaeological data have been interpreted. We are also refining our views of chronology, subsistence, resource utilization, and past human activities. With this information, we are slowly filling in pieces of the puzzle. Not surprisingly, the more we look, the more we find.

People have lived in New Hampshire for the past 10,000 years. During this time, they did not roam aimlessly across the landscape but made choices on when and where to settle and on the types of activities best suited for each place. Today, the archaeological record allows interpretation of these choices, but the record is beset with problems. Fine chronological resolution is often absent, especially where stratigraphy is mixed or compressed and when temporally diagnostic artifacts are not preserved. Many sites contain multiple occupation phases, which are often mixed or merged. Regional boundaries, territories, and the spatial organization of human activity are generally vague and often arbitrarily defined. Site formation processes—including how artifacts enter the archaeological record and their subsequent movement or preservation by man or nature—introduce biases.

Historic and modern land use has obscured or obliterated huge tracts of the prehistoric landscape, eliminating the opportunity to acquire important data (see Zvelebil et al. 1992: 196–197). Despite problems and biases, we can examine changes in the way people used places over

Source: Victoria Bunker, "New Hampshire's Prehistoric Settlement and Chronology," *New Hampshire Archeologist* 33–34, no. 1 (1994): 20–28.

time and can discuss some aspects of prehistoric settlement patterns in New Hampshire. Since reconstruction of prehistoric cultural systems is notoriously difficult because of limits in the archaeological data, our investigation of settlement is based largely on study of the landscape. This involves viewing the environmental qualities which may have made particular places or features attractive to humans in the past. While this is not necessarily the best nor the only way to study settlement patterns, it is an approach which archaeologists have used in New Hampshire to date.

CHRONOLOGY

Archaeologists have divided New Hampshire's prehistory into several broad chronological periods based on data from archaeological sites, artifact collections, and analogues from sites elsewhere in New England and the Northeast. Radiocarbon dating and detailed artifact analysis have refined chronological sequences, but temporal resolution has not yet been obtained for New Hampshire prehistory. Our chronological framework is very broad, and there are vast gaps for every cultural period. Unfortunately, much of our classification is based on single artifact types rather than entire artifact assemblages. This has introduced a significant interpretive bias such that sites without diagnostic artifacts cannot be placed in time. We have also developed a tendency to view past cultures in terms of the projectile points or pots people made, a highly dangerous situation which does not accommodate past peoples' rich diversity in material and nonmaterial culture.

The periods recognized in New Hampshire include the Paleo-Indian (ca. 11,000–9,000 B.P., years before present);

Early (9,000–8,000 B.P.), Middle (8,000–6,000 B.P.), and Late (6,000–3,000 B.P.) Archaic; Early (3,000–2,000 B.P.), Middle (2,000–1,000 B.P.), and Late (1,000–400 B.P.) Woodland; and Contact (400–200 B.P.).

The Paleo-Indian period marks the earliest known human occupation of New Hampshire. The period is represented largely by the presence of scattered diagnostic artifacts, primarily in the form of fluted points or edge tools, such as an Eden point discovered on the Merrimack River (Berry 1937) or fluted points discovered on the Saco River (Sargent and Ledoux 1973). A complete Paleo-Indian assemblage, or tool kit, has been recognized at only one site (the Whipple site) in the state (Curran 1980 and Curran 1994), and analysis is underway on another site in the Merrimack Valley (Stinson 1988). Only a single radiocarbon date for this period has been obtained in New Hampshire; this is a date of 9,615 ± 225 B.P. from Weirs Beach on Lake Winnipesaukee (Bolian 1980: 124). During this period, the population was probably quite small, relied on hunting for subsistence, was highly mobile, and fashioned tools from a variety of materials, including cherts from distant sources. The distribution of known finds suggests that the Paleo-Indians focused their settlement around a mosaic of streams and wetlands, including those which formed in the drainage basins of proglacial lakes. Lake shores, lake outlets, and high river terraces were also selected for occupation. The diversity of resources in these settings would have been attractive to a highly mobile population and may partially account for the wide distribution of sites and materials seen today (Nicholas 1983; Spiess 1992).

The Early Archaic is believed to represent a transition to settling in. Diagnostic bifaces are rare but include the

Bifurcate Base, Kirk, and Dalton point types, commonly recognized in southern New England (Johnson and Mahlstedt 1984). A nonbifacial tool kit has been recently recognized throughout northern New England during the Early Archaic period (Robinson et al. 1992). Quartz is the primary stone tool material in this tool kit, which consists of a variety of steep and beaked unifacial edge tools, cores, and flakes. Other tools include a diverse range of ground stone tools, such as full-channeled gouges and ground stone rods. Bifaces are rare and may have been manufactured of wood or bone (Robinson 1992). In New Hampshire, several eighth millennium components have been defined at deeply stratified sites, such as the Eddy site at Amoskeag Falls and the Wadleigh Falls site on the Lamprey River, where quartz cores, edge tools, and cobble tools form the artifact assemblages (Bunker 1992; Maymon and Bolian 1992). Early Archaic peoples appear to have occupied lake shores and lake outlets as well as river terraces, particularly those associated with major falls.

The Middle Archaic is characterized as a period of broad regionalism. People lived in widely distributed locations. Settlement along major waterways and lakes is believed to reflect a reliance on aquatic resources, such as anadromous fish. Highly visible Middle Archaic components have been recognized at major falls along large rivers. The Neville site at Amoskeag Falls has served as a base line for interpreting Middle Archaic sites elsewhere in the state (Dincauze 1976). We have also begun to recognize Middle Archaic sites in other locations along river tributaries, on secondary perennial streams, and on high terraces away from main rivers (Bunker and Potter 1993; Potter 1993; Starbuck 1981). One feature of the Middle Archaic is an increased usage of volcanic stone tool materials from

regional sources such as the Ossipee Mountains or the Boston Basin. Stone tool materials were transported as cores or preforms to locations where they were reduced to final biface form. Quartz continued to be utilized as a stone tool material and was probably most often quarried from vein sources. Neville (ca. 7,500 B.P.) and Stark (ca. 7,000 B.P.) complexes define the earlier years of the Middle Archaic, while the Merrimack complex (ca. 6,000 B.P.) defines the transition into the Late Archaic period.

The Late Archaic is typically defined in New England by three prominent traditions: the Small Stemmed, the Laurentian, and the Susquehanna, or Broad Blade. The material culture of the Small Stemmed tradition typically includes small triangular or stemmed bifaces. The material culture of the Laurentian tradition typically includes bifaces of the Otter Creek, Vosburg, and Brewerton types, defined from sites in New York state, as well as ground stone tools and cobble tools such as adzes, plummets, gouges, and ulus. The material culture of the Broad Blade tradition typically includes Susquehanna and Perkiomen bifaces, defined from sites outside New England, as well as broad implement blades such as the Atlantic, Wayland Notched, and Mansion Inn types, defined from sites in southern New England. By the end of the period, the Orient Fishtail point is the prominent biface. Large implement blades are widely associated with the Late Archaic (Johnson and Mahlstedt 1984). Burial ceremonialism is an important feature of the period; for example, ritual breakage, or "killing," of Susquehanna bifaces is known from a site in Litchfield along the Merrimack River, and cremation burials were practiced (Bunker 1988: 27–28). Also during the Late Archaic, steatite is used for the manufacture of stone bowls.

Diverse stone tool materials characterize the Late Archaic. Locally available lithics were heavily utilized and include quartz from vein and cobble sources, crystal quartz, argillicious materials, and volcanics (Boisvert 1992; Bunker and Potter 1993). Materials from greater distances include quartzites, cherts, and volcanics. Volcanic materials utilized during this period originated from regional source areas, including the Ossipee Mountains of New Hampshire, Mt. Kineo in Maine, and the Blue Hills, Attleboro, and North Shore locales of Massachusetts.

The exact relationships of the major Late Archaic traditions have yet to be untangled; many sites contain artifacts assigned to two or more traditions, suggesting that cultural boundaries were not clear-cut. Late Archaic period sites are found virtually everywhere in New Hampshire along both major and minor water features; throughout New England, the Late Archaic exhibits a strong riverine orientation (Dewar and McBride 1992: 248). People probably practiced a subsistence economy based on hunting, fishing, shellfish collecting, and plant gathering. Culture contact beyond the immediate geographic locale is reflected in morphological and functional artifact diversity, an influx of exotic stone tool materials, and the practice of ceremonial ritualism. These wide culture contacts, mobility, and diversity characterize the Late Archaic.

The cultural dynamism of the Late Archaic continued into the Woodland period. The Woodland is considered "cosmopolitan" (Dincauze 1976: 132) in contrast to the preceding Archaic period. This period is marked by the debut of ceramics in the material culture. In the neighboring state of Maine, the period is known as the Ceramic rather than the Woodland to emphasize a continuation of a hunting-gathering lifestyle with the adoption of ceramics (Spiess 1991). While the tradi-

tional view of the Woodland includes a horticultural economy, horticulture was not a primary subsistence factor in New Hampshire. Instead, people continued their reliance on wild foods, with domesticated plants playing only a minor role very late in the period. For example, only a single kernel of prehistoric flint corn has been discovered in the entire Merrimack Valley of New Hampshire (Bunker 1988). The Early, Middle, and Late Woodland periods are subdivided on the basis of ceramic style and technology, as well as typological differences in formal stone tools. The age of the first appearance of pottery is continuously being pushed back in time; new dates from the Beaver Meadow Brook site and the Eddy site now place the first pottery in the Merrimack Valley at 3,150 ± 125 B.P. (Howe 1988: 82) and 3,315 ± 90 B.P. (Bunker 1986). Regional interaction increased through the Woodland period as is evident in ceramic decorative techniques and the use of diverse stone tool materials, including exotic cherts. Bifaces diagnostic of the Early Woodland are Meadowood and Rossville; for the Middle Woodland, they are the Jack's Reef pentagonal and stemmed types as well as Woodland Lanceolate bifaces; and for the Late Woodland, they are large triangles of the Levanna type (Johnson and Mahlstedt 1984). A "bewildering diversity" (Dincauze 1976: 132) of lithic materials characterizes the Woodland period, with stones from nonlocal sources strongly represented in the archaeological record. Sites are located along streams, rivers, and the coast throughout the Woodland. The appearance of large storage features at sites in prominent riverine or coastal locations suggests new storage technology by the Late Woodland. This may coincide with population growth, nucleation, or increased sedentism.

The Contact period, with the arrival

of European traders, fishermen, explorers, and surveyors, marks the end of prehistory. The archaeological assemblage includes items of both native and European origin. European materials were often transformed to suit native needs, such as copper kettles cut into effigy pendants or ballast flint used for stone tool manufacture. By the mid-1600s, contacts had extended far into the interior; for example, a fort was built by English carpenters on Lake Ossipee as protection against the Mohawk (Colby 1975: 146). The native population neared extinction during this period from war and disease. Dean Snow (1980: 34) has estimated that the local Western Abenaki population was reduced by 98 percent from 10,000 to 250 individuals. Survivors often abandoned their traditional lands and moved north to join the community at St. Francis, Quebec. While Contact period sites are notoriously ephemeral, sources indicate that trading centers, villages, and forts were located on the coast and along major rivers (Robinson and Bolian 1987; Bunker 1988; Starbuck 1982; Thomas 1979). Sheltered locations or isolated hilltops were also selected for habitation, perhaps to escape the pressures of war, disease, or land acquisition as Europeans encroached.

ANTHROPOLOGICAL FRAMEWORK

New England archaeologists have long believed that the "distribution of natural resources conditions the location of human settlements" (Thorbahn and Cox 1988: 174), or that environmental factors are "deterministic" for settlement, subsistence, and technology (Ritchie and Funk 1973: 2). This approach focuses on the economic reasons for people's movement and settlement and incorporates

environmental change, seasonal food availability, and fluctuations in biological (e.g., plants, fish, shellfish, and game animals) productivity. Generally this approach views the most desirable settlement locations as those which exhibited either a mix of resources or easy access to several ecological zones with diverse resources.

Site types and their distribution are usually thought to reflect prehistoric economic systems; movement to resources is viewed as necessary for subsistence and survival. Snow (1980: 14–15) has described most prehistoric New England community patterns as a continuum between "central-based wandering" or "semipermanent sedentary" patterns. Snow also uses the "restricted wandering" pattern to discuss the earliest New England sites (Snow 1980: 129). These patterns were first defined in 1955 (Beardsley et al. 1955) as tools for visualizing and interpreting human communities and their mobility.

The restricted wandering community pattern is defined as "communities that wander about within a territory that they define as theirs and defend against trespass, or on which they have exclusive rights to food resources of certain kinds. Movement within the territory may be erratic or may follow a seasonal round, depending on the kind of wild food resources utilized" (Beardsley et al. 1955: 136) The central-based wandering community pattern is defined as "a community that spends part of each year wandering and the rest at a settlement or 'central base,' to which it may or may not consistently return in subsequent years" (Bearsley et al. 1955: 138). The semipermanent sedentary community pattern is defined as "a community, which can be identified with a village, that establishes itself in successive locations, occupying each for a period of years. The population is stable and continuously sedentary, but able to be so only by moving the village periodically" (Bearsley et al. 1955: 140). This approach acknowledges that "economic, sociopolitical, and ceremonial interrelationships" are significant but that improved subsistence is key to evolution (Beardsley et al. 1955: 134). Thus, the model is deeply rooted in human exploitation of natural resources, establishing a perception of the reasons prehistoric people moved across the landscape.

People had many ways of accommodating resource variety and fluctuations. People could choose "focal" or "diffuse" adaptations when resources were plentiful or scarce (Snow 1980: 15). Storage and mobility are two mechanisms for smoothing fluctuations in resource variability (Snow 1980: 15). Mobility allows people to gain "space utility" of resources by using a wider area than that in which the resource is actually available (Binford 1978: 138). Storage allows people to gain "time utility" from resources by storing and using resources for a longer time than they are actually available (Binford 1978: 138). Economic and seasonal activity is not the sole determinant of settlement patterns (Dewar and McBride 1992: 228), and New England sites rarely fit neatly into community pattern definitions because available data are generally insufficient. In particular, the high resolution data necessary to define single annual rounds, finely tuned component ages, or specific examples of occupations linked through each of four seasons simply do not exist (Dewar and McBride (1992: 229). Instead, we are only able to study "remnant settlement patterns," the product of many processes both natural and cultural (Dewar and McBride 1992: 230). What we view in the archaeological record is the product of individual people during individual seasons at individual locations. The clarity of the record is obscured by preservation and

discovery factors and by our ability to read past human sequences and choices.

Economic and seasonal factors work well in explaining observed archaeological site locations. They are relatively clear to archaeologists in the form of tool kits with defined functions, seasonal plant or animal remains, and settings in landscapes with certain known or likely resources (e.g., landform, favorable aspect, elevation, surface water, plant or animal communities). They also correlate relatively well with ethnographic data from New England and other areas beyond our region. Another factor, however, is equally responsible for past settlement—people.

People have many reasons for making decisions about the favorability of a site. Social or political boundaries, the distance to the next occupied location, or taboos are important determinants. Because humans tend to change their environment, the effects of recent past habitation can alter site attractiveness. A site may become less attractive if recent occupants used up all the firewood and left waste or parasites behind. A site may become more attractive if recent occupants altered the setting to attract game or left behind structures or caches (Dewar and McBride 1992: 232–233). If a strong and stable resource is available, people may have had no effect on it, and a location may be repeatedly occupied. People also schedule their use of resources, monitoring depletion or generation, so that reoccupation can be planned without negative effect. These variables are crucial in identifying a settlement pattern, but they are accessible only to ethnographers. Archaeologists rarely observe this variability and only view the surviving traces.

Trends and patterns are still evident in the archaeological record, even though the full agency responsible may not be visible. Some places may be occupied only once; others may be reoccupied many times. The variation observed in the "spatial congruence" of sites may reflect certain human choices and effects. Sites may be "concentrated," "localized," or "dispersed" due to varying degrees of impact by subsequent occupants in a single location (Dewar and McBride 1992: 234). Certain places on the landscape must have been so rich, special, or unique as to invite persistent occupation; other locations may not have been attractive at all and never occupied.

PREHISTORIC SITE SETTING

There are archaeological sites with components datable to all periods of prehistory throughout New Hampshire. Site locations are known from a variety of sources, including accounts in local and regional histories; artifacts in private collections or public institutions; and accounts of professional or avocational archaeologists recorded in statewide site survey files maintained by the New Hampshire Archeological Society and the New Hampshire Division of Historical Resources or reported in published and unpublished sources. There are certain biases in the data base which reflect archaeological activity rather than actual prehistoric settlement. Most of the known sites are located within the lakes region, in the Merrimack Valley, or on the New Hampshire seacoast. This reflects the vigor of amateur archaeologists, the focus of several university projects, and the locations of greatest contemporary growth, which prompted cultural resources management surveys. The extensive farmlands in these areas also provided nineteenth- and twentieth-century artifact collectors with easy access to surface finds in plowed fields. Site locations are less well known in other portions of the state due to less

intensive study. These areas include the Connecticut River valley, the White Mountains, eastern rivers such as the Saco, Ossipee, Salmon Falls, or Piscataqua, and the North Country.

Variation in prehistoric site setting through time is not visible. The lack of radiocarbon dates and the absence of temporally diagnostic artifacts at many sites is partially responsible. Continuity in settlement choice through time is also responsible. Generally, the entire New Hampshire landscape was available for occupation in early postglacial times. Fluctuations in stream and sea level and climatic changes (with accompanying changes in vegetative and animal communities) may have made some locations more accessible or more desirable for settlement than others. New Hampshire sites share a number of attributes, and certain features of the landscape witnessed more occupation than others. There are general trends, unique cases, and exceptions to every rule.

Most prehistoric people located themselves near surface water features. These features vary in size and type, including the ocean, major rivers and their tributaries, estuaries, seasonal and perennial streams, wetlands, springs, ponds, and lakes. People occupied islands, estuary heads, and locations where two or more features intersect (e.g., stream and river confluences, lake outlets, or stream and wetland junctions), and they lived near falls and rapids. Wetlands are now recognized as an important feature for prehistoric peoples (Nicholas 1992). People lived along shorelines or stream and river margins where no differentiating factors are apparent today. Sites are often found in protected settings, in coves or bays, or out of the wind; sites are rarely found on open beaches. Sites are found on high terraces and bluffs with commanding vistas of river valleys below.

Sites are generally located on well-drained soils, not on poorly drained soils. In the coastal area, where soils of good and poor drainage are interfingered, sites are positioned on the soils of better drainage even when poorly drained soils occur only a few meters away. Sites are generally located on stone-free soils, usually those formed in alluvial or outwash deposits—the soils which are commonly associated with stream or river valleys. Sites are less frequently positioned on till-based soils, unless these are the soils along the margins of a water feature. Sites with alluvial soils typically exhibit deep cultural stratigraphy, often extending a meter or more below ground surface, with site remains periodically buried by flooding. Site deposits on outwash or till soils exhibit shallow or compressed cultural stratigraphy. This is due to the absence of additional sediment deposition to separate cultural episodes. The way sites are positioned on an irregular surface, a slope, a terrace margin, a knoll, or a shoreline may be the most telling of human choices.

Sites are not generally found on very steep slopes or very rocky landscapes. Yet there is evidence that hilltop and mountain locations were attractive, as were caves or rock shelters. These settings may have provided lookouts, may have been easily defensible, or may have been near stone well suited for the manufacture of tools.

With increasing distance from prominent landscape features, site size, artifact quantity, and number of occupations decreases. That is, sites with the largest area, highest artifact density, and greatest number of occupations are located in distinctive settings. These include major river channels, particularly at falls or river confluences, the interface of tidal estuaries and fresh water, and the outlets of lakes. It is easy to speculate that reliable, predictable, and abundant food resources would have been readily available at such locations, making them desirable for occupation by large groups of people. These might include fish runs at Amoskeag Falls, or the Weirs, or equal access to coastal and interior fish, game, and shellfish at seacoast sites. It then becomes easy to imagine people congregating at these places during certain seasons and dispersing to other places during other times of the year. Perhaps this did happen. Perhaps other factors were equally responsible for the persistence we see in the archaeological deposits at certain spots. Perhaps major falls along a river would have been a barrier to travel and a natural stopping place, or perhaps they were natural focal points. Perhaps river confluences were landmarks and access routes to interior highlands. Perhaps certain spots marked cultural, political, or social boundaries; others may have been centers for congregating or trading; others may have been defensible or offered vantages; and yet others may have been neutral zones between tribal entities.

Most of New Hampshire's prehistoric sites are multicomponent. People visited the same location many times in the past, often at intervals of thousands of years. While the same site location was repeatedly selected, individual components are not always precisely spatially congruent—often components are horizontally separated by tens of hundreds of meters. Some sort of continuity in attractiveness must have existed for these places. At some locations, the range of activities was nearly identical even though habitation was separated by thousands of years. For example, plant food processing was repeated at the Smolt site in Litchfield from the Archaic through the Woodland (Kenyon 1983), and manufacture of bifaces from cores or preforms was repeated at the Mason site in Pembroke throughout the Archaic (Bunker and Potter 1993). Does this reflect conservatism? tradition?

adaptive and technological stability? resource availability? or chance?

FUTURE DIRECTIONS

Because large sites and sites with many artifacts are highly visible, they have naturally become the focus of archaeology in New Hampshire. When the entire prehistoric landscape is considered, the role of these sites will be less dominant, and a more complete view of settlement pattern will emerge. To make these patterns visible, one key variable must be refined—time. With a temporal scale as broad as the one we now have, understanding the relationship of New Hampshire's many sites is next to impossible. This is coupled with the constraints of poor preservation, weak ethnography, incomparable data samples, and lack of evidence for seasonality. It is no wonder that environmental and economic models—the easiest to understand and simplest to apply—are so often used to interpret our prehistoric sites.

Despite gaps in our knowledge, simply looking for more sites will not be sufficient. Instead, we must better interpret the sites we already have recorded. We can stretch our research questions to include cultural, social, and political issues and look for settlement causes beyond annual rounds based on food or resource availability. A first step would be to study single component sites, where activities are not blurred by repeated occupations over several time periods. At multiple-occupation sites, we need to recognize components and define their relationship to contemporaneous locations in the same immediate landscape. Another starting place would be to investigate more sites at greater distances from prominent natural features. At interior, upland, or backland sites we are likely to have better temporal,

seasonal, and functional resolution. We can also turn to less-developed areas of the state where preservation of the full range of sites is less likely to have been compromised by modern and historic development. A more thorough review of ethnographic data in sixteenth- and seventeenth-century accounts may give insights, as might critical reading of romanticized Indian tales of the nineteenth century. Although historic accounts are often flawed by the views of the teller, they are usually based on traditions which have their roots in reality. In all attempts, we must remain sensitive to biases in interpretation from preservation or data accessibility.

Finally, we need to remember that when using archaeological data we can only view the remnants of what must have been a rich and integrated social system. Given the great time depth of our sites, we can begin to understand dynamics, changes, and past choices for settlement throughout the ancient New Hampshire landscape.

References

Beardsley, Richard, Preston Holder, Alex Krieger, Betty J. Meggers, John Rinaldo and Paul Kutsche
1955 Functional and Evolutionary Implications of Community Patterning. Seminars in Archaeology: 1955. *Society for American Archaeology, Memoir*, vol. 11: 129–155.

Binford, Lewis
1978 Jochim: Hunter-Gatherer Subsistence and Settlement: A Predicative Model. *American Antiquity*, vol. 43(1): 137–138.

Boisvert, Richard
1992 X-Ray Diffraction Analysis of Lithics from West Branch Brook Site 27-CA, Madison, NH. *New Hampshire Archeological Society Newsletter*, vol. 8(2): 7–8.

Bolian, Charles
1980 The Early and Middle Archaic of the

Lakes Region, New Hampshire. *Occasional Publications in Northeastern Anthropology*, vol. 7: 115–134.

Bunker, Victoria
1986 The Eddy Site. Field notes on file at Phillips Exeter Academy.
1988 Archeological Survey of Litchfield, New Hampshire. Report on file at NH Division of Historical Resources.
1992 Stratified Components of the Gulf of Maine Archaic Tradition at the Eddy Site, Amoskeag Falls. *Occasional Publications in Maine Archaeology*, vol. 9: 135–148.

Bunker, Victoria, and Jane Potter
1993 Archeological Research Study: Data Recovery at the Mason Site. Draft report in preparation for Stone and Webster Engineering Corporation, Boston, Massachusetts.

Colby, Solon
1975 *Colby's Indian History*. Center Conway: Walkers Pond Press.

Curran, Mary Lou
1980 *Studying Human Adaptation at a Paleo-Indian Site: A Preliminary Report*. Research Report 18, University of Massachusetts, Amherst.

Dewar, Robert, and Kevin McBride
1992 Remnant Settlement Patterns. In *Space, Time, and Archaeological Landscapes*, ed. by J. Rossignol and L. Wandsnider. New York: Plenum Press, pp. 193–226.

Dincauze, Dena F.
1976 *The Neville Site: 8000 Years at Amoskeag*. Peabody Museum Monograph No. 4. Cambridge, MA.

Howe, Dennis E.
1988 The Beaver Meadow Brook Site: Prehistory on the West Bank at Sewall's Falls, Concord, New Hampshire. *The New Hampshire Archeologist*, vol. 29(1): 49–107.

Johnson, Eric, and Thomas Mahlstedt
1984 *Guide to Prehistoric Site Files and Artifact Classification System*. Massachusetts Historic Commission, Boston, MA.

Kenyon, Victoria
1983 The Smolt Site: Seasonal Occupation in the Merrimack Valley. *The New Hampshire Archeologist*, vol. 24.

Maymon, Jeffrey, and Charles Bolian
1992 The Wadleigh Falls Site: An Early and Middle Archaic Period Site in Southeastern New Hampshire. *Occasional Publications in Maine Archaeology*, vol. 9: 117–134.

Nicholas, George
1979 The Cohas Brook Site (NH 45–24), Manchester, New Hampshire: a Preliminary Report. *The New Hampshire Archeologist*, vol. 20: 1–30.

Potter, Jane
1993 Phase II Intensive Archeological Survey, Nashua Project. Report on file at NH Division of Historical Resources.

Ritchie, William, and Robert Funk
1973 *Aboriginal Settlement Patterns in the Northeast*. Memoir 20, New York State Museum and Science Service. Albany, NY.

Robinson, Brian
1992 Early and Middle Archaic Period Occupation in the Gulf of Maine Region: Mortuary and Technological Patterning. *Occasional Publications in Maine Archaeology*, vol. 9: 63–116.

Robinson, Brian, and Charles Bolian
1987 A Preliminary Report on the Rocks Road Site (Seabrook Station): late Archaic to Contact Period Occupation in Seabrook, New Hampshire. *The New Hampshire Archeologist*, vol. 28(1): 19–51.

Robinson, Brian, James Petersen and Anne Robinson, eds.
1992 Early Holocene Occupation in Northern New England. *Occasional Publications in Maine Archaeology*, Number Nine.

Sargent, Howard, and Francois Ledoux
1973 Two Fluted Points from New England. *Man in the Northeast*, vol. 5: 67–68.

Snow, Dean R.
1980 *The Archaeology of New England*. New York: Academic Press.

Spiess, Arthur
1991 Ceramic Period Study Unit. Manuscript on file at Maine Historic Preservation Commission, Augusta, Maine.
1992 Late Paleoindian Context. Manuscript on file at Maine Historic Preservation Commission, Augusta, Maine.

Starbuck, David R.

1981 *NH 31-20-5. A Middle Archaic Site in Belmont, New Hampshire.* State of New Hampshire, Department of Public Works and Highways.

1982 Excavations at Sewall's Falls (NH 31-30) in Concord, NH. *The New Hampshire Archeologist*, vol. 23: 1–36.

Stinson, Wesley

1988 Division of Historical Resources, Archeology in Merrimack. *New Hampshire Archeological Society Newsletter*, vol. 4(2): 3–4.

Thomas, Peter

1979 In the Maelstrom of Change. The Indian Trade and Cultural Process in the Middle Connecticut River Valley: 1635–1655. Ph.D. Dissertation, Dept. of Anthropology, University of Massachusetts, Amherst.

Thorbahn, Peter, and Deborah Cox

1988 The Effect of Estuary Formation on Prehistoric Settlement in Southern Rhode Island. In *Holocene Human Ecology in Northeastern North America*, ed. by George Nicholas. New York: Plenum Press, pp. 167–184.

Zvelebil, Marek, Stanton Green and Mark Macklin

1992 Archaeological Landscapes, Lithic Scatters, and Human Behavior. In *Space, Time, and Archaeological Landscapes*, ed. by J. Rossignol and L. Wandsnider. New York: Plenum Press, pp. 193–226.

2

Ancient Lifeways at the Smyth Site

Donald W. Foster,
Victoria B. Kenyon, George P. Nicholas II

The Smyth site represents a unique set of archaeological resources which has now, unfortunately, been destroyed. Although the data base recovered through the Smyth site excavation is not complete, increasingly sophisticated archaeological methods have allowed the recovery of more information from the data than was previously thought possible. While there are problems in the data base, the available evidence has been approached as objectively as possible. It is hoped that the examination of the Smyth site will promote a greater public awareness of New Hampshire's cultural resources and will help preserve its fragile mantle of archaeological sites.*

History and Excavation

"The Indians tell us of a beautiful river far to the south which they call the Merrimack," wrote the Sieur De Monts from the banks of the St. Lawrence in 1604, and thus did this important river make its first appearance in the annals of recorded history.

The river is formed in the White Mountains by the confluence of the Pemigewasset and Winnipesaukee rivers and empties into the Atlantic Ocean 110 miles (171.5 km) away. In Manchester—approximately halfway between the mountains and the ocean—are the largest of the Merrimack's many series of falls

The description, analysis, and write-up of the Smyth Site materials took place at the Department of Anthropology, the Phillips Exeter Academy. Major funding for the laboratory analysis has been provided by a Federal Historic Preservation Survey and Planning Grant-in-aid, administered by the State of New Hampshire Historic Preservation Office, contract number 93327. Funds supporting the preparation of this manuscript were provided by the Norwin and Elizabeth Bean Foundation.

Source: Donald W. Foster, Victoria B. Kenyon, George P. Nicholas II, "Ancient Lifeways at the Smyth Site, NH38-4," *New Hampshire Archeologist* 22, no. 2 (1981): 1–17.

and rapids. This area of the river, as well as the surrounding countryside, was called by the Indians *Namoskeag*, or "fishing place."

The river served as a highway for travel from the Atlantic Ocean to the White Mountains. When the first European settlers arrived (a few years before the town of Derryfield was officially chartered in 1751) to take advantage of the area's abundant resources, it was not surprising that they found evidence all about them of the Indians who had fished, trapped, hunted, and camped for centuries in this same fertile valley. When the Europeans first arrived, the Indian populations had already been greatly depleted. Early records indicate that in 1616 an epidemic of an unknown disease broke out among the Indians along the coast. The actual disease and its cause have never been definitely determined, yet whatever it was, its effects were devastating (Hoornbeek 1978). It has been estimated that 19 out of every 20 Indians died before the disease ended four years later in 1620. This disease may have slowly made its way up the Merrimack and affected the population at Amoskeag.

Although both oral tradition and history agree that the Amoskeag area was of great importance to the native peoples, the historical records are scanty. For the most part, the early settlers had little desire or leisure time in which to examine and record the culture of these people. It was not until the 1800s that Americans began to take an interest in the "noble savage." By that time, however, only a handful of accounts were on record, and from what oral traditions were left, it was difficult to separate truth from fiction. Who were these Indians who first appeared in written records? Of the preceding thousands of years there was little known.

In 1967, archaeologists—both amateur and professional—were presented with a unique opportunity to find some of the answers to this perplexing question. It was learned that the Amoskeag bridge was to be replaced with a new and much larger structure with new approaches. In addition, the entire block lying between West Salmon, River, and West North streets would be leveled to provide a parking lot for the New Hampshire Insurance Group building. This meant that the entire bluff above the river would be demolished. Several smaller Indian sites had already been excavated throughout the state. However, it had long been known that on this bluff overlooking Amoskeag Falls was one of the largest prehistoric sites along the Merrimack River.

The site of the main area to be excavated was located on a large dune built up about 13,000 years ago. As the late Wisconsin ice sheet receded, large amounts of sand and gravel were deposited over the region; prior to the establishment of initial vegetation, large amounts of sand were blown up from the river and deposited over the bedrock.

The first archaeological inquiry at Amoskeag took place in 1930 when Warren K. Moorehead of the Robert S. Peabody Foundation obtained permission to sink test pits around the estate. Some of these were placed in Mrs. Smyth's treasured flower gardens. These test pits showed evidence of Indian occupation down to depths of 4.5 feet below the surface (Moorehead 1931).

It was the late Solon Colby who first learned in 1966 that plans for the new bridge also included the destruction of the bluff on which the Smyth mansion stood. He felt certain that this site was the most heavily utilized settlement in New Hampshire and that the cultural materials buried there would show great antiquity (Colby 1975). He obtained permission from the New Hampshire Insurance Company, owners of the land, for the NHAS (New Hampshire Archeological Society) to begin excavations the following year in an effort to extract as much information as possible before the site was destroyed forever. Thus, in the summer of 1967, the NHAS with only a small handful of volunteers began the excavation of the south lawn of the Smyth estate.

The excavation at Amoskeag proceeded slowly due to one burdensome (and yet necessary) restriction agreed upon by both the insurance company and the NHAS: "No excavations could be left open after sundown, as these would constitute hazards to people wandering over the area" (Colby 1975, 58). The few volunteers, able to work only on weekends, had to spend a great deal of their time backfilling their pits before leaving the site at the end of each day, only to laboriously dig them out again at the beginning of each new day. It was soon recognized by Colby and by Eugene Winter, the director of the society's dig, that more workers were needed.

In the summer of 1968, students from Franklin Pierce College, under the direction of Howard Sargent, with matching funds from the college, the New Hampshire Bureau of Public Roads, and the Manchester Historic Association, began a large-scale formal salvage operation of the portion of the site to be destroyed by the new bridge approach. With the increased help able to work five days a week and the ability to hire security guards 24 hours a day, seven days a week, it was possible to excavate more efficiently. The NHAS proceeded to excavate the large area of the south lawn and along the knoll northwest of the Smyth mansion.

Excavated materials were screened through four-to-the-inch wire mesh. The lack of clear-cut strata led the excavators to use arbitrary three-inch vertical levels for recovering materials. The five-foot squares were taken down using trowels with some shoveling.

All archaeological work ended on the Smyth site in 1969 when construction for the new bridge made it impossible to continue excavations. The Smyth mansion was quickly turned into a heap of rubble, and the entire bluff was bulldozed and leveled off, leaving only a parking lot and a paved approach to the new Amoskeag bridge. Yet much information was gathered during that brief period of excavation. ...

HISTORIC CONTEXT

Historic period modification of the natural landscape at the Smyth site has complicated the archaeological record. The land was once a part of the General John Stark farm. Deep plowmarks seen in the excavation profiles may be attributed to early farming by Stark.

Further disturbances of the archaeological context occurred on the property during the nineteenth century. In 1866, Governor Frederick Smyth bought ten acres of land, which was then covered with willows, elms, and birches, upon which to construct his estate, "The Willows":

> The land was undulating, and consisted of one prominent ridge overlooking river and falls, east of which crept a valley, and still farther east arose to the level of Elm Street. With the exceptions named, the plot was a barren sand bank, relieved by an unsightly swamp [Poore and Eaton, 449–54].

In order to improve the landscape, Smyth went to great lengths:

> A hedge of spruce was set about the entire lot, and after several years of labor in ditching, draining, grading, and top-dressing, the land assumed a new aspect. The sandy hill became a field of living green, the waters of the

swamp were collected into a pond, the underlying ledge which cropped out here and there was fringed with creeping vines and made to do duty in adding grace to the scenery, and everywhere was seen harmonious growth [*ibid.*].

The house was constructed, and the grounds were arranged:

> Many pieces of classic and modern statuary are placed in favorable situations, fountains play to cool the summer air, and rustic seats invite one to rest under wide-spreading willows [*ibid.*].

Outbuildings, including a windmill, a workmen's house, and a stable, were also constructed.

Recognition of these nineteenth-century disturbances is essential in evaluating the archaeological context of the Smyth site and in reconstructing the landscape and the resources available to prehistoric occupants. Evidence of these historic activities was recognizable in the archaeological record. Material remains, including ceramics, nails, bottle glass, kaolin pipes, and other household items, were recovered in the topsoil across the entire excavated area. Other materials were related to the construction and landscaping of the estate, notably brick and mortar fragments in excavation units near the house and granite "flakes" from statuary base finishing in areas of the south lawn.

Stratigraphically, both the John Stark plow zone and the Frederick Smyth grading and filling were recognized during the excavation. A thick, dark topsoil level was present in most excavation units.* This level contained historic as well as prehistoric materials. Apparently the grading and filling operation associated with the

house foundation construction and the pond dredging used soils bearing prehistoric cultural remains. One further subsurface historic disturbance included a trench to the north of the house; this may have been constructed to house the cables running between the house and the windmill.

PREHISTORIC CONTEXT

From available information it has been possible to make some inferences concerning the original landscape of the Smyth site and its natural and cultural stratigraphy. The bluff was probably well drained and dry, partially formed by wind-deposited sediments. The "unsightly swamp" which Governor Smyth dredged was located on the easternmost portion of the bluff approximately 200 feet from the edge of the terrace. Clearly, this natural feature made the site attractive to the prehistoric occupants. Fresh water could be obtained without descending the steep slope to the river. Furthermore, a variety of small mammals and reptiles from the marsh environment would have provided food for the residents of the site.

Once the river cut through to bedrock the falls probably provided the primary impetus for settlement. The site exhibits the heaviest occupation during the Middle Archaic and Middle Woodland periods. Neighboring areas of the Merrimack were probably intensively occupied during other time periods.

The natural stratigraphy of the Smyth site has been difficult to reconstruct due to the effects of intermittent human occupation over a 10,000-year period. The top 15 inches of the profile consists of dark brown, sandy loam. The remaining profile

---

*In some excavation units it was necessary for the Society members to dig through more than 20 or more inches of fill before the original topsoil was exposed.

differs in color but not in texture. The dark color of the topsoil is the result of plowing and the admixture of organic materials in recent times. Below the plow zone, soils are generally lighter in color. Their variable staining may be due to prehistoric occupation.

Discrete stratigraphic cultural levels cannot be identified below the plow zone at the Smyth site. Examination of the vertical distribution of lithic artifacts below the plow zone reveals the mixed nature of the cultural stratigraphy throughout the site. The greatest number of artifacts (representative of all time periods) comes from a 12-inch band lying between levels 6 and 9 (from 15 to 27 inches below the surface). This may be the result of slow deposition over the years. However, there is a great deal of soil buildup over many portions of the site—up to four feet—suggesting substantial soil deposition by wind or possibly flood. The occurrence of a heavy artifact-bearing level is a function of lateral displacement of artifacts during repeated occupation, or of site intrusion.

Additionally, intensive mixing of cultural levels is evident. Often Woodland artifacts are noted at greater depths than Archaic materials. It is unlikely that this is a function of either excavation bias, as it occurs regularly, or the continued manufacture of Archaic tool forms during the Early Woodland times. Instead, Woodland site intrusions, perhaps in the form of deep pits or other features, appear to be the cause. Vertical inversion of the artifacts is not the only explanation. Horizontal displacement of materials from prehistoric excavations—large pits—may also contribute to this pattern.

While a number of features have been identified, we suspect that many others were missed and not recorded during the excavation. Fire-cracked rock has been found distributed throughout the site with the bulk located outside of those areas where features have been recorded. Furthermore, charcoal has been recovered from nearly every excavation unit. The abundance of features suggested by the data indicates that site disturbance during prehistoric times was a common occurrence.

In an attempt to clarify the presence of cultural stratification and occupation floors, densities and frequencies of artifacts were examined. However, no significant patterns were identified. Furthermore, a series of horizontal and vertical scatter maps revealed no readily visible clusters of lithic artifacts, either by raw material, function, or chronological type.

In order to determine the existence of well-defined areas of tool manufacture on the site, correlation coefficients were calculated for cores, bifaces, and debitage by raw material types for each three-inch level within the excavation units. The findings of this test show no pattern, that is, the cores, debitage, and bifaces do not appear to have been deposited together, and the knowledge of the depositional context of one type does not help predict another.

An examination of horizontal and vertical distribution of debitage by raw material and pottery by weight and temporal association has further confirmed extensive prehistoric disturbance. Vertical and horizontal mixing, compact stratigraphy along with abundant features, and the large quantity of cultural material suggest intensive and repeated site use. ...

CHRONOLOGY

Paleo-Indian (10,000–8,000 B.P.)

Three artifacts associated with the Paleo-Indian period have been identified in the lithic sample. These include two fluted points and one removed base. While

Paleo-Indian tool kits are known to include many more artifact types, only the fluted points have been recognized in the Smyth site sample. As such, they are somewhat isolated contextually and offer only minimal indication that a Paleo-Indian occupation existed at Amoskeag. The likelihood of such an occupation is strengthened by the presence of other fluted points recovered from the Neville site (Dincauze 1976, 118–19). It should be recognized in this regard, however, that the local landscape 10,000 years ago would have been considerably different.

Early Archaic
(8,000–7,000 B.P.)

The typical diagnostic artifact for the Early Archaic period is the presence of bifurcate base points. Several bifurcates have been found in the Merrimack River valley (see Sargent 1976), however, none have been identified in the materials from the Smyth site. The Early Archaic is poorly known due to the paucity of diagnostic artifacts. While some researchers believe that a population hiatus accounts for the apparent low density of Early Archaic sites (Salwen 1975), others believe that the low density is more apparent than real, a function of our inability to recognize the full artifactual assemblage of the period (Starbuck 1977, Dincauze and Mulholland 1977). Unfortunately, the data from the Smyth site are insufficient to resolve this problem.

Middle Archaic
(7,000–6,000 B.P.)

The Middle Archaic is represented at the Neville site where three biface types have been defined (Dincauze 1976). These include the Stark, Neville, and Merrimack point types. Through comparison of Smyth site bifaces to those from the Neville site, a similar Middle Archaic assemblage has been recognized. In addition to these three types, the "Neville Variant," renamed the Amoskeag point, has been identified in the Smyth site sample. Identification of this point as a separate type has been done on the basis of its representation in the sample; the quantity of Amoskeag points is roughly equivalent to the number of Stark and Neville types. Stylistically, it is intermediate between the Stark and Neville points. The range of variation of the Amoskeag points is discrete enough to warrant separate treatment. Middle Archaic bifaces represent 60 percent of the typed lithics in the sample.

Late Archaic
(6,000–3,500 B.P.)

During the Late Archaic in New England, at least three cultural traditions manifest themselves, each with distinctive bifacial tool types. These are the Small Point tradition, the Susquehanna tradition, and the Laurentian tradition (Dincauze 1975b, Turnbaugh 1975). The Susquehanna and Laurentian traditions represent influences from outside New England: the Susquehanna River valley to the southwest and New York state to the west. The Small Point tradition represents a local tradition based on a quartz industry and appears to carry over into the Early Woodland period. All manifestations of the Late Archaic period have been found in the Smyth site assemblage. Included in the Small Point tradition are Squibnocket and Small Stemmed point types; in the Laurentian are the Brewerton, Normanskill, Otter Creek, and Vosburg point types; in the Susquehanna are the Susquehanna and Atlantic point types. Also present are Orient points representing a merging of Broad Blade and Small Stemmed styles along with steatite bowl fragments. Late Archaic point types constitute 31 percent of the temporally diagnostic biface sample. The Orient Fishtail type predominates with a virtual absence of Small points and Susquehanna points. Similarly, Laurentian items are present in low numbers, suggesting minimal interaction among Smyth site residents and groups to the west.

Early Woodland
(3,500–2,000 B.P.)

The Early Woodland time period is most easily recognized at the Smyth site by the presence of pottery, namely the Vinette I type, the earliest appearance of which is dated to 841 B.C. in New York state (Ritchie 1962). Also included are Rossville points and Stubenville points, representing 1 percent of the sample, and Meadowood points, which also account for 1 percent of the sample.

The scarcity of Early Woodland sites in the Northeast has been explained by a number of researchers in terms of a population decline related to changing environmental conditions and food resources (cf. Braun 1974). The inability to recognize artifactual materials associated with this time period, especially tool types which carried over from the Late Archaic, may account for some of the difficulty in the recognition of Early Woodland sites. If this is true, the relatively low proportions of Early Woodland materials at the Smyth site suggest a less-intensive occupation at this location on the east bank of the Amoskeag area. The question of an Early Woodland population hiatus cannot be resolved using the Smyth site data.

Middle Woodland
(2,000–1,000 B.P.)

During the Middle Woodland, a more intensive occupation of the site is apparent. Pottery associated with the Middle Woodland is abundant and is represented by stamped decorative motifs (Ritchie 1969).

Uniformity in the decorative techniques of Middle Woodland pottery is present throughout the New England area. These include use of stamped and cord-impressed decoration, dentate stamp, rocker stamp, punctation, scallop shell stamp, and cord-wrapped stick impression (Petersen 1980, Ritchie 1969, and Dincauze 1975a). All of these Middle Woodland decorative elements were present among the Smyth site pottery sample. The major lithic artifact type associated with the Middle Woodland occupation at the Smyth site is the Jack's Reef point, a point type established from New York state sites (Ritchie 1971). However, these occur in very low frequencies; only 2 percent of the biface assemblage has been assigned a Middle Woodland association.

Late Woodland
(1,000–500 B.P.)

The Late Woodland period has traditionally been characterized by the development of sedentary occupations based on crop cultivation. Horticulture is the primary mode of subsistence and is associated with large villages. Warfare and pallisaded settlements commonly appear. While these characteristics may have been present in some areas of the Northeast, it is doubtful that horticulture was an important food source in New England during the Late Woodland period. Studies by Ceci (1979) and Bourque (1973) and a closer examination of ethnohistorical documents suggest that horticulture and the development of large village settlements in the Northeast were responses to the contact situation rather than a previously established prehistoric settlement pattern.

There is no evidence from the Smyth

site that horticulture was practiced. Nor is there any evidence for permanent residence at the site. The Late Woodland occupation of the site appears instead to have been limited. Although a small proportion of Late Woodland pottery, with its incised decorative motifs and castellated forms, is present, influences from areas outside the Merrimack River valley appear to have been minimal. Late Woodland points also appear infrequently; the major point type for this period is the Levanna (Ritchie 1971) and represents only 6 percent of the sample.

Contact (500 B.P.)

The Contact period marks the beginning of European cultural influences. A series of plagues all but obliterated the Native American population in New Hampshire.

The presence of Contact period artifacts—sheet metal cutouts, beads, and points (Willoughby 1935)—indicates that the Amoskeag area was occupied during this period. Several beads and a bird-shaped metal cutout were recovered during the NHAS excavations in disturbed topsoil levels. Their original context may have been some distance from earlier occupation loci. There is the possibility that a trading post was located in the vicinity.

Many activities of Native Americans in the Amoskeag area were observed and described by European settlers in the seventeenth century. According to traditional accounts, the inhabitants at Amoskeag spent much time fishing; in the spring and autumn they would gather at the falls. Potter (1856, 56) claims that Passaconaway (chief of the Pennacook during the early English settlement) would spend the growing season in Concord (Penacook) while he established his principal "royal residence" at "Namaoskeag, upon

the bluff immediately east of the falls" where the Pennacook Federation would gather for meetings, councils, and feasting. Marshall (1942, 360) also claims that a large population had settled on the bluffs where the Smyth estate later stood.

Colby (1975, 52) contends that when the fish arrived at the falls about the middle of May, the Indians had already planted their crops elsewhere. They would come to Amoskeag, stay for two or three weeks, fish, and cure their catch. They would then return to their villages, leaving Amoskeag deserted. He feels, however, that occasionally the Pennacook tribe transferred its headquarters to Amoskeag during the fishing season and that the main village was situated on the "hill-bluff" on the east side of the river.

Archaeological data have failed to confirm the existence of a permanent village at Amoskeag. To the contrary, materials from the Late Woodland and Contact periods are minimal in comparison with those from the preceding Middle Woodland period.

SUMMARY

The artifactual remains from the Smyth site excavations indicate that the site was occupied throughout prehistory. Artifact totals suggest that the Middle and Late Archaic and the Middle Woodland periods exhibit the most abundant remains. Bifaces confirm this pattern for the Archaic and pottery for the Woodland. Bifaces from all prehistoric periods known in New England have been identified in the excavated material, including samples from the Paleo-Indian, Archaic, and Woodland periods.

During periods for which artifact representation is low, occupation at the site may have been equally intensive. As stated above, the lack of evidence confirming intensive occupation during these time periods might be the result of poor preservation. It might also be the case that different locations of the east bank became popular during different time periods and that the general Amoskeag area was continuously occupied.

References

Ahler, S. A.
1971 Projectile Point Form and Function at Rodgers Shelter, Missouri. *American Archaeological Society Research Series 8.*
1979 Functional Analysis of Nonobsidian Chipped Stone Artifacts, in *Lithic Use-Wear Analysis*, B. Hayden, ed. New York: Academic Press, pp. 301–328.

Ahler, S. A., and B. R. McMillan
1976 Material Culture at Rodgers Shelter, in *Prehistoric Man and His Environment*, W. R. Wood and R. B. McMillan, eds. New York: Academic Press, pp. 163–199.

Bourque, B.
1973 Aboriginal Settlement and Subsistence of the Maine Coast. *Man in the Northeast* 6: 3–20.

Braun, D.
1974 Explanatory Models for the Evaluation of Coastal Adaptation in Prehistoric Eastern United States. *American Antiquity* 39 (4): 582–596.

Callahan, E.
1979 The Basics of Biface Knapping in the Eastern Fluted Point Tradition. *Archaeology of Eastern North America* 7 (1): 1–179.

Ceci, L.
1979 Maize Cultivation in Coastal New York: The Archaeological, Agronomical, and Documentary Evidence. *North American Archaeologist* 1 (1): 45–74.

Colby, S.
1975 *Colby's Indian History*. Center Conway, NH: Walker's Pond Press.

Dincauze, D.
1975a Ceramic Sherds from the Charles River Valley. *Bulletin of the Archaeological Society of Connecticut* 39: 5–17.
1975b The Late Archaic Period in Southern New England. *Arctic Anthropology* 12 (2): 23–34.
1976 The Neville Site: 8,000 Years at Amoskeag. *Peabody Museum Monographs*, no. 4, Harvard University.

Dincauze, D. and M. Mulholland
1977 Early and Middle Archaic Site Distributions and Habitats in Southern New England. *Amerinds and Their Paleoenvironments in Northeastern North America*. Annals of the New York Academy of Science 288: 439–457.

Foster, D.
1978 Review. The Neville Site: 8,000 Years at Amoskeag, Manchester, New Hampshire. Dena Dincauze. *Historical New Hampshire* 33 (1): 62–67.

Greiser, S. T., and P. D. Sheets
1979 Raw Material as a Functional Variable in Use-Wear Studies, in *Lithic Use-Wear Analysis*, B. Hayden, ed. New York: Academic Press, pp. 289–296.

Hayden, B., ed.
1979 *Lithic Use-Wear Analysis*. New York: Academic Press.

Hoornbeek, B.
1978 An Investigation into the Cause or Causes of the Epidemic Which Decimated the Indian Population of New England, 1616–1619. *New Hampshire Archeologist* 19: 35–46.

Keeley, L. H.
1980 *Experimental Determination of Stone Tool Uses: A Microwear Analysis*. Chicago: University of Chicago Press.

Marshall, H.
1942 Some Ancient Indian Village Sites Adjacent to Manchester, N.H. *American Antiquity* 7 (4): 359–363.

Moorehead, W. K.
1931 *The Merrimack Archeological Survey*. Salem, Mass.: The Peabody Museum.

Nicholas, G. P.
1979 Variability in the Late Archaic: A Lithic Analysis. *American Archaeology Research Report Series 12*, University of Missouri-Columbia.
1981 Prehistoric Utilization of Crystal Quartz in Northern New England. *New Hampshire Archeologist* 22 (1): 49–64.

Petersen, J.
1980 The Middle Woodland Ceramics of the Winooski Site, A.D. 1–1000. New Series, Monograph #1, The Vermont Archaeological Society.

Poore, B. P., and F. P. Eaton
1885 *Sketches of the Life and Public Services of Frederick Smyth of New Hampshire.* Manchester, NH: John B. Clarke, Printer.

Potter, C.
1856 *History of Manchester.* Manchester, NH.

Ritchie, W. A.
1962 The Antiquity of Pottery in the Northeast. *American Antiquity* 27 (4): 583–584.
1969 *The Archaeology of New York State.* New York: The Natural History Press.
1971 *A Typology and Nomenclature for New York Projectile Points.* New York State Museum and Science Service. Bulletin 384.

Salwen, B.
1975 Post-Glacial Environments and Cultural Change in the Hudson River Basin. *Man in the Northeast* 10: 43–70.

Sargent, H.
1976 *A Preliminary Archeological Reconnaissance in the Winnipesaukee River Basin: Part I.* Copy on file at the New Hampshire State Historic Preservation Office.

Starbuck, D.
1977 Post-glacial Environments and Culture Change in the Hudson River Basin. *Man in the Northeast* 13: 96–99.

Turnbaugh, W.
1975 Toward an Explanation of the Broadpoint Dispersal in Eastern North American Prehistory. *Journal of Anthropological Research* 31: 51–68.

Willoughby, C.
1935 *Antiquities of the New England Indians.* Cambridge: The Peabody Museum, Harvard University.

Winter, E.
1975 The Smyth Site at Amoskeag Falls: A Preliminary Report. *New Hampshire Archeologist* 18: 5–8.

3

The Neville Site:
8,000 Years at Amoskeag

Dena F. Dincauze

The Neville site in Manchester, New Hampshire, was located near the lip of the Amoskeag Falls, an important fishery since their formation about 8,000 years ago. The site's low elevation (205 feet) and location at the head of a north-south trending valley places it at the margin of the seaboard lowland, within the transitional forest of central New England. Materials recovered by excavation in 1968 were donated by the excavators to the Peabody Museum of Harvard University, along with the field records. The report describes and analyzes the excavated materials and features. The study was directed toward three specific goals: 1) demonstration of the validity of the stratigraphy, 2) description and dating of the cultural sequence, and 3) definition of diachronic patterns of site utilization.

The site was established on a river terrace above the flood plain of the river, coincident with or shortly later than the formation of the falls. The surface of the site was aggraded throughout the duration of prehistoric occupation by wind-deposited sediments. Five major stratigraphic divisions (strata 1–5) have been defined. Three of these are further subdivided. Stratum 5 formed above the oldest living floor; it has two subdivisions (A and B) and apparently accumulated within the eighth millennium B.P. Stratum 4 also has two divisions; the interface at 4A/B, dated to 6,000 B.P., is the last living floor with Middle Archaic cultural materials. Stratum 3 was accumulated between 4,000 and 3,500 years ago. Stratum 2 was a plow zone formed in the late eighteenth and early nineteenth centuries, which incorporated and mixed living floors of the last 3,400 years of prehistory. Stratum 1 (A–D) was overburden resulting from mid–nineteenth-century construction activities and plowing.

Morphological, functional, and technical attributes of major artifacts and artifact classes are summarized in text, tables, and plates [in the 1976 monograph]. In all cases where numbers are large enough for

Source: Dena Ferran Dincauze, "The Neville Site: 8,000 Years at Amoskeag," *New Hampshire Archeologist* 18 (1975): 2–4. This was a prepublication synopsis of her 1976 report bearing the same title.

demonstration, distinct artifact classes have discrete and coherent stratigraphic distributions. Three types of Middle Archaic stemmed projectile points are defined: the Neville, Stark, and Merrimack styles. Late Archaic and Woodland projectile points are predominantly types familiar in southern and central New England. Twelve types of scrapers are defined; five of these occur only in Middle Archaic assemblages and include three ancient, very conservative forms. Middle Archaic flake knives and spokeshaves are other conservative artifact classes. Ground stone tools in the Middle Archaic levels of the site include winged atlatl weights and full-grooved axes. Several classes of rough stone tools in Middle Archaic levels differ from later forms. Ceramics below stratum 2 were intruded in pits; no stratigraphy of ceramic styles was possible because of mixture in the plow zone. It was possible to document some contrasts in feature form and function among the several strata.

Microchemical analysis of a soil column confirms natural and cultural stratigraphic units and supports the hypothesis that the site was predominantly a late-spring fishing station, particularly in the Middle Archaic period. High levels of mercury in the soils of strata 4B and 5 are interpreted as evidence for initial large amounts of organic waste from anadromous fish. Eight of twelve radiocarbon samples are reasonably congruent with their stratigraphic positions, providing a coarse chronology for the five strata which accumulated since at least 7,740 years ago. The four incongruent dates probably result from sampling error, most likely misinterpretations of pit proveniences. Artifact assemblages are summarized by stratigraphic units, with some further subdivision possible in strata 4A and 3 on the basis of Late Archaic assemblages previously defined elsewhere. The result is a sequence of three Middle Archaic and at

least three Late Archaic assemblages, spanning 4,200 or more years, overlaid by a mixed stratum containing Terminal Archaic, Woodland, and Contact materials.

A few Paleo-Indian and Early Archaic artifacts were recovered in secondary contexts at the site, testifying to earlier occupations elsewhere in the locality. Food procurement and processing, general maintenance, and stone tool manufacturing were major activities during the Middle Archaic occupations of the site, until 6,000 B.P. Until that time, the site appears to have been a base camp occupied during spring fish runs by peoples of a single evolving cultural tradition. Diachronic changes in lithic raw materials indicate increasing familiarity with and dependence upon regional and local resources. Use of the site ceased for an unmeasured duration of time after 6,000 B.P., and when it was resumed peoples of a different cultural tradition, with mid-continental affinities, were involved. During the Late Archaic period the range of activities at the site was restricted in comparison with what had been before. The site appears to have been a member of more complex settlement patterns, a special-purpose site where a limited number of tasks were performed. The range of functional classes of artifacts from Terminal Archaic and Woodland occupations was even more restricted. The ceramics are mostly of regional and local styles.

The conclusions derived from this study have significance for the prehistory of 1) the locality, 2) the southern New England region, and 3) the Atlantic coastal area. A case has been made for human utilization of seasonal runs of fish at Amoskeag for almost 8,000 years. Colonization and subsequent local adaptation can be dimly perceived. The site sequence has added to southern New England's culture history 2,000 years of Middle Archaic complexes and contributed to

clarification of Late Archaic cultural relationships and sequence. The apparent
abrupt termination of Middle Archaic
occupations, a period of site abandon-
ment, and the subsequent appearance of
an unrelated cultural tradition pose major
problems which will have to be resolved by
regional research. Regional studies are also
needed to test and amplify the adaptive
processes hypothesized from this study,
specifically, the suggestion that increasing
complexity of settlement pattern is a sys-
temic reflection of increasing population
density needs to be rigorously tested in
several regional habitats. The many specific parallels observed between the Middle Archaic complexes of New Hampshire
and North Carolina imply a large, ancient
culture area along the east coast. An
Atlantic slope macrotradition, embracing
several Archaic traditions of the east coast,
is proposed.

PART II

CONTACT ERA

4

An Investigation into the Cause or Causes of the Epidemic Which Decimated the Indian Population of New England, 1616–1619

Billee Hoornbeek

BACKGROUND

One of the mysteries associated with the settling of New England is the nature of the epidemic that decimated the coastal Indian tribes (1616–19). As Daniel Denton describes the situation in his 1670 journal (quoted in Smith 1973), "[H]ow strangely they have decreased by the Hand of God ... and it hath generally been observed that where the English come to settle, a Divine Hand makes way for them."

The sources available for analyzing this epidemic are limited. The earliest accounts were written by those who only viewed the aftermath of the devastation. Cotton Mather wrote, "[T]hey were consumed in such vast multitudes that our first planting found the land almost cov-ered with their unburied carcasses." Later reports were based on the recollections of the survivors and the accounts recorded by early chroniclers. The credibility of these sources is suspect because of the medical knowledge at that time.

The situation is analogous to that described by Henry F. Dobyns (1976: 11) for demographers attempting to reconstruct prehistoric populations in the New World: "One either uses such data as may be available and learns something, however inadequate, or abjures such data and learns nothing." It may not be possible to pinpoint the exact pathogen which caused the epidemic, but with the available information, it is possible to rule out a number of suspects.

It is impossible to reconstruct a

Source: Billee Hoornbeek, "An Investigation into the Cause or Causes of the Epidemic Which Deci-mated the Indian Population of New England, 1616–1619," *New Hampshire Archeologist* 19 (1976–77): 35–46.

disease experience by considering only the pathogen and the consequences. Its impact, spread, and tenacity must be assessed in light of the people and their culture, their native disease profile, and the pathogen vector. In a lecture delivered on April 7, 1977, Dr. Jerome Rose, physical anthropologist at the University of Arkansas, listed fourteen possible categories of disease which could have been present in the precontact New World:

1. bacillary and amoebic dysentery
2. viral influenza and pneumonias
3. various arthritides
4. rickettsial fevers
5. viral fevers
6. protozoans
7. American tripanomiasis
8. roundworm, hookworm
9. postulated trempanemus
10. nutritional disorders
11. streptococcus and staphylococcus
12. salmonellas
13. some form of typhus*
14. tuberculosis†

The continental climate (hot, humid summers and cold winters) of New England and the dispersed villages of the inhabitants would have further limited the disease experience. From the above the possible infective agents would include:

1. bacillary and amoebic dysentery
2. viral influenza and pneumonias
3. arthritides
4. viral fevers
5. protozoans
6. roundworm
7. nutritional disorders
8. streptococcus and staphylococcus
9. salmonellas

William H. McNeill (1976) attributes the lack of epidemic diseases in the New World to the scarcity of domesticated animals. He believes many of the epidemic diseases were transferred from cattle to man (smallpox, tuberculosis, undulant fever, etc.). The only precontact domesticate in New England, however, was the dog.

The symptoms the Indians exhibited are described by Daniel Gookin (cited in Cook 1973), who wrote in 1692: "I have discoursed with old Indians who were then youths, who say that the bodies all over were exceedingly yellow, describing it by a yellow garment they showed me, both before they died and afterwards." Captain Dermer, in a letter written in 1619 to Samuel Purchas (quoted in *ibid.*, 487) says, "Their disease the plague, for we might perceive the sores of some that had escaped, who described the spots of such as usually die."

At least two of the deaths ascribed in the literature to the 1616–19 epidemic (Cook 1973) did not actually occur until years after the end of the epidemic. Cook (1973: 487) quotes William Bradford's description of the death of Squanto in November 1622 and attributes it to the same pathogen. According to Sir Ferdinando Gorges (1880: 105), the population of Squanto's village had been ravaged by the epidemic; he was either the only or one of a very few survivors. This is offered as one of the reasons for his joy when the pilgrims arrived. Squanto had spent some three years in England previous to this time, having been captured and transported by some of the early traders. From all accounts, he either did not suffer the malady or had survived it. Cook (1973: 488) relates that Dr. Samuel Fuller, the

---

*This is controversial and based upon the fact that the Aztecs had a name for the disease and their pictorial art depicts the symptoms of spots and nosebleeds.

†Also controversial and based on Allison's work with the Peruvian mummies.

first New England physician, died of the disease. This is again a post-1620 death, and there is no evidence to connect it with the epidemic.

M. K. Bennett (1955: 370) described the culture of the New England Indians in the precontact period of the seventeenth century:

The tribes were spread, though thinly, all along the coast from Eastport, Maine, to the extreme tip of southern Connecticut. Each tribe had its proper domain, consisting of a little cleared land for the gardens; much open swamp and densely wooded jungle along streams and lakes, where there were fishing stations; and such parklike upland forest, wherein the undergrowth was burned off annually in order to provide grazing for deer and open ground for the winter hunting.... The Indian cornfields were limited to eastern Connecticut, Rhode Island, central and eastern Massachusetts, and a fringe not more than about 50–75 miles inland from the coasts of New Hampshire and Maine. Their presence tended to coincide with the lower land elevations, seldom above 500 feet; with the area where the average number of days in a year without killing frost exceeds 120 and usually 130; and with the area south of the isotherm of 66°F mean summer (June–August) temperature— an approximate northern limit for corn. The most north-easterly ancient field of corn to which I have found reference was at Meductic, on the upper St. John River in New Brunswick; but there (in 1689) the corn seems not to have ripened and was customarily harvested in the milk,* boiled, and dried in order to preserve.

From this description and other accounts of the area (Cook, 1973, 1976) a picture emerges of small villages strung thinly along the coast in the spring and summer at fishing stations and cornfields. The people dispersed to sheltered areas back from the coast in the winter to hunt in the areas they had burned. With the exception of an apparent depopulation of the southern coastal area between A.D. 0 and A.D. 100 (Dincauze 1974, Braun 1976), the population in the area had been remarkably stable for some 4,000 years.

At the time of European contact, corn, beans, and squash were an integral part of the diet. Animal protein was provided by wild game, dogs, fish, and shellfish. The actual northern boundary of this subsistence pattern is unknown. A description of the Popham Colony, located at the mouth of the Kennebec, makes no mention of cornfields. It would appear, therefore, that the people of the northern areas were more dependent on hunting and gathering, because the growing season was too short for the varieties of corn available at that time (Bennett 1955).

There are conflicting opinions as to when Europeans first set foot on New England soil. The town of Greenland, New Hampshire, was named by those who firmly believed the Norsemen had landed there. The Cabots are credited with the discovery of the New England coastline in 1497. Sebastian Cabot sailed the length of the eastern seaboard in 1508 or 1509. Although there is no mention of going ashore on these early voyages, it is hardly conceivable that they would sail along in sight of land and not at least get some fresh water.

David B. Quinn (1974: 46) maintains it is probable that men from Bristol, England, were sailing to the Newfoundland fisheries as early as 1491. By 1520 it is recorded that they were sailing annually,

This was done before the corn had ripened to the stage where it produces viable seed.

as were the Spanish, Portuguese, and French fishing fleets. In 1583 Hayes reported planting the flag for the queen (in August 1583, at the harbor of St. John's in Newfoundland) before a crowd of Portuguese, French, and English sailors (Quinn 1974: 237).*

Colonization of New England was being promoted in the 1570s. The first attempt at English colonization was the Popham Colony, which existed from August 29, 1607, until May 1608. This colony failed, but by this time fishermen and fur traders were spending a portion of each year on the mainland of New England as well as on the islands along the coast.

In 1605 Samuel de Champlain mentions that the Indians of Newfoundland were bringing their furs to the coast every spring to trade with the Europeans (Champlain 1778). Commercial activity of this sort suggests established trade and not initial contact.

The earliest sustained contact with the Europeans in the Northeast was on the Atlantic coast of Canada. The first account of Indian disease is from this region. The Jesuit "Relations" in 1616 reports that the Indians "are astonished and often complain that since the French mingle and carry on trade with them they are dying fast, and the population is thinning out. For they assert that before this association and intercourse, all their countries were very populous and they tell how one by one the different coasts, according as they have begun to traffic with us, have been reduced by disease" (Crosby 1972: 14).

To date those who have wrestled with the problem have taken a simplistic and/or catastrophic viewpoint. They have relied on the old records and accounts, mixed the symptoms of various time periods, and attempted to link these with Old World epidemic diseases. Two principal theories are advanced: smallpox (Shrewsbury 1949, reported in Cook 1973: 489) and bubonic and pneumonic plague (Williams 1909, Cook 1973). The theory of yellow fever, which was derived from the statement of Gookin (see above), has been discounted since the infection raged through at least two winters, and Cook (1973: 489) maintains, "no mosquito-borne infection can withstand a New England winter."

Smallpox is a highly contagious viral infection which caused great loss of life in the New World as well as the Old (Crosby 1972). The pathogen is transmitted through contact with an infected person or their clothing, bedding, dust, or other inanimate objects associated with the person (Dollar 1976: 17). The victim can transmit the disease from the end of the incubation period (8 to 14 days) throughout the active span of the infection (8 to 12 days). Clyde D. Dollar, in his research into the high plains epidemic (1976), reported that it was possible for a person to be contagious for several weeks or months after recuperation began, but his clothing and bedding would remain infectious for months. There are, however, a number of reasons to discount it as the causal virus in the 1616–19 epidemic:

Later Indian reaction to this pathogen is well documented in the New England area (Cassedy 1969), and the Indians themselves discriminated between this epidemic and the smallpox epidemic which began in 1633.

The smallpox epidemic of 1633 attacked

*John Rut created the first extensive English mapping of the New England coastline in 1527, but the Verrazzano brothers of France presented their map of the area to Henry VIII prior to that date. Hakluyt credits them with having made three trips to the area by this time (Quinn 1974: 172).

Indians of all ages with no apparent discrimination. Had the earlier pathogen been smallpox those Indians that survived would have been immune.

None of the post-1620 accounts of Indians make any mention of pockmarks.

The only Europeans who were in contact with the Indians of New England during the years of the epidemic were adult males. Most of them would have already survived smallpox and would not have been infectious carriers.

During this period the crossing of the Atlantic from east to west required about three months. Given the age and sex structure of the crews, it is unlikely that an epidemic on board ship could have been sustained for a sufficient length of time to reach the New World.

Most modern writers (Cook 1973, Duffy 1974, Bennett 1955, Dobyns 1976, Crosby 1972) suggest that it could have been bubonic and/or pneumonic plague. Cook (1973; 489) believes that "there are no facts that clearly negate the possibility that the epidemic of 1616–1619 was some type of bubonic or pneumonic plague." He does admit that the word was used at that time to designate any highly contagious febrile infection but cites the fact that reference was constantly made to *the* plague as if it were well recognized. A number of facts need to be examined in light of this assumption.

Bubonic plague (*Pasteurella pestis*) is carried by burrowing rodents. It is spread to humans by the fleas which live on the rodents and then bite people, which infects them. Six species of fleas are known to transmit the disease, but two species are the most frequent carriers. Of the two species *Xenophylla choopis* transmits about 90 percent of the pathogens.

The disease starts with an infected rodent. Fleas domicile in the rodent nests. When the flea bites an infected rodent it

takes in the bacillus (approximately 12 percent of the time). The bacillus quickly becomes established in the flea's stomach; it multiplies until the stomach is filled and, although the flea continues to bite in an attempt to get nourishment, no food (blood) can get into the stomach to be digested. This results in what is referred to as a "blocked flea." The host rodent dies (of plague) and the starving flea, still seeking food, is forced to seek another host. It is only when this situation occurs that the fleas will bite other animals (Pollitzer 1954).

The animal which would have spread the pathogen to the New World would have been *Rattus rattus*, the ship or house rat. There seem to be three factors necessary for an epidemic:

1. a large congregation of people—the data from the 1720 plague in Europe document the fact that maintaining the plague over a period of time requires large towns and cities
2. a large population of infected rats
3. a large population of fleas

The infection of human populations is preceded by the infection and death of large populations of rats that are hosts to vast numbers of fleas. Champlain and Marc Lescarbot mention rats escaping from the ships to the shore, but there is no further mention of these rodents. These would have been *R. rattus*, the rodent responsible for the spread of the plague in Europe. But even granting that rats came ashore from all of the ships that were plying the coast, the conditions were not right for a population explosion.

There is a direct correlation between the number of people in a community and the ability of the plague to create an epidemic. *R. rattus* is a so-called domestic rat that subsists on human garbage and stored food. The paucity of dwellings that would have provided food and protection against the winters would have kept the population to a minimum during this period. Only later, when the Europeans began building substantial dwellings and warehouses, would the necessary conditions have been established to encourage a rapid growth of the rat population. The fact that the Europeans lived in the houses where the Indians were dying (Cook 1973) also argues against the plague. They would not knowingly have exposed themselves to infection by this dreaded killer.

Pneumonic plague can be ruled out on similar grounds. Pneumonic plague develops from bubonic. The pathogen infects the lungs and is then passed from person to person. Pneumonic plague is always fatal under primitive conditions (Pollitzer 1954). Consequently, the epidemic could not have been bubonic nor pneumonic plague. It is possible that a plague could have been introduced by a ship docking during this period. However, cultural and environmental conditions would not have supported a three-year epidemic.

Other infectious diseases have been suggested, including measles, typhoid, and typhus. Two factors limit their probability: (1) the infection had to be maintained on board ship for three months and still be virulent upon arrival in the New World, and (2) the disease had to have the ability to maintain itself in a population which resided in villages of limited size.

One possible source of contamination which has been largely overlooked is chicken pox. Frank Fenner (1968) describes it as a human viral infection that requires a very small (less than 1,000) population to ensure its survival. Chicken pox virus has the ability to remain latent in the human body for years. At this point it becomes shingles (zoster). The vesicles of shingles contain chicken pox virus (Fenner 1968: 58).

In considering the type of pathogen which might have been responsible for the epidemic there are a number of factors which require consideration:

At the time the disease reached epidemic proportions, the Indians were not under any demographic stress. The Europeans present were few in number and did not constitute a threat.

The only change in the cultural pattern was the marketing (trading) of furs. The presence of cornfields and caches of corn as noted by William Bradford in 1620 (reported in Bennett 1955) would suggest that the fur industry was not interfering with horticulture. The nutritional level should not have been appreciably altered. The pelts being traded were principally beaver. From archaeological evidence (Hoornbeek n.d., Bolian n.d.) it is obvious that the Indians of New England ate beaver, thus the pelt animals would have been a source of protein.

The Indians did not maintain large permanent "towns" with substantial dwellings containing hundreds of people.

There is no record of a European having the disease during the 1616–19 period.

The Indians did maintain trade routes, but they were not analogous to the large caravans of the Old World. In the winter, the depth of the snow, the iced-over rivers, and the cold would have rendered intervillage contact infrequent and sporadic.

The ancestors of the American Indian left the Old World long before the modern disease pattern was established. They had been isolated for a period of 20,000 to 60,000 years. The history of the Old World bears ample testimony to the widespread depopulation which occurred when long-range contacts brought new diseases. The Indians' plight was even worse. Through a minimum of 200 generations there had been no contact with any of the plants, animals, or pathogens of the Old World.

When considering the source of the contamination, it is important to look at the parameters of the epidemic region. The northern line of the area is less clearly drawn than its southern boundary, which ran along the east shore of Narragansett Bay. Cook (1973) thinks that it did not extend more than 20–30 miles inland and did not extend up the rivers. Bennett (1955) sets the limits at 50–60 miles inland, the edge of the uplands and the approximate limits of known areas of corn horticulture. The Pennacook of the Concord, New Hampshire, area were decimated by war with the Mohawk before 1620. Cook (1976: 14) quotes Edward Ballard as postulating that "the plague" might also have been a factor. The initial infection had to occur at some spot or spots within this area. Considering the experience of the Canadian Indians it seems certain that Europeans were the vectors. The other possible source would have been Indians who came from the north into the area carrying the pathogen.

Another possibility which must be considered would be zoonoses (internal and external parasites of other animals). This would have required an infection of the game animals, in which case the Europeans would also have been victims. The extent of contact between the Canadian Indians and the Indians south of the Penobscot, which is the hypothetical limit of the disease, is not known. Extensive contact among the tribes within the parameters must be assumed if a single source is accepted. From the account of Europeans living with the Indians in Maine, it is certain that the epidemic was present in the winter of 1617–18. I have been unable

to find the source of the parameter dates, 1616–19. All of the authors agree on these dates but provide no references. Nor are there any references to the region in which the epidemic was first manifest.

Two French ships are known to have been wrecked off the coast of Massachusetts between 1614 and 1619. One ship was wrecked in Massachusetts Bay. This one was burned by the Indians and all the crew members were slain. The other ship ran aground off Cape Cod. In this wreck some of the crew members reached shore where they were captured by the Indians and enslaved. Most of them died in captivity, but two were later ransomed by Captain Dermer and described their captivity (Morton 1883). They told of mistreatment and of the arrogance of the Indians, but no mention was made of disease. Cook (1973, 1976) postulates that this could have been the source of the epidemic. In view of the widespread European-Indian contact during this period and the lack of evidence to substantiate the presence of disease among the captives, this appears to be an unwarranted assumption.

DISCUSSION

The fact that an epidemic swept through the villages of the New England Indians between 1616 and 1619 appears to be indisputable. There is ample documentation of the fact that the Indian tribes suffered large-scale population loss. The available records and the demographic information do not substantiate the premise that it was either the plague or smallpox. The only common disease which cannot be removed from consideration is chicken pox, which can be maintained in a small population and which can reoccur in those who have had the disease in the form of shingles (zoster). The authors cited all take the view that it was a European epidemic disease which spread from a single source. In assuming this position they have failed to deal with three problems:

1. The Canadian Indians were complaining of disease in the villages which had trade and intercourse with the Europeans.
2. The immunity of the Europeans to the disease.
3. The 10,000-year isolation of the Indians.

In view of these facts the idea of one source of contamination and only one pathogen becomes untenable. It would appear that sustained contact was all that was necessary to trigger outbreaks of deadly illness among the Indians.

The presence of a European epidemic disease would surely have killed off a number of the white men present during the epidemics. They were no doubt a hardy group who were immune to a great number of diseases, but universal immunity does not seem remotely possible. The early accounts make mention of deaths and suffering among the crews of the ships and the traders but little mention is made of contagious disease.

The 200-generation isolation should not be ignored. The widespread depopulation of the Old World upon contact with new diseases is well documented. Only the strongest survived. Those lacking sufficient immunity were eliminated from the gene pool. (Could the paucity of the O blood group in the Old World be a result of this selective process?) Equating the symptoms manifested by the Indians in response to a new disease with the symptoms of the Europeans could also be an error. Due to the long-term isolation their reaction would be more violent and perhaps deviant.

Conclusions

In conclusion, the literature to date does not adequately support the assumptions made. The source and the identity of the pathogen or pathogens will probably never be satisfactorily solved. In view of the records that are available, it would seem more reasonable to postulate that the Europeans were spreading a pathogen or pathogens which were adapted and endemic to their culture. It is recorded that contact with the Europeans spread illness and death all through the New World (Crosby 1972). This contamination could still be a part of our culture, and the Indians may have also become adapted. The best definition of the disease is probably that of Bradford: an infectious fever.

References

Bennett, M. K.
1955 The Food Economy of the New England Indians 1605–1675. *The Journal of Political Economy* 63 (5): 369–97

Bolian, Charles E.
n.d. *Faunal Analysis of Seabrook Station Site.*

Bradford, William
1899 *Bradford's History of Plimoth Plantation.* Printed under the direction of the Secretary of the Commonwealth, by order of the General Court, Boston.

Braun, David P.
1974 Explanatory Models for Evolution of Coastal Adaptation in Prehistoric Eastern New England. *American Antiquity* 39 (4): 582–96.

Cassedy, James H.
1969 *Demography in Early America.* Cambridge: Harvard University Press.

Champlain, Samuel de
1878 *Voyages of Samuel De Champlain.* Boston: Prince Society, vol. 12.

Cook, Sherburne F.
1973 The Significance of Disease in the Extinction of the New England Indians. *Human Biology* 45 (3): 485–8.

1976 The Indian Population of New England in the 17th Century. *University of California Publications in Anthropology*, vol. 12, Berkeley.

Crosby, Alfred W., Jr.
1972 *The Columbian Exchange*. Westport, CT: Greenwood Press.

Dincauze, Dena F.
1974 Introduction to Archaeology of the Greater Boston Area. *Archaeology of Eastern North America* 2 (1): 39–66.

Dobyns, Henry F.
1976 *Native American Historical Demography*. Bloomington: Indiana University Press.

Dollar, Clyde D.
1976 The High Plains Smallpox Epidemic of 1837–38. *Western Historical Quarterly* 8 (1): 15–38.

Duffy, John
1953 *Epidemics in Colonial America*. Baton Rouge: Louisiana State University Press.

Fenner, Frank
1968 The Effects of Changing Social Organization on the Infectious Diseases of Man, in *The Impact of Civilization on the Biology of Man*, S. V. Boyden, ed. Toronto: University of Toronto Press.

Gorges, Sir Fernando
1880 *Memoirs of Sir Fernando Gorges*. Boston: Prince Society.

Hoornbeek, Billee M.
n.d. *Faunal Analysis of Hunt's Island*.

Mather, Cotton
1911 *Diary of Cotton Mather, 1681–1724*. Boston: Collections of the Massachusetts Historical Society.

McNeill, William H.
1976 *Plagues and Peoples*. New York: Anchor Press.

Morton, Thomas
1883 *New England Canaan of Thomas Morton*. Boston: Prince Society, vol. 14.

Pollitzer, R.
1954 *Plague*. Geneva: World Health Organization.

Quinn, David B.
1974 *England and the Discovery of America*. New York: Knopf.

Rose, Jerome C.
n.d. *Lecture in Medical Anthropology*. Spring 1977.

Smith, Carlyle S.
1973 *Archaeology of Coastal New York*.

Williams, H. U.
1909 The Epidemic of the Indians in New England 1616–20, with remarks on Native American Infections. *Bulletin of the Johns Hopkins Hospital*, November, pp. 340–49.

5

The Manners, Customs, and Some Historical Facts About the Indians of Northern New England (Excerpts from Explorers and Missionaries, 1524–1657)

Compiled by Harlan A. Marshall

Sources: Harlan A. Marshall, comp., "The Manners, Customs, and Some Historical Facts about the Indians of Northern New England," a typed manuscript from the 1940s in the Manchester Historic Association files. A copy of an earlier (and less accurate version) is also in the New Hampshire Room files of the Manchester City Library. In the margin of the first page of the latter, a librarian's note indicates that it was a "gift from the author"; the date 1-9-1950 follows. The Endecott letter and Eliot's 1647 and 1648 letters come from Marshall's manuscript "John Eliot: Apostle, Friend, and Adviser of the Indians of Central New England," which provides more complete versions. Unfortunately Marshall, who died in 1970, did not include any information regarding the sources he used other than what is contained in his introductory paragraphs and at the beginning of each citation.

David Stewart-Smith, who is familiar with the primary sources of New England Native American history, has tried to trace the sources of Marshall's citations. Marshall's text, however, does not always correspond exactly to the text in the sources identified below. Many of the differences, no doubt, are due to Marshall's cutting and pasting, but it may be that his material comes from sources other than these.

The Verrazano (14–16, 18–19), Brereton (43–45), Gosnold (35, 42), Pring (56–59), Champlain (74–76, 79–81, 88), Smith (213, 240–41), and Levett (268, 282–83) citations can be found in Winship 1905. The quotations from Mourt can be found in the *Massachusetts Historical Society Collections*, 2d ser., vol. 9, 1832 (but Marshall specifically refers to the edition published by Cheever and one "under a later date"). Josselyn's quotes can be found in the same collection, 3d ser., vol. 3, 1833. Many of Eliot's letters can also be found there, in the 3d ser., vol. 4, 1834; his last letter is in the 1st ser., vol. 2, 1793. The Endecott letter and the quote from Gookin (1st ser., vol. 1, 1792) are also in that source. The Gorges, Wood, Williams, Winthrop, Willoughby, and Morton citations come probably from their own works. The source for Biard is probably Ruben Gold Thwaites, ed., *The Jesuit Relations and Allied Documents*, 73 vols. (Cleveland: Burrows, 1896–1901). The source of the Bradford references was undetermined.

In assembling the material for this work the writer has made an earnest effort to bring together subject matter which will prove of value to the student or interested reader by collecting quotations from the writings of early explorers and missionaries with reference to the Indians living in the northern New England area in the interval from 1524 to 1657.

Especial research by the perusal of a great many of the works of early writers has been made to find bits of information bearing on this subject. The purpose is to give a picture of Indian life of this period rather than a complete history of the same.

Included in this work are brief summaries of the lives of John Eliot, the apostle to the Indians, and Daniel Gookin, magistrate and historian. A few of the letters of John Eliot are included which show his deep love for and great efforts to improve the condition of the natives. Some of the brother missionaries working with Eliot were Thomas Mayhew, Thomas Shepard, Edward Winslow, and Henry Whitfeld.

Among the early explorers and adventurers who visited this territory during the interval mentioned above were Giovanni da Verrazano, John Brereton, Bartholomew Gosnold, Martin Pring, Samuel de Champlain, Pere Biard, John Smith, Sir Ferdinando Gorges, Governor William Bradford, Christopher Levett, William Wood, Roger Williams, Gov. John Winthrop, Gabriel Sagard, Thomas Morton, John Josselyn, and Governor John Endecott.

The territory of central New England occupied by the Indians during the 1524–1657 period was divided among the following tribes: Abenaki, Pennacook, Nipmuc, and Massachusett.

Among the books, letters, and articles most consulted in preparing this work are *Antiquities of the New England Indians* by Charles C. Willoughby; *Sailors' Narratives of Voyages Along the New England Coast, 1524–1624* by George Parker Winship; *A Description of New England* by Captain John Smith; *The Journal of the Pilgrims at Plymouth* (Mourt's Relation) published by George B. Cheever; *New England's Prospect* by William Wood; *Winthrop's Journal* by John Winthrop; *An Account of Two Voyages to New-England* by John Josselyn; *New English Canaan* by Thomas Morton; and *Historical Collections of the Indians of New England* by Daniel Gookin. The collections of the Massachusetts Historical Society were found to be invaluable in the completion of this work.

The following quotations, arranged in chronological order, are presented with the hope that a satisfactory idea may be gained of the conditions under which the natives were living at the time of the arrival, and for several decades thereafter, of the first white settlers in Maine, New Hampshire, and Massachusetts. Prior to the arrival of the Pilgrims in 1620, several explorers visited this section of New England, and their discoveries pertinent to this manuscript are herein supplied together with the findings of other pioneers up through the year 1657.

Giovanni da Verrazano, the Florentine explorer, arrived on the New England coast in 1524. He spent fifteen days either in Buzzard's Bay, Narragansett Bay, or Boston Harbor and was much interested in the natives with whom he came in contact. He writes:

> There were amongst these people two Kings of so goodly stature and shape as is possible to declare, the eldest is about 40 yeares of age, the second was a yong man of 20 yeares old. Their apparell was on this manner—the elder had upon his naked body a harts skin wrought artificialie with divers braunches, his head was bare, with the hair tied up behind with divers knottes. About his neck he had a large chaine

garnished with divers stones of sundrie colours. The yong man was almost apparelid after the same manner. This is the goodiest people, and of the fairest conditions, that wee have found in this our voyage....

The women are of like confomitie and Beawtie, very handsome and well favored, they are as well mannered as anye women of good education. There are also of them whiche weare on their armes verie riche skinnes of leopards or lynx. They adorn their heades with divers ornaments made of their own haire, whiche hange downe before on both sides of their breasts, others use other kinds of dressing themselves....

Turkey and eagle feathers were worn in the hair by men. A headdress of upright feathers was sometimes worn fashioned like a coronet, broadwise like a fan, or like a turkey cock's train....

We sawe their houses made in circular or rounde fourm 10 or 12 foote in compasse.... They moove the foresaide houses from one place to another according to the commoditie of the place and season, wherein they will make their abode and only taking of the cover, they have other houses builded. The Father and whole familie dwell together in one house in great number: in some of them we saw 25 or 30 persons....

We also saw many plates of wrought copper which they esteem more than gold, which for the color (yellow) they make no account of, for that among all other is accounted the basest. They make most account of azure and red. The things they esteemed most of all those which we gave them were bells, crystals of azure color, and other toys to hang at their ears and about their necks.

John Brereton in 1602 saw among the Indians of Massachusetts:

Great store of copper, some very red, and some of a paler colour (brass) none of them but have chaines, ear-rings, or collars of this metal: they head some of their arrows herewith much like our broad arrow heads, very workmanly made. Their chaines are many hollow pieces cemented together, each piece of the bigness of one of our reeds, a finger in length, ten or twelve of them together on a string, which they wear about their necks: their collars they wear about their bodies like bandeliers a handful broad, all hollow pieces, like the other, but somewhat shorter, four hundred pieces in a collar, very fine and evenly set together. Besides these they have large drinking cups made like sculls and other thin plates of copper, made much like our boar spear blades, all of which, they so little esteem, as they offered their fairest collars and chains for a knife or such like trifle, but we seemed little to regard it.

Brereton in writing of the Indians of Massachusetts mentions their use of firestones:

They strike fire in this manner; every one carrieth about him in a purse of sewed leather, a mineral stone and with a flat emery stone tied fast to the end of a little stick, gently he striketh on the mineral stone and within a stroke or two, a spark falleth upon a piece of touchwood (much like our sponge in England) and with the least spark he maketh a fire presently.

In *Sailors' Narratives* we find that in 1602 Bartholomew Gosnold came to anchor on the New England coast near some islands; he gives the following account of his adventures there and on the shore of Maine:

Coming to an anchor under one of them which was about three or four leagues from the Maine, we went ashore and going round about it, we found it to be four English miles in compasse without house or inhabitant, saving a little old house made of boughes, covered with barke, an old piece of weare of the Indians, to catch fish and one or two places where they had made fires. But the second day after coming from the Maine, we espied nine canoes or boats, with fifty Indians in them, coming toward us from this part of the Maine, where we two daies before, landed; and being loth they should discover our fortification, we went out on the sea-side to meet them and coming somewhat neere them, they all sat down upon the stones, calling aloud to us to doe the like a little distance from them.

Their Lord or Captaine which sat in the midst of them, presently rose up and tooke a large beaver skin from one that stood about him, and gave it unto me. These people are of tall stature, broad and grim visage, of a blacke complection, their eie-browes painted white; their weapons are bowes and arrowes.

These people, as they are exceeding courteous, gentle of disposition, and well conditioned, excelling all others that we have seen; so for shape of bodie and lively favour, I think excell all the people of America; of stature much higher than we; of complexion or colour, much like darke olive; their eie-browes and haire blacke, which they weare long, tied up behind in knots, whereon they pricke feathers of fowles, in fashion of a crownet: some of them are black thin bearded: they make beards of the haire of beasts.

In 1603 Martin Pring went ashore at Plymouth Harbor; he gives the following description of his discoveries:

During our abode on shore, the people of the countrey came to our men sometimes ten, twenty, fortie, or three-score and at one time one hundred and twentie at once. We used them kindly, and gave them divers sorts of our meanest merchandize. They did eat pease and beanes with our men. Their owne vituals were most of fish.

Their weapons are bows of five or sixe foot long of wich-hazell, painted black and yellow, the strings of three twists of sinewes, bigger than our bow strings. Their arrowes are of a yard and an handfull long not made of reeds, but of a fine light wood very smooth and round with three long and deepe black feathers of some eagle, vulture or kite, as closely fastened with some binding matter, as any of ours can glue them on. Their quivers are full a yard long, made of rushes wrought about two handfulls broad above and one handfull beneath with prettie workes and compartiments, diamant wise of red and other colours....

Passing up a river we saw certaine cottages together, abandoned by the Savages, and not farre off we beheld their gardens and one among the rest of an acre of ground, and in the same was sowne tobacco, pompions, cowcumbers and such like; and some of the people had maiz or Indian wheate among them. In the fields we found wild pease, strawberries very faire and bigge gooseberries, raspices, hurts, and other wild fruits.

Samuel de Champlain visited the coast of Maine in the year 1605. He describes the manners and customs of the natives:

These savages shave off the hair far up on the head, and wear what remains very long, which they comb and twist behind in various ways very neatly, intertwined with feathers which they attach to the head. They paint their faces black and red, like the other savages which we have seen. They are an agile people, with well formed bodies. Their weapons are pikes, clubs, bows and arrows, at the end of which some attach the tail of a fish called the signoc, others bones, while the arrows of others are entirely of wood. They till and cultivate the soil, something which we have not hitherto observed. In the place of ploughs, they use an instrument of very hard wood, shaped like a spade.

The Champlain explorers then made their way to the mouth of a river (now known to have been the Merrimack) and the narrative continues:

Then they drew within the first mentioned bay a river which we had passed, which has shoals and is very long. We found in this place a great many vines, the green grapes on which were a little larger than peas, also many nut trees, the nuts on which were no larger than musket-balls. The savages told us that all those inhabiting this country cultivated the land and sowed seeds like the others, whom we had before seen.

The following information refers to a visit to an island in Boston Harbor by this same party:

Having sailed seven or eight leagues, we anchored near an island, whence we observed many smokes along the shore, and many savages running up to see us. We gave some knives to present to them, with which they were greatly pleased, and danced several times in acknowledgement. All along the shore there is a great deal of land cleared up and planted with Indian corn. The country is very pleasant and agreeable, and there is no lack of fine trees. The canoes of those who live there are made of a single piece and are very liable to turn over if one is not skillful in managing them. We had not before seen any of this kind. They are made in the following manner. After cutting down, at a cost of much labor and time, the largest and tallest tree they can find, by means of stone hatchets, they remove

the bark, and round off the tree except on one side, where they apply fire gradually along its entire length; and sometimes they put red-hot pebble-stones on top, when the fire is too fierce, they extinguish it with a little water, not entirely, but so that the edge of the boat may not be burnt. It being hollowed out as much as they wish, they scrape it all over with stones, which they use instead of knives. These stones resemble our musket flints....

There were also several fields entirely uncultivated, the land being allowed to remain fallow. When they wish to plant it, they set fire to the weeds, and then work it over with their wooden spades. Their cabins are round, and covered with heavy thatch made of reeds. In the roof there is an opening of about a foot and a half, whence the smoke from the fire passes out.

Regarding historic Indian fortifications in New England, Champlain refers to a fort on the right bank of the Saco River near its mouth. He notices a square enclosure containing a single house:

The savages dwell permanently in this place, and have a large cabin surrounded by palisades made of rather large trees placed by the side of each other, in which they take refuge when their enemies make war upon them.

In one of his writings Champlain mentions a girl with her hair very neatly dressed with a skin, colored red, and bordered on the upper part with little shell beads. A portion of it hung down behind, the rest being braided in various ways.

The following description of Indian wigwams in the state of Maine by Pere Biard was written in the year 1613:

The women go to the woods and bring back some poles which are stuck into the ground in a circle around the fire, and at the top are interlaced, in the form of a pyramid, so that they come together directly over the fire, for there is the chimney. Upon the poles they throw some skins, matting or bark. At the foot of the poles, under the skins, they put their baggage. All the space around the fire is strewn with leaves of the fir tree, so they will not feel the dampness of the ground; over these leaves are often thrown some mats; upon this they stretch themselves around the fire with their heads resting upon their baggage. They are very warm around that little fire, even in the greatest rigors of the winter. In summer the shape of their houses is changed; for then they are broad and long, that they may have more air; then they nearly always cover them with bark, or mats made of tender reeds, finer and more delicate than those of straw, and so skillfully woven that when they are hung up the water runs along their surface without penetrating them.

Captain John Smith in *A Description of New England* states: "In the moneth of April, 1614 with two ships from London, I chanced to arrive in New England which stretcheth from Pennobscot to Cape Cod." Two years later, in 1616, he writes: "The country of Massachusetts ... is the paradise of all these parts.... For heere are many isles all planted with corn groves, mulberries, salvage gardens and has many good harbors.... The Sea Coast as you pass, shews you all along large corn fields and great troups of well proportioned people."

The Journal of the Pilgrims at Plymouth (Mourt's Relation) published by George B. Cheever provides an excellent description of the wigwams and their furnishings as seen by the Pilgrims at Cape Cod in 1620:

The houses were made with long Sapling trees, bended and both ends stucke into the ground; they were made round, like unto an Arbour, and covered downe to the ground with thicke and well wrought matts, and the doore was not over a yard high, made of a matt to open; the chimney was a wide open hole in the top, for which they had a matt to cover it close when they pleased; one might stand and goe upright in them, in the midst of them were foure little trunches knockt into the ground and small stickes laid over, on which they hung their Pots and what they had to seeth; round about the fire they lay on matts, which are their beds. The houses were double matted, for as they were matted without, so were they within, with newer & fairer matts. In the houses we found wooden Bowles, Trayes & Dishes, Earthen Pots, Hand baskets made of Crab shells, wrought together; also an English Paile, it wanted a bayle, but it had Iron eares: there was also Baskets of sundry sorts, bigger and some lesser, finer and some courser: some were curiously wrought with blacke and white in pretie works, and sundry other of their household stuffe: we found also two or three Deeres heads, one whereof had been newly killed, for it was still fresh; there was also a company of Deeres feete stuck up in the houses, Harts hornes, and Eagles clawes, and sundry such like things there was: also two or three Baskets full of parched Acornes, peeces of fish, and a peece of broyled Hering. We found also a little silke grasse, and a little Tobacco seed, with some other seeds which wee knew not; without was sundry bundles of Flags, and Sedge, Bullrushes, and other stuffe to make matts.

In *The Journal of the Pilgrims* under a later date, we find this record of the first personal conversation held with the natives:

The first intelligible word uttered from the man's lips being the sweet English word, "welcome!" which, from a savage in the wilderness, must have seemed a miracle. This stark naked barbarian, whose name was Samoset, of the Massasoits, had learned enough English from various fishermen, at different times, to hold a broken conversation, and he was a man free in speech considering the limited extent of his acquisitions. He spoke, among other things, of the pestilence. He told us that about four years ago, all the inhabitants died of a[n] extraordinary plague, and there is neither man, woman, nor child remaining, as indeed we have found none; so as there is none to hinder our possession, or to lay claim unto it.

In the year 1622, Sir Ferdinando Gorges, having formed an intimacy with Captain John Mason, governor of Portsmouth, in the county of Hants jointly with him procured from the council a grant of a large extent of country, which they called Laconia, extending from the Merrimack River to Sagadahock in Maine. About the same time (1623) a settlement was begun at the Piscataqua River by Captain Mason and several other merchants, among whom Gorges had a share. Another venture of Gorges was the obtaining from the Crown of a confirmation of his own grant, which was styled the Province of Maine. In order to entertain a just view of Gorges we must consider him both as a member of the Council of Plymouth, pursuing the general interest of American plantations and, at the same time, as an adventurer undertaking a settlement of his own in a particular part of the territory, which was subject to the jurisdiction of the council. In his paper "A Brief Narration of the Original Undertakings of the Advancement of Plantations into the Parts of America," Gorges writes:

As for that of New England, where I am chiefly interested, by reason of the time and means I have spent in the prosecution of that business. At our first discovery of those coasts, we found it very populous, the inhabitants stout and warlike, the country plentiful in grain and other fruits and roots, besides deer of all sorts and other animals for food, with plenty of fish and fowl.

Governor William Bradford, in a letter dated September 8, 1623, says the natives could obtain of these traders:

Not toys and trifles but good substantial commodities as ketkels, hatchets and clothes of all sorts; yea the French do store them with Biskay boats, fitted both with sails and ores with which they can either row or sail as well as we; also with powder and shot, for fowling and other services. Also I know upon my knowledge many of the Indians to be as well furnished with good ketkels, both strong and of a large size as many farmers in England.

Native pottery, therefore, went out of use in parts of New England at an early date, for good kettles were sold to the Indians by Dutch and French traders soon after the first explorers came to New England. The following account of a transaction and its important bearing upon the future trade relations with the New England tribes comes from a report written by Governor Bradford:

This year the Dutch sent againe unto them [the English] from their plantation both kind leterss, and also diverse comodities, as sugar, linen cloth, Holland finer & courser stufes &c. and did perswade them they would find it so at Kenebeck; and so it came to pass in time, though at first it stuck, & it was 2 years before they could put of this small quantity, till ye inland people knew of it; and afterwards they could scarce ever gett enough for them, for many years together.

Christopher Levett, while exploring the coast of Maine in 1624, came to the mouth of a large river (probably the Saco):

This river, as I am told by the Savages cometh from a great mountaine called the Christall hill, being as they say 100 miles in the country, yet is it to be scene at the sea side, and there is no ship arrives in New England, either to the west so farre as Cape Cod, or to the east so far as Monbiggen, but they see this Mountain the first land, if the weather be cleere.

With reference to the religious beliefs of the natives the writer continues:

I find they have two Gods, one they love; and the other they hate. The God they love, they call Squanto, and to him they ascribe all their good fortunes. The God they hate they call Tanto, and to him they ascribe all their evil fortunes, as thus when any is killed, hurt or sicke, or when any dyes, they say Tanto carries them to his wigwam, that is his house, and they never see them more. I have asked them where Squanto dwells, they say they cannot tell but up on high, and will poynt upwards. And for Tanto, they say farre west, but they know not where.

And to say something of the Countrey: I will not doe therin as some have done to my knowledge speak more then is true: I will not tell you that you may smell the corne fields before you see the Land, neither must men thinke that corne doth grow naturally (or on the trees) nor will the deare come when they are called, or stand still and looke on a man, untill he shute him, not knowing a man from a beast, nor the fish leape into the kettle, nor on the drie land, neither are they so plentifull, that you may dipp them up in baskets, nor take Codd in netts to make a voyage, which is no truer: then that the fowles will present themselves, to you with

spitts through them. But certainely there is fowle, Deare, and Fish enough for the taking if men be diligent, there be also Vines, Plume trees, Cherry trees, Strawberies, Gooseberies, and Raspes, Walnuts, chestnut, and small nuts, of each great plenty; there is also great store of parsley, and divers other holesome Earbes, both for profit and pleasure, with great store of Saxifrage, Cersa-perilla, and Anni-seeds.

William Wood traveled through northern New England in 1629; in *New England's Prospect* we find the following interesting items from his pen:

Their black haire is naturall, yet it is brought to a more jetty colour by oyling, dying, and daily dressing. Sometimes they weare it very long, hanging down in a loose dishevel'd womanish manner; otherwhile tied up hard and short like a horse taile, bound close with a fillet, which they say makes it grow the faster: they are not a little phantasticall or customsick in this particular; their boyes being not permitted to weare their hair long till sixteene yeares of age, and then they must come to it by degrees; some being cut with long foretop, a long locke on the crowne, one at each side of his head, the rest of his haire being cut even with the scalpe: the young men and souldiers weare their haire long on the one side, the other side being cut short like a screw; other cuts they have as their fancie befools them, which would torture the wits of a curious Barber to imitate. But though they be thus wedded to the haire of their head, you cannot wooe them to weare it on their chinnes where it no sooner growes, but it is stubbed up by the rootes....

Upon their cheekes certaine pourtraitures of beasts, as Beares, Deeres, Mooses, Wolves, &. some of fowls as or Eagles, Hawkes, &. which be not a superficiall painting, but a certaine incision, or else a raising of their skin by a small sharpe instrument, under which they conveigh a certain kind of black unchangeable inke, which makes the desired forme apparent and permanent. Others have certaine round Impressions downe the outside of their armes and brests, in forme of mullets or spur-rowels, which they imprint by searing irons: whether these be foiles to illustrate their unparalleld beauty (as they deem it) or Armes to blazon their antique Gentilitie, I cannot easily determine: but a Sagamore with a Humberd in his eare for a pendant, a black hawke on his occiput for his plume, Mowhackees (purple beads) for his gold chaine, good store of Wampompeage (white beads) begirting his loynes, his bow in his hand, his quiver at his back, with six naked Indian spatterlashes at his heels for his guard, thinkes himself little inferiour to the great Cham: hee will not stick to say, hee is all one with King Charles....

In the Summer these Indian women, when Lobsters be in their plenty and prime, they drie them to keepe for Winter, erecting scaffolds in the hot sunshine, making fires likewise underneath them, by whose smoake the flies are expelled, till the substance remain hard and drie. In this manner they drie Basse and other fishes without salt, cutting them very thinne to dry suddainely, before the flies spoile them, or the rain moist them, having a special care to hang them in their smoakie houses, in the night and dankish weather....

Their bowes they make of handsome shape, strung commonly with the sinnewes of Mooses; their arrowes are made of young Elderne, feathered with feathers of Eagles wing and tailes, headed with brasse in shape of a heart or triangle, fastened in a slender peece of wood six or 8 inches long, which is framed to put loose in the pithie Elderne, that is bound fast for riving: their arrowes be made in this manner

because the arrow might shake from his head and be left behind for their finding, and the pile onely remaine to gaule the wounded beast....

[They] use no other weapons in warre than bowes and arrowes, saving that their Captaine have long speares, on which if they returne conquerors they carrie the heads of their chiefe enemies that they slay in the wars: it being the custome to cut off their heads, hands, and feete, to beare home to their wives and children, as true tokens of their renowned victorie....

Their Sturgeon netts be not deepe, not above 30, or 40, foote long, which in ebbing low waters they stake fast to the ground, where they are sure the Sturgeon will come, never looking more at it, till the next low water....

It is custome for their Kings to inherite, the sonne always taking the Kingdome after his fathers death. If their be no sonne, then the Queene rules; if no Queene, then the next to the bloodroyall....

These Forts some be fortie or fiftie foote square, erected of young timber trees, ten or twelve foote high, rammed into the ground, with undermining within, the earth being cast up for their shelter against the dischargements of their enemies, having loopholes to send out their winged messengers....

Of these swamps, some be ten, some twenty, some thirty miles long, being preserved by the wetneese of the soile wherin they grow; for it being the custome of the Indians to burne the wood in November, when the grass is withered, and leaves dryed, it consumes all the underwood, and rubbish, which otherwise would over grow the Country, making it unpassable, and spoile their much affected hunting: so that by this means in those places where the Indians inhabit, there is scarce a bush or bramble, or any cumbersome underwood to bee seene in the more champion ground. Small wood growing in these places where the fire could not come is preserved.

Roger Williams came to Massachusetts in 1631. Later he sailed for England as agent for that colony. During this voyage he composed his *Key into the Language of America,* a part of which reads as follows:

The Indians are ignorant of Europes Coyne. Their owne is of two sorts; one white, which they make of the stem or stocke of the Periwincle, and of this sort six of their small Beads (which they make with holes to string the bracelets) are currant with the English for a Peny. The second is black, inclining to blew, which is made of the shell of a fish, which some English call Hens, and of this sort three make an English peny. They that live upon the Sea side generally make of it, and as many make as will. The Indians bring downe all their sorts of Furres, which they take in the countrey, both to the Indians and to the English for this Indian Money. This Money the English, French and Dutch, trade to the Indians, six hundred miles in several parts (North and South from New England) for their Furres and whatsoever they stand in need of from them. Their white they call Wompam (which signifies white) their black Suckauhock signifying black. Both amongst themselves, as also the English and Dutch, the blacke peny is two pence white; the black fathom double or two fathom of white. They hang these strings of money about their necks and wrists; as also upon the necks and wrists of their wives and children.

Williams tells us that the Indians generally delighted in clams, and in winter and summer:

At low water the women dig for them: this fish and the naturall liquors of it, they boile and it makes their broth and their Nasaump (which is a kind of thickened broth) and their bread seasonable and savoury in stead of Salt....

The women of a family will commonly raise two or three heaps of corn of twelve, fifteene or twentie bushells a heap, which they drie in round broad heaps; and if she have helpe of her children or friends, much more....

Generally all the Men throughout the Countrey have a tobacco-bag with a pipe in it, hanging at their back, sometimes they make such great pipes both of wood and stone, that they are two foot long, with men or beasts carved, so big or massie, that a Man may be hurt mortally by one of them; but these commonly come from the Mohawks, or the men eaters, three or foure hundred miles from us: They have excellent Art to cast our Pewter and Brass into very neate and artificiall Pipes.

Williams also gives us this interesting account of an Indian boat builder:

I have seen a native go into woods with his hatchet, carrying only a basket of corne and stones to strike fire. When he has felled his tree (either chestnut or pine) he maketh his a little hut or shed of the bark of it. He puts fire, and follows the burning of it in the midst, in many places. His corne he boils, and hath the brook by him, and sometimes angles for a little fish. So he continueth burning and hewing until he hath, in ten or twelve days, finished, and getting hands, launched his boat.

Governor John Winthrop, in the spring of 1631, set up the frame of a house at Newtown and shortly thereafter had an interview with an Indian chief whose name was Chickatabot, who visited the governor with voluntary professions of friendship. Winthrop describes his first talk with the chief:

Chickatabot came with his chiefs and squaws, and presented the governor with a hogshead of Indian corn. After they had all dined, and had each a small cup of sack and beer, and the men tobacco, he sent away all his men and women. (Though the governor would have stayed them in regard of the rain and thunder.) Himself and one squaw and one sannup stayed all night; and being in English clothes, the governor set him at his own table, where he behaved himself as soberly, &c., as an Englishman. The next day after dinner he returned home, the governor giving him cheese, and pease, and a mug, and other things.

Winthrop's Journal contains the following narrative concerning the Merrimack Valley chief Passaconaway:

Upon the warrant which went to Ipswich, Rowley, and Newbury, to disarm Passaconamy, who lived by Merrimack, they sent 40 men armed the next day, being the Lord's day. But it rained all the day, as it had done divers days before, and also after, so as they could not go to his wigwam, but they came to his son's and took him, which they had warrant for, and a squaw and her child, which they had no warrant for, and therefore order was given so soon as we heard of it, to send them home again. Upon the intelligence of these unwarranted proceedings, and considering that Passaconamy would look at it as a manifest injury, we sent Cutshamekin to him to let him know that what was done to his son and squaw was without order, and to show him the occasion whereupon we had sent to disarm all the Indians. He returned answer that he knew not what was to become of his son and his squaw (for one of them was run into the woods and came not again for ten days after, and the other was still in custody), if he had them safe again, then he would come to us.

Charles C. Willoughby, author of *Antiquities of the New England Indians*, in his description of pottery making, has this to say about the art as practiced in this area:

I am inclined to accept the following process followed by certain Canadian tribes, and described in [Gabriel] Sagard's *History of Canada* written in 1636, as being much like that in vogue in New England: "They are skilful in making good earthen pots which they harden very well on the hearth, and which are so strong they do not, like our own, break over the fire when having no water in them. But they cannot sustain dampness nor cold water so long as our own, since they become brittle and break at the least shock given them; otherwise they last very well. The Savages make them by taking some earth of the right kind, which they clean and knead well in their hands, mixing with it, on what principle I know not, a small quantity of grease. Then making the mass into the shape of a ball, they make an indentation in the middle of it with the fist, which they make continually larger by striking repeatedly on the outside with a little wooden paddle as much as is necessary to complete it. These vessels are of different sizes, without feet or handles, completely round like a ball, excepting the mouth, which projects a little."

Thomas Morton in his *New English Canaan* describes the manners and customs of the New England Indians in detail:

The Natives of New England gather poles in the woodes and put the great end of them in the ground, placinge them in forme of a circle or circumference, and bendinge the topps of them in form of an arch, they bind them together with the Bark of Walnut trees, which is wondrous tuffe, so that they make the frame round on the top for the smoke of their fire to assend and passe through; this they cover with matts, some made of reeds and some of longe flagges, or sedge, finely sowed together with needles made of the splinter bones of a Cranes legge, with threeds made of their Indian hemp, which they grow naturally, leaving several places for dores, which are covered with mats which may be rowled up and down again at their pleasures, making use of the severall dores, according as the winde fitts.

The fire is always made in the middle of the house, yet sometimes they fell a tree that groweth neere the house, and by drawing in the end there of, maintaine the fire on both sides, burning the tree by Degrees shorter and shorter, until it is all consumed; for it burneth night and day. Their lodging is made in three places of the house about the fire: they lye upon planks, comonly about a foot or 18 inches above the ground, raised upon railes that are borne up upon forks; they lay mats under them, and Coats of Dears skinnes, otters, beavers, Racownes and of Beares hides, all which they have dressed and converted into good leather, with the hair on, for their coverings, and in this manner they lye as warme as they desire. In the day time either the kettle is on with fish or flesh or else the fire is employed in roasting of fishes, which they delight in.

They are willing that anyone shall eate with them, Nay, if anyone shall come into their houses and there fall asleep, when they see him disposed to lye downe, they will spread a mat for him of their own accord, and lay skinnes for him and let him lye. If they sleepe until their meate be dished up, they will fetch a wooden bowl of meate and wake him saying, Cattup keene Meckin: That is, If you be hungry, there is meate for you, where if you will eat you may. Likewise, when they are

minded to remoove they carry away the mats with them. They use not to winter and summer in one place, but after the manner of the gentry of Civilized natives, remove for their pleasures; sometimes to their hunting places, and sometimes to their fishing places and at the Spring, when fish come in plentifully. They have meetinges from several places, where they exercise themselves in gaminge and playing of juglinge trickes and all manner of Revelles, which they delighted in.

Their skinnes they convert into very good lether. Some of these skinnes they dress with the haire on, and some with the haire off; the hairy side in winter time they weare next to their bodies, and in warm weather they weare the haire outwardes. They make likewise some Coates of the Feathers of Turkies, which together with twine of their own makinge, these garments they weave like mantels knit over their shoulders and put under their arme. Mantels made of Beares skinnes is an usuall wearinge among the Natives that live where the Beares doe haunt; they make shooes of Mose skinnes. They also make shoes of Deeres skinnes, and of such Deeres skinnes as they dress bare, they make stockinges that comes within their shoes and is fastned above at their belt. Those garments they alwayes put on when they go huntinge, to keep their skinnes from the brush of the shrubs. A girdle of their making, they raped around about their middles, to which girdle is fastned a bagg, in which his instruments be with which hee can strike fire upon any occasion. Thus with their bow in their left hand, and their quiver of arrows at their back, hanging one on their left shoulder, they will runne away a dog trot until they come to their journey end.

Although these people have not the use of navigation yet do they barter for such commodities as they have, and have a kinde of beads insteede of money to buy with all such things as they want, which they call Wampampeak. It is of two sorts, the one is white, the other is of violet coloure. These are made of the shells of fishe. The white with them is as silver with us, the other as our gould: and for these beads they buy and sell, not only among themselves, but even with us. The skinnes of beasts are sould and bartered, to such people as have none of the same kinde in the parts where they live. Likewise they have earthen potts of divers sizes, from a quarte to a gallon to boil their vitels in; very strong, though they be thin like our Iron potts. They have dainty wooden bowles of maple, of highe price amongst them and these are dispersed by bartering one with the other.

If we doe not judge amisse of these Salvages in accounting them witches, yet out of all question we may be bould to conclude them to be but weake witches, such of them as wee call by the names of Powahs. Papasiquineo the Sachem or Sagamore, is a Powah of great estimation among all kinde of Salvages there: hee is at their Revels (which is the time when a great company of Salvages meete from severall parts of the country, in amity with their neighbours) hath advanced his honor in his feats or jugling tricks. Likewise as seen by our English, in the heat of all summer to make Ice appeare in a bowle of faire water; first having the water set before him; hee begunne his incantation according to their ususal accustome, and before the same has bin ended a thick of Clowde has darkned the aire and on a sodane, a thunder clap hath bin heard that has amazed the natives; in an instant he hath shewed a firme peece of the Ice to flote in the middest of the bowle in the presence of the vulgar people which doubtles was done by the agility of Satan.

The Salvages are accustomed to set fire of the Country in all places where they come, and to burne it twize a yeare, vis: at the Spring and the fall of the leafe. The reason that mooves them to doe so, is because it would be all a coppice wood, and the people would not be able in any wise to passe through the Country out of a beaten path. The burning of the grasse destroyes the underwoods, and soscorcheth the elder trees that it shrinkes them, and hinders their grouth very much: so that hee that will looke to finde large trees and good tymber, must not depend upon the help of a wooden prospect to find them on the upland ground; but must seeke for them (as I and others have done) in the lower grounds, where the grounds are wett, for the Salvages, by this custome of theirs, have spoiled all the rest: for this custome hath been continued from the beginninge. And this custome of firing the Country is the meanes to make it passable; and by that meanes the trees growe here, and there as in our parks: and makes the Country very beautiful and commodious.

John Josselyn, in his work *An Account of Two Voyages to New-England* (made in 1638 and 1663), relates the following facts regarding the natives of northern New England:

As for their persons they are tall and handsome timber'd people, black eyed which is accounted the strongest for sight, and generally black hair'd both smooth and curl'd wearing it long. No beards, or very rarely, their teeth are very white, short and even, they account them the most necessary and best parts of man. The Indesses that are young, are some of them very comely, having good features, their faces plump and round, and generally plump of their Bodies. For apparel before the English came amongst these people, was the skins of wild Beasts with the hair on, Buskins of Deers-skin or Moose drest and drawn with lines into several works, the lines being coloured with yellow, blew or red. Pumps too they have, made of tough skins without soles. In the winter when the snow will bear them, they fasten to their feet their snow shooes which are made like a large Racket, lacing them with Deers-guts and the like. The men continue their old fashion going bare headed, excepting some old men amongst them. They are very proud as appeareth by their setting themselves out with white and blue Beads of their own making, and painting of their faces with the above mentioned colours.

Their houses which they call Wig-wams, are built with Poles pitcht into the ground of a round form for most part, sometimes square, they bind down the tops of their poles, leaving a hole for smoak to go out at, the rest they cover with the bark of Trees, and line the inside of their Wigwams with mats made of Rushes painted with several colours, one good post they set up in the middle that reaches to the hole in the top, with a staff before it at a con-venient height, they knock in a pin on which they hang their Kettle, beneath that they set up a broad stone for a back which keepeth the post from burning; round by the walls they spread their mats and skins where the men sleep whilst their women dress their victuals, they have comonly two doors, one opening to the South, the other to the North, and according as the Wind sits, they close up one door with bark and hang a Dears skin or the like before the other. I have seen half a hundred of their Wigwams together in a piece of ground and they shew prettily....

Delicate sweet dishes too they make of Birch-Bark sowed with threads drawn from Spruse or white Cedar-Roots, and garnished on the out-side with flourist works, and on the brims with glistering quills taken from the Porcupine, and dyed, some black, oth-ers red, the white are natural, these they make of all sizes from a dram cup to a dish containing a pottle, likewise Buck-ets to carry water or the like, large Boxes too of the same materials....

The Bass and Blue-fish they take in harbours, and at the mouth of barr'd Rivers being in their Canows, striking them with a fishgig, a kind of dart or staff, to the lower end wherof they fas-ten a sharp jagged bone with a string fastened to it, as soon as the fish is struck they pull away the staff, leaving the bony head in the fishes body and fasten the other end of the string to the Canow: Thus they will hale after them to shore half a dozen or half a score great fishes.

Josselyn says that lobsters were taken in large bays:

When it is low water, and the wind still, going out in their Birchen-Canows with a staff two or three yards long, made small and sharpen'd at one end, and nick'd with deep nicks to take hold. When they spye the Lobster crawling upon the Sand in two fathom water, more or less, they stick him towards the head and bring him up. I have known thirty Lobsters taken by an Indian lad in an hour and a half, thus they take Flouke and Lumps. Lobsters the Indians dry as they do Lampres and Oysters.... The Oysters are long shel-l'd, I have had of them nine inches long from the joynt to the tow, containing Oysters, that were to be cut into three pieces before they could get them into their mouths.

Daniel Gookin, author of *Historical Collections of the Indians of New England*, was born in the county of Kent. He came early to North America and at first estab-lished himself in Virginia. In 1644 he removed with his family to New England and settled in Cambridge. Soon after his arrival he was appointed captain of the military company in Cambridge. Later he became one of the magistrates of the Massachusetts Colony and still later was employed in the civil government and conduct of the Indians in Massachusetts Colony by order of the General Court. The first of Daniel Gookin's writings, later brought together to form his *Historical Collections,* were probably penned soon after his arrival in Massachusetts in 1644, and additions were made to it at various times for several years thereafter. The following descriptions of the manners and customs of the natives are taken from these collections:

> They are much addicted to idleness especially the men who are disposed to hunting and fishing. In their removals from place to place for their fishing and hunting at the several seasons the women carry the greatest burden. They also prepare all the diet. The houses for wigwams are built with small poles fixed in the ground, bent and fastened together with barks of trees oval or arbour wise on the top. The best sort of their houses are covered very neatly tight and warm with barks of trees slipped from their bodies at such season when the sap is up and made into great flakes with pressures of weighty timbers when they are green and so become dry they will retain a form suitable for the use they prepare them for. The meaner sort of wigwams are covered with mats they make of a kind of bulrush. These houses are made of several sizes some twenty some forty feet long and broad. Some I have seen of sixty or a hundred feet long and thirty feet broad. In the smaller they made a fire in the center of the house and have a hole on the house to let out the smoke. Upon the Floor they spread mats and sometimes bear skins also skins of deer. These are large enough for three or four persons to lodge upon. One may either draw nearer or keep at more distance from the heat of fire for their mattresses are six or eight feet broad.
>
> Their food is generally boiled maize or Indian corn mixed with kidney beans or sometimes without. Also they frequently boil in this fish and flesh of all sorts either new taken or dried as shads, eels, alewives or any other sort of fish. But they dry mostly those sorts before mentioned. These they cut in pieces bones and all and boil them in the aforesaid pottage. I have wondered that they were not in danger of being choaked with fish bones but they are so dextrous to separate the bones from the fish in their eating that they are in no hazard. Also they boil in this furminty all sorts of flesh they take in hunting as venison, beavers flesh, moose, otter & rackoon. Cutting this flesh in small pieces and boiling it as aforesaid. Also they mix with the said pottage several sorts of roots as artichokes, ground nuts and other roots also pompkin, squashes and several sorts of nuts as acorns, chestnuts and walnuts. Also they beat their maize into meal, they make bread baking it in the ashes, covering the dough with leaves. Sometimes they make of their meal a small sort of cakes and boil them. They make also a certain sort of meal of parched maize. This they call nokake. It is sweet and hearty after which he drinks water. If on a journey they put this nokake in a basket or bag for their use.
>
> Their household stuff is little. The pots are made of clay or earth almost in the form of an egg the top taken off. Their dishes and spoons also ladles are made of wood very smooth and artificial of a sort of wood not subject to split. Their pails to fetch their water in are made of birch barks doubled up that it hath four corners and a handle. Some of these will hold two or three gallons and they will make one of them in an hours time. They keep the door into the wigwams always shut by a mat falling there on as people go in and out. If the smoke beat down at the lower pole they hung a little mat in the way of a skreen on the top of the house, which they can with a cord turn to the windward side which prevents the smoke. In the

greater houses they make two, three or four fires at a distance from another. I have often lodged in their wigwams and found them as warm as the best English houses. In their wigwams they make a kind of couch or mattress firm and strong, raised about a foot high, first covered with boards that they split out of trees.

From the tree where the bark grows they make several sorts of baskets. Some will hold four bushels or more and so downward to a pint. In these baskets they put their provisions. Some of their baskets are made of rushes, some of bents others of maize husks and silk grass, a kind of hemp or barks of trees. Some are neat with portraitures of birds, beasts, fishes and flowers upon them in colors. Also they make mats for covering their houses and doors as well as to sleep and sit upon. The baskets and mats are made by the women, their dishes, pots and spoons by the men. Of latter years since the English came some of them get tin cups and little palls, chests of wood and glass bottles. Their drink was formerly water but of late years some of them planted orchards of apples and make cider.

The Indian clothing in former times was of the same matter as Adams was, skins of beasts also some had mantles of the feather of birds. To this day some of them wear their old kind of clothing. Later they sell their skins of furs to the English, Dutch and French and buy them a kind of cloth called duffels or trucking cloth about a yard and a half wide made of course wool. In this sort of cloth two yards make a mantle or coat for men and women. Their ornaments especially the women's are bracelets, neck laces and head bands also several sorts of beads especially of black and white wompon which is most esteem among them.

Their weapons are bows and arrows, clubs and tomahawks made of wood with a sharpened stone fastened therin.

For their water passage they make boats or canoes either of great trees made hollow which they do by burning them and after with lots of scraping, smoothing and shaping them. Some I have seen will carry twenty persons being forty or fifty feet in length and broad as the tree. They make another sort of canoes of birchen bark which they close together sewing them with a kind of bark and smearing the places with turpentine of the pine tree. These kind of canoes are neatly made being strengthned in the inside with some thin timbers and ribs, yet they are so light that one man will carry one of them upon his back several miles. When they go hunting some take their canoes on their backs while others carry their arms and food. These canoes are easy to overset but the Indians are so used to them that they seldom overturn.

They used to oil their skins and hair with bears grease and then paint their faces with vermilion or other red and powder their heads. Also they use black and white paints and make one part of their face of one color and another of another. The women especially do thus and some men also especially when they are marching to their wars. The women in time of mourning after death of their husbands or kindred do paint their faces all over black and so continue many days. The men in their wars do use turkey or eagle feathers stuck in their hair, as it is put up in a roll. Others wear deer shuts, made in the fashion of a cock's comb died red crossing the head like a half moon.

And also they delight much in dancing at which time he that danceth (for they dance singly the men and not the women) the rest singing, which is their chief music, will give away in his frolick all that ever he hath gradually, some to one and some to another according to fancy and affection. And then when he hath stripped himself of all he hath and is weary another succeeds and doth like. So one after another night after night, resting and sleeping in the days and so continue sometimes a week together. And at such dancing and feasting and reveling which are used mostly after the ingathering of their harvests all their neighbors, kindred and friends meet together. They use great vehemency in the motion of their bodies in their dances and sometimes the men dance in greater numbers in their war dances.

They are much given to hospitality in their way. If any strangers come to their houses they will give him the best lodging and diet they have. The strangers must be first served by themselves. The wife makes ready and by her husbands direction delivers to the strangers according to their quality or his affection.

Their chief Sachem or Sagamore is their law but yet a Sachem hath some chief men that he consults with as his special counsellors. Their Sagamore doing not any weighty matter without the consent of his great men or petty Sagamores.

Their religion is as other gentiles are. Some for their God adore the Sun, others the moon, and some the Earth. Others the fire and like vanities. Yet generally they acknowledge one great supreme doer of good and they call him Woonand or Mannitt. Another that is the great doer of evil they call Mattand which is the Devil and him they fear more than they love their chief God. There are among them certain men and women whom they call powows. These are partly witches and partly physicians and make use of herbs and roots for curing the sick. These with their spells, mutterings seem to do wonders. They use strange motions of their bodies insomuch that they will sweat until they foam and this will continue for some hours stroking and hovering over the sick. Sometimes broken bones have been set, wounds healed and sick recovered.

John Endecott came early to New England and was one of the founders of Salem, the oldest town in the colony of Massachusetts Bay. To protect themselves against the Indians, a military company was organized by the settlers, and Endecott was placed in command. Later he was chosen governor of Massachusetts and became the center of several religious controversies. Although the commander of an expedition against the Indians, Governor Endecott was much concerned regarding the spread of the gospel among them. The following letter, showing this concern, was written by him in the year 1651:

Much honoured and beloved in the Lord Jesus.

I esteeme it not the least of God's mercies that hath stirred up the hearts of any of the people of God to be instrumentall in the inlarging of the Kingdoms of his deare Sonne here amongst the Heathen Indians, which was one end of our coming hither, and it is not frustrated.

To speak truly I could hardly refrain tears from very joy to see their diligent attention to the work first taught by one of the Indians, who before his exercise prayed for the manner devoutly and reverently. His prayer was about a quarter of an houre or more, as we judged it. Mr. Eliot taught in the Indian tongue about three quarters of an hour as neer as I could guesse; the Indians which were in number men and women neer about one hundred, seemed the most of them so to attend him, as if they would loose nothing of what was taught them. After all this there was a Psalme sung in the Indian tongue, and Indian meeter, but to an English tune, read by one of themselves, that the rest might follow, and he read it very distinctly without missing a word as we could judge, and the rest sang chearfully, and prettie tuneablie. I rode on purpose thither being distant from my dwelling about thirty-eight or forty miles, and truly I account it one of the best Journeyes I made these many years. Some few dayes after I desired Mr. Eliot briefly to write me the substance of the Indian Exercise, which when he went thither again, namely to Naticke, where Indians dwell, and where the Indian taught, he read what he remembered of it first to their School Master who is an Indian, and teacheth them and their Children to write, and I saw him write also in English.

To tell you of their industry and ingenuitie in building of an house after the English manner, the hewing and squaring of their tymber, the sawing of the boards themselves, and making of a Chimney in it, making of their ground-sells, and wall-plates, and mortising, and letting in the studds into them artificially, there being but one English man a Carpenter to shew them, being but two dayes with them is remarkeable. They have also built a Fort there with halfe trees cleft about eight or ten inches over, about ten or twelve foot high, besides what is intrencht in the ground, which is above a quarter of an acre of ground as I judge. They have also built a foot bridge over Charles River, with Ground-sells and Spurres to uphold it against the strength of the Flood and Ice in Winter; it stood firme last Winter, and I think it will stand many Winters. They have made Drummes of their owne with heads and brases very neatly and artificially, all which shews they are industrious and ingenuous. And they intend to build a Water-Mill the next Summer, as I was told when I was with them. Some of them learnt to mow grasse very well. I shall no further trouble you with any more at this time concerning them.

Boston the 27th.
of the Eight. 1651.

Your loving Friend
in all service of Christ,

John Endecott

The self-sacrifice and hard work performed by the early missionaries in converting the natives to Christianity is well known. These men of God put self-interest aside and worked unceasingly for the welfare of the Indians. The most noted of these early workers in the vineyard was the Indian apostle John Eliot. This noted preacher was born in the year 1604 and died in 1690. After leaving the University of Cambridge Eliot became a teacher. In 1631 he arrived at Boston and the following year was settled as a teacher of the church in Roxbury.

Later he performed his marvelous work among the natives which included not only the religious phase, but an attempt to found a settlement in Massachusetts for them as well as instruction in the use of the white man's tools. Preacher Eliot's versatility was unbounded for he instructed the Indians in the use of the scythe and also showed them how to construct houses and bridges. The women wished to learn to spin, and again it was the Indian apostle who provided them with spinning wheels. It should be noted that John Eliot was almost alone in his endeavors to provide for the maintenance of the Indians in their native locations in New England instead of driving them from their old haunts.

The following letters written by Eliot give a good idea of the volume of work performed by this devoted missionary. In what follows, the apostle's desire to visit the Indian village at Amoskeag Falls is clearly indicated. However sickness prevented the journey and although on several occasions he expressed the wish to reach the falls at Amoskeag, there is nothing in any of his letters to show that he actually did so. The reference in one of them to talks between Eliot and Passaconaway leads one to the conclusion that Eliot may have journeyed as far as the falls to please the chief, but this is only conjecture.

Worthy Sir,

I perceive our Western Indians up into the Inland do more earnestly embrace the Gospel. Shawannon the great Sachym of Nashawog doth embrace the Gospel, and pray unto God. I have been foure times there this summer, and there be more people by far, than be amongst us; and sundry of them do gladly hear the word of God, but it is near 40 miles off, and I can but seldom goe to them, whereat they are troubled, and desire I should come oftener, and stay longer when I come.

There is a great fishing place upon one of the Falls of Merimack River called Pautucket, where is a great confluence of Indians every Spring, and thither I have gone these two years in that season, and intend so to doe the next Spring (if God will).

This Spring I did there meet old Papassaconnaway, who is a great Sagamore, and hath been a great Witch in all men's esteem (as I suppose yourself have often heard) and a very politick wise man. The last yeare he and all his sonnes fled when I came, pretending feare that we would kill him. But this yeare it pleased God to bow his heart to heare the word; I preached out of Malachi 1.11.

After a good space, this old Papassaconnaway speak to this purpose, that indeed he had never prayed unto God as yet, for he had never heard of God before, as now he doth. And he said further, that he did believe what I taught them to be true. And for his own part he was purposed in his heart from thenceforth to pray unto God, and that hee would perswade all his sonnes to do the same, pointing at two of them who were present, and naming such as were absent. His sonnes present especially his eldest sonne (who is Sachim at Wadchuset) gave his willing consent to what his father had promised, and so did the other who was but a youth. And this act of his was not only a present notion that soon vanished, but a

good while after he spake to Capt. [Simon] Willard, who tradeth with them in these parts for Bever and Otter Skins, &c. that he would be glad if I would come and live in some place thereabouts to teach them, and that Capt. Willard would live there also; and that if any good ground or place that hee had would be acceptable to me, he would willingly let me have it. I doe endeavour to engage the Sachims of greatest note to accept the Gospel, because that doth greatly animate and encourge such as are well affected, and is damping to those that are scoffers and opposers; for many such there be, though they dare not appear so before me.

There is another great fishing place about threescore miles from us, whither I intend (God Willing) to go next Spring, which belongeth to the forenamed Papassaconnaway; which journey though it be like to be both difficult and chargeable for horse and men, in fitting provisions, yet I have sundry reasons which bow and draw my heart thereunto. I desire your prayers to the Lord for me and for them, that the Lord would open my mouth to speak in his Name to their understandings, that with their hearts they may embrace that message which I shall bring unto them.

Roxbury this 12.
of Nov. 1648.

Yours to be commanded
in Jesus Christ,

John Eliot

In concluding this manuscript a few more excerpts and letters which bear testimony to the zeal of their author are included:

(1) When I went to Pautuket another fishing place, wherefrom all parts about they met together, thither came divers of these Sowahegan Indians and

heard me teach, and I had conference with them, and among other things, I asked whether Sowahegan Indians were desirous to pray to God; they answered; yea, I asked how many desired it; they answered wamu, that is, All, and with such affection as did much affect those Christian men that I had with me in company.

(2) I had, and still have, a great desire to go to a great fishing place, Namaske upon Merimak; and because the Indians way lyeth beyond the great river which we cannot passe with our horses, nor can we go to it on this side the river, unless we go by Nashaway, which is about, and bad way, unbeaten, the Indians not using that way; I therefore hired a hardy man of Nashaway to beat out a way and to mark trees, so that he my Pilot me thither in the Spring, and he hired Indians with him and did it and in the way passed through a great people called Sowahegen Indians, some of which had heard me at Pautuket, and at Nashaway, and carried home such tydings, that they were generally stirred with a desire that I would come and teach them, and when they saw a man come to cut out a way for me that way, they were very glad; and when he told them I intended to come that way the next Spring they seemed to him full of joy, and made him very welcome. But in the Spring, when I should have gone, I was not well, it being a very sickly time, so that I saw the Lord prevented me of that journey.

(3) The Chief Sachim of this place Pautuket and of all Mermak is Papassaconnaway whom I mentioned unto you gave up himself and his sons to pray unto God. This man did this year show very great affection on to me and to the work of God; he did exceeding earnestly invite me to come and live there and teach them; he used many arguments, many whereof I have forgotten: but this was one, that my coming thither but once in a year did them but little good because they soon forgot what I taught. Such elegant arguments as these did he use, with much gravity, and affection; and truly my heart much yearneth toward them, and I have a great desire to make our Indian Town that way; yet the Lord by the eye of Providence seemeth not to look thither partly because there is not a competent place of due encouragement for subsistence which would spoil the work, and partly because our Indians which are our first and chief materials are loth to go northward.

The following quotation comes from a friend of the apostle:

I had almost forgot to tell you of Mr. Eliot going up the Country lately with Mr. Flint, Captain Willard of Concord, and sundry others, towards Merrimath River unto that Indian Sachim Passaconnaway.

Daniel Gookin relates that the Reverend Eliot preached to the natives of Wamesit, also called Namkeke, and that the Wamesits were located at the junction of the Merrimack and Concord rivers. Apparently the locations of the Namaoskeag or Namoskek at Amoskeag Falls and the Wamesit or Namkeke site to the south were sometimes confused, possibly because both sites were noted fishing places:

Much respected and beloved in our Lord Jesus.

For the work of the Lord among the Indians, I thank his majesty he still smileth on it, he favoureth and blesseth it; through his help that strengthenth me, I cease not in my poor measure to instruct them; and I do see that they profit and grow in knowledge of the truth, and some of them in the love of it which appeareth by a ready obedience to it.

When grasse was fit to cut, I sent

some Indians to mow and others to make some hay at the place, because we must oft ride thither in the Autumn when grasse is withered and dead, and especially in the Spring before any grasse is come and there is provision for our horses, this work was performed well, as I found when I went up to them with my man to order it. We must also of necessity have an house to lodge in, meet in, and lay up our provisions and clothes, which cannot be in Wigwams. I set them therefore to fell and square timber for an house, and when it was ready, I went, and many of them with me, and on their shoulders carried all the timber together &. These things they cheerfully do, but this also I do, I pay them wages carefully for all such works I set them about, which is good encouragement to labor. I purpose, God willing, to call them together this Autumne to break and prepare their own ground against the Spring, and for other necessary works, which are not a few, in such an enterprize.

There is a great river which divideth between their planting grounds and dwelling place, through which, though they easily wade in Summer, yet in the Spring its deep, and unfit for daily passing over, especially of women and children; therefore I thought it necesary, that this Autumne we should make a foot Bridge over, against such time in the Spring as they shall have daily use of it; I told them my purpose and reason of it, wished them to go with me to do that work, which they chearfully did, and with their own hands did build a Bridge eighty foot long, and nine foot high in the midst, that it might stand above the floods; When we had done I cald them together, prayed, and gave thanks to God, and taught them out of a portion of Scripture, and at parting I told them, I was glad of their readinesse to labour.

At one time they gave [Mr. Cotton] twenty bushels of corne, at another time more than six bushels; two

hunting dayes they killed him fifteen Deeres; they brake up for him two acres of Land, they made for him a great house or Wigwam, they made twenty rod of fence for him with a Ditch and two Railes about it, they paid a debt for him of 3.li. 10.s. only some others were contributors in this money; one of them gave him a skin of Beaver of two pound, at his returne from building, besides many dayes works in planting corne altogether.

If the Lord please to prosper our poor beginnings, my purpose is, so far as the Lord shal enable me to give attendance unto the work, to have schoole exercises for all the men by daily instruction of them to read and write.

Roxbury this 21. 50. of the 8th.
Yours in our Lord Jesus,
John Eliot

Deare Brother,

At your desire I have wrote a few things touching the Indians which at present came to my mind, as being some of those passages which took principal impressions in my heart, wherein I thought I saw the Lord, and said the finger of God is here.

Their young men, who of all the rest, live most idlely and dissolutely, now begin to goe to service, some to Indians, some to English; and some of them growing weary, break out of their services so that some propounded what they should doe to remedy that evil. They desired that they might have a Court among them for government, at which motion wee rejoyced, seeing it came from themselves, and tended so much to civilise them; the good Lord prosper and bless it.

They moved also as you know for a School, and through God's mercy a course is now taken that there be Schooles at both places where their children are taught. You know likewise that wee exhorted them to fence their ground with ditches, stone walls, upon the banks, and promised to helpe them with Shovels, Spades, Mattocks, Crows of Iron; and they are very desirous to follow that counsell, and call upon me to help them with tools faster than I can get them, though I have now bought pretty store, and they (I hope) are at work. The women are desirous to learn to spin, and I have procured wheels for sundry of them, and they can spin pretty well. They begin to grow industrious, and find something to sell at Market all the year long; All winter they sell Brooms, Staves, Elepots, Baskets, Turkies. In the Spring, Cranberies, Fish, Strawberries; in the summer Hurtleberries, Grapes, Fish; in the Autum they sell Cranberies, Fish, Venison & they find a good benefit by the Market, and grow more and more to make use thereof; besides sundry of them work with the English in Hay time and Harvest, but yet it's not comparable to what they might do, if they were industrious, and old bought must be bent a little at once; if we can set the young twiggs in a better bent, it will bee God's mercy.

Deare Brother I can go no further, a weary body, and sleepy eyes command me to conclude. If I have not satisfied your desire in this letter, let me understand it from you and I shall be willing to do my indeavour: and thus with my deare love remembered to your self and your beloved and desiring your prayers for God's grace and blessing upon my spirit and poor indeavours, I take leave at this time and rest.

Roxbury this 24th.
of Septemb. 1647.

Your loving Brother
in our Saviour Christ,

John Eliot

To Major Atherton at his house in Dorchester:

Much honoured and beloved in the Lord.

Though our poor Indians are much molested in most places in their proceedings in way of civility yet the Lord hath put it into your hearts to suffer us to proceed quietly at Ponkipog, for which I bless God and thank yourself and all the good people of Dorchester. And now that our proceedings may be the more comfortable and peaceable my request is that you would please to further these two motions. First that you would please to make an order in your town secretly and record it in your town records, that you approve and allow the Indians of Ponkipog, there to sit down and make a town, and to enjoy such accommodations, as may be competent to maintain God's ordinances among them another day. My second request is that you would appoint fitting men, who may, in a fit season, bound and lay out the same and record that also and thus commending you to the Lord, I rest.

Roxbury this 4th. of the 4th. 57.

Yours to serve in the
service of Jesus Christ,

John Eliot

6

Monuments and Relics of the Indians

Jeremy Belknap

In describing any country, it is natural to make some inquiry concerning the vestiges of its ancient inhabitants. It is well known that the original natives of this part of America were not ambitious of perpetuating their fame by durable monuments. Their invention was chiefly employed either in providing for their subsistence, by hunting, fishing, and planting, or in guarding against and surprising their enemies. Their houses and canoes were constructed of light and perishable materials. Their mode of traveling was to take all possible advantage of water carriage, and to shorten distances, by transporting their birchen canoes across the necks of land which were convenient for the purpose. Their manner of taking fish was either by entangling them in wears, or dipping for them in scoopnets, or striking them with spears. They took quadrupeds in traps or pit-falls, or shot them, as well as birds, with arrows. For the construction of their canoes and houses they used hatchets, chissels, and gouges of stone. To cook their meat, they either broiled it on coals, or on a wooden grate, or roasted it on a forked stick, or boiled it in kettles of stone. Their corn was pounded in mortars of wood, with pestles of stone. Their bread was either baked on flat stones set before a fire, or in green leaves laid under hot ashes. Clam-shells served them for spoons, and their fingers for knives and forks. They had no sharper instruments than could be formed of stones, shells, and bones. Of these the two last are perishable by age; but of the first, relics are frequently found in the places of their former residence, generally in the neighbourhood of water falls, and other convenient fishing places. The manner of finding them is by plowing or digging. The most of those which have been discovered have come to light by accident, and a few only are so perfect as to merit preservation.

The hatchet is a hard stone, eight or ten inches in length and three or four in breadth, of an oval form, flatted and rubbed to an edge at one end; near the other end is a groove in which the handle was fastened; and their process to do it

Source: Jeremy Belknap, *The History of New Hampshire* (1791), vol. 2 (New York: Sources of Science, 1970), 63–72.

was this: When the stone was prepared, they chose a very young sapling, and, splitting it near the ground, they forced the hatchet into it, as far as the groove, and left nature to complete the work by growth of the wood, so as to fill the groove and adhere firmly to the stone. They then cut off the sapling above and below, and the hatchet was fit to use.

The chissel is about six inches long and two inches wide, flatted and rubbed sharp at one end. It was used only by the hand, for it would not bear to be driven. The gouge differs from the chissel only in being hollow at the edge. With these instruments they felled trees, cut them into proper lengths, scooped them out hollow for canoes, trays, or mortars, and fashioned them to any shape which they pleased. To save labor, they made use of fire, to soften those parts of the wood which were to be cut with these imperfect tools; and by a proper application of wet earth or clay, they could circumscribe the operation of the fire at their pleasure.*

Their pestles are long, cylindrical or conical stones, of the heaviest kind; some of which have figures, rudely wrought, at the end of the handle.

Their kettle is nothing more than a hole, either natural or artificial, in a large stone; but their mode of boiling in it would not readily occur to a person who had seen a kettle used no other way than with a fire under it. Their fire was made by the side of the kettle, and a number of small stones were heated. The kettle being filled with water and the food placed in it, the hot stones were put in, one after another, and by a dextrous repetition of this process, the meat or fish was boiled.

Of arrow-heads, there is found a greater number than of any other instrument; and they are of all sizes from one to five inches in length; pointed and jagged, with a notch on each side, at the lower end, to bind them to the shaft, the end of which was split to let in the head. Children were early taught the use of the bow, and many of the arrow-heads which are found seem to have been fit only for their use.

Another implement of stone is found, the use of which is to us undetermined. It is shaped like a pear, with a neck, and was probably suspended by a string. Some suppose it was hung to a net, and that many of them placed at the lower edge served the purpose of weights to sink it.

Some specimens of sculpture have been found, but they are not common. In the museum of the Academy of Arts and Sciences, there is an imitation of the head of a serpent, at the end of a long stone pestle, found at Wells, in the county of York. There is, in the possession of a gentleman in New-Hampshire, a piece of bone, on which is engraven the bust of a man, apparently in the agonies of death. The countenance is savage, and the work is well executed. This bone with the figure on it was found at the shore of the little bay in the river Pascataqua.

In the places of their habitations are sometimes found circular hearths of flat stones, which were laid in the middle of their wigwams. Their mode of lodging was with their feet to the fire. This custom is adopted by people who lie abroad in the woods, and by others at home. It is accounted both a preventative and a remedy for a cold.

The cellars in which they preserved

---

*"I have seen a native," says Roger Williams, "go into the woods with his hatchet, carrying only a basket of corne, and stones to strike fire. When he hath felled his tree [either a chestnut or pine] he maketh him a little hut or shed of the bark of it. He puts fire, and follows the burning of it in the midst, in many places. His corne he boils, and hath the brooke by him, and sometimes angles for a little fish. So he continueth burning and hewing, until he hath, in ten or twelve days, finished, and getting hands, launched his boat."

their corn are sometimes discovered in the new settlements, and their graves are frequently seen. Most of the skeletons appear to be in a sitting posture, and some remains of the instruments which were supposed necessary to their subsistence, ornament, or defence in the "country of souls" are found with them, particularly the stone pipe for smoking tobacco, of which there are several varieties. In a piece of intervale land near the Ossapy pond is a *tumulus*, or mound of earth, overgrown with pine, in which, at the depth of two feet, several skeletons have been discovered, buried with the face downward.* At Exeter, about two years ago, the remains of an infant skeleton were dug up. It was in a perpendicular position, and had been inclosed with a hollow log. Some strings of wampum were found near it and several spoons, apparently of European manufacture.

The remains of their fields are still visible in many places; they were not extensive, and the hills which they made about their corn stalks were small. Some pieces of baked earthen ware have been found at Sanborn-town and Goff's-town, from which it is supposed that the Indians had learned the potter's art; but of what antiquity these remnants are, and whether manufactured by them or not, is uncertain.

The paths which served them for carrying places between rivers or different parts of the same river are frequently discovered in the cutting of roads or laying out of new townships. Probably some hints might be taken from this circumstance, to expedite and facilitate our inland navigation.

In their capital fishing places, particularly in great Ossapy and Winipiseogee

rivers, are the remains of their wears, constructed with very large stones. At Sanborntown there is the appearance of a fortress consisting of five distinct walls, one within the other, and at Hinsdale there is something of the same kind; but these are vastly inferior, both in design and execution to the military works found in the country of the Senekas and in the neighbourhood of the Ohio.

I have heard of two specimens of an Indian *Gazette*, found in New-Hampshire. One was a pine tree, on the shore of Winipiseogee river, on which was depicted a canoe with two men in it. This is supposed to have been a mark of direction to those who might come after.† The other was a tree in Moultonborough, standing by a carrying place, between two ponds. On this tree was carved the history of one of their expeditions. The number of the killed and prisoners was represented by so many human figures; the former were marked with the stroke of a knife, across their throats, and even the distinction between the males and females was preserved.§

Some of their modes and customs have been learned by our own people and are still retained. In the river Pascataqua, lobsters and flat fish are struck with a spear; and the best time for this kind of fishing is the night. A lighted pitch-knot is placed on the outside of a canoe, which not only attracts the fish, but gives the fishermen direction where to strike. The river is sometimes illuminated by a multitude of these floating lights. The Indian scoopnet is shaped like a pocket, the edge of which is fastened to a wooden bow, at the end of a long pole. With these are caught salmon, shad, alewives, smelts, and lampreys. Frost-fish are taken with

MS. letter of Wentworth Cheswell, Esq.

†*Woodman's MS. letter.*

§*Shaw's MS. letter.*

wooden tongs, and black eels in cylindrical baskets, with a hole, resembling mouse traps made of wire.

The *culheag*, or log-trap, is used for taking wolves, bears, and martins. Its size varies, according to the bulk or strength of the animal. It is a forceps, composed of two long sticks, one lying on the other, connected at one end and open at the other. Near the open end is made a semicircular, covered enclosure, with short stakes, driven into the ground on one side of the logs which are firmly secured by another stake, on the opposite side. In this enclosure is placed the bait, fastened to a round stick, which lies across the lower log, the upper log resting on the end of a perpendicular pointed stick, the other end of which is set on the round stick. The animal having scented the bait, finds no way to come at it, but by putting his head between the logs. As soon as he touches the bait, the round stick on which it is fastened rolls; the perpendicular gives way; the upper log falls and crushes him to death in an instant, without injuring his skin.

To take martins, the hunters make a great number of these traps, at the distance of about a quarter or half a mile from each other; they scent the whole space between the traps, by drawing a piece of raw flesh on the ground; this scent guides the animal to the trap, which is baited with the same. The hunters visit the traps once in a day and retire to their camp with the prey. There are two seasons for this species of hunting, namely, in December and March.

Beavers are taken in iron spring traps. The Indians have learned to use these traps, in preference to their own.

The use of snow-shoes was learned at first from them. The shape and construction of them are well known. The stick which projects behind acts as a spring, and sets the man forward at every step; by which means, one who is used to this mode of travelling can walk on the snow more expeditiously than on the ground.

We are indebted to them for the method of preserving the flesh of animals in snow. This is very useful to people who raise or buy large quantities of poultry for the market. They fill the hollow parts and pack them in a cask with snow, which, whilst it remains undissolved, preserves the flesh in its original sweetness. The Indians had another way of preserving flesh, by cutting it from the bone and drying it in smoke; but this is now seldom used, unless the meat has been previously cured with salt, the use of which was unknown to the savages.

Their mode of catching ducks is still used in those places where this species of game abounds. In the month of August, the old ducks shed their feathers, and the young, being unfledged, are not able to fly. During this period they swim on the water and may be driven into small creeks, whence they cannot escape. They are then easily caught in great numbers and preserved for winter by salt or smoke.

We have also learned from the natives to dress leather with the brains and fat of the animal, which render it extremely soft and pliable.* They have an art of dying hair in various colors, which are bright and permanent. I know not whether they have communicated this knowledge.

Some of their modes of cookery have

---

*A lather is made of the brains and the soft fat or marrow in which the skin is soaked; it is then dried in smoke; afterward washed and soaked in warm water, till the grain is open then wrung out, dried by a slow fire, rubbed and stretched as long as any moisture remains in it. It is then scraped with a circular knife, and becomes very soft and delicate. Hearne.

been adopted and are retained. Their roasted and boiled ears of green corn, their *samp* and *homony*, which consist of corn bruised and soaked or boiled, their *noke-hike*, which is corn parched and pounded, their *suckatash*, which is a mixture of corn and beans boiled, are much used and very palatable. One of the most delicate of their dishes was *upaquontop*, or the head of a bass boiled, and the broth thickened with homony. The lip of a moose and the tail of a beaver, prepared in this manner, were among their greatest luxuries. They prepared a very agreeable liquor by infusing the meal of parched corn in warm water and sweetening it with the sugar of maple.

Their cultivation was extremely imperfect. The only objects of it were corn, beans, pumpkins, and squashes, which were planted by their women with the aid of no instruments but stones and clam-shells and no manure but fish. Yet, their judgment of the proper season for planting cannot be amended. It was when the leaves of the white oak are as big as the ear of a mouse. Their method of girdling trees to kill them, that the land might be opened for planting, is used by some people in their first essays of husbandry. It is not only a lazy fashion and quite inex-cuseable where axes may be had, but the ground needs clearing as often as the trees or branches are broken off by the wind.

The virtues of many herbs, roots, and barks, with which the country abounds, were well known to the natives, and some traditionary knowledge of this kind has been preserved, though much is lost for want of a more certain mode of preservation than human memory. Some of their medicinal operations are still practiced; but most of them are disused, being super-seded by professional improvements. They raised a blister by burning *punk*, or touch-wood, on the skin. They applied roots, boiled soft, in the form of a poultice to the throat or other parts, when swelled or inflamed. They relieved a person chilled with cold by pouring warm water down the throat. They attempted the cure of fevers by sweating in a covered hut, with the steam of water poured on hot stones, and then plunging into cold water. For pains in the limbs they had another mode of sweating. A number of sods were heated, and the patient, wrapped in a mat, was laid on some and covered with others, till the heat of the turf was supposed to have extracted the pain. The offices of physician and priest were united in the same person, and a variety of mysterious rites accompanied his operations.

They had a knowledge of poisons and antidotes and could so prepare themselves that the most venomous serpents would avoid them, or prove harmless in their hands. This knowledge has seldom been communicated and is always treated as mysterious.

I wish it could not be said that some of their superstitious notions have been transferred and propagated. The idea that lonely mountains and rocks are inhabited by departed spirits and other invisible and imaginary beings is not yet worn out. Certain charms and spells, which are supposed to be effectual preservatives or cures in cases of witchcraft, are still in use among the vulgar; though perhaps some of these traditions may owe their origin to the superstition of our European ancestors, descended from the remoter savages of Britain, Ireland, and Germany. Their notions, however pitied by some and ridiculed by others, are still deeply engraven on the minds of many and are maintained with an inflexibility which would do them honor if the cause were worthy of defence. So strong are these impressions that the same persons, whose intrepidity in scenes of real danger is unquestionable, often render themselves miserable by the apprehension of evils, which exist only in their imagination.

7

The History of Manchester

Chandler E. Potter

The voyagers to the coast of New England, in the early part of the seventeenth century, found the same divided among several tribes of Indians, all speaking radically the same language—Algonkin. Captain John Smith, of these early voyagers, gives the most minute account of these tribes. He says:

The principall habitations I saw at Northward, was Pennobscot, who are in warres with the Terentines, their next Northerly neighbors. Southerly up the Rivers, and along the Coast, wee found Mecadacut, Segocket, Pemmaquid, Nusconcus, Sagadahock, Satquin, Aumughcawgen, and Kenabeca: to those belong the Countries and people of Segotago, Pauhuntanuck, Pocopassum, Taughtanakagnet, Wabigganus, Nassaque, Mauherosqueck, Warigwick, Moshoquen, Waccogo, Pasharanack, &c. To those are alied in confederacy the Countries of Aucocisco, Accominticus, Passataquak, Augawoam, and Naemkeck, all those for any thing I could perceive, differ little in language or any thing, though most of them be Sagamos and Lords of themselves, yet they hold the Bashabes of Pennobscot the chiefe and greatest amongst them. The next is Mattahunt, Totant, Massachuset, Paconekick, then Cape Cod, by which is Pawmet, the Iles Nawset and Capawuck, neere which are the shoules of Rocks and sands that stretch themselves into the maine Sea twenty leagues; and very dangerous, betwixt the degrees of 40 and 41.*

Most of these tribes named by Smith occupied the same relative positions for more than a century after the country was permanently settled by the English.

West of Cape Cod were the powerful tribes of the Narragansets† and Pequots; while in the country, upon the rivers and lakes, were several powerful tribes; the Nipmucks, in the interior of Massachusetts, and New Hampshire, and occupying the valley of the Merrimack, in New Hampshire, and Massachusetts; and the Norridgewocks seated upon the

*See Mass. Hist. Coll. Vol. iii, third series, p. 20.

†Narraganset is from Nanrantsouack and means a carrying-place. Norridgewock is also a corruption of the same word. (See Mem. Amer. Acad. New Series, Vol. I, pages 272 and 373.)

Source: Chandler E. Potter, The History of Manchester (Manchester, NH: C. E. Potter, 1856), 22–31.

branches of the Kennebec, and the lakes in the northern interior of Maine. This last tribe was called Abnakis by the French and was principally noted for their adherence to the French interests and their inroads upon the English settlements, which their connection with the French led them to undertake.

East of the Penobscot were the Scootucks, or Passamaquoddies, inhabiting the Scootuck or St. Croix River and the shore of Passamaquoddy Bay; the Milicetes in the valley of the river St. John; and the Micmacs, occupying the rest of New Brunswick and the peninsula of Nova Scotia.

The Micmacs were, and still are, a warlike people. Living mainly upon the sea shore, athletic, of powerful frame, and most expert canoe-men, they were fond of warlike expeditions and often were a source of fear and anxiety to their western neighbors, under the dreaded name of Tarratines. They even extended their war expeditions against the tribes of Massachusetts, within the knowledge of the English, and in some of the earliest stipulations between the tribes of New Hampshire and Massachusetts and their English neighbors mention is made of their dread of the Tarratines.

When Captain Smith coasted along the shore of New England, in 1614, making the island of Monheagan the centre of his operations, the Penobscot tribe was one of the most powerful in New England. They were under the control of a Bashaba, or Chief, who held the tribes of Maine as far west as the Saco as tributary, or subject to him. He was then at war with the Tarratines, and in 1615, that warlike people sent an expedition against him, with such secrecy and consequent success as that they took him by surprise, and put him and his family to death.

Divisions arose as to the succession to the Bashaba, of which the Tarratines

taking the advantage soon overpowered the other tribes of Maine and extended a war of extermination along the coast of Massachusetts. Hand in hand, as it were, with war, stalked pestilence, so that in 1620, the tribes upon the sea coast, from the St. Croix to Cape Cod, had become greatly depreciated in numbers; and some places had become almost entirely depopulated.

Speaking of this depopulation, Captain Smith says, "They had three plagues in three years successively neere two hundred miles along the Sea coast, that in some places there scarce remained five of a hundred … but it is most certaine there was an exceeding great plague amongst them; for where I have seene two or three hundred, within three years after remained scarce thirty."

Whatever this disease may have been, it seems to have extended little farther south than Cape Cod and to have been limited in violence, at least, among the tribes of the interior, so that the Pilgrims in 1620 and for many years subsequent, had but little to fear from the once powerful tribes upon the seashore north of Cape Cod; but on the contrary, had to use every precaution and much vigilance against the power of the southern tribes and those of the interior, which had been less afflicted by disease and war.

At this period, the most powerful tribes of the interior, and probably of New England, north of the Pequots, had their residence in the valley of the Merrimack, upon the productive falls and fertile meadows of that beautiful river. These meadows, or "intervales," as they are usually called, are basins made up of alluvial and vegetable deposits and were, doubtless, once covered with water, which has gradually passed away through the Merrimack, that continually deepening its channel, has burst the rocky barriers of these bays, or lakes, and left their former beds dry and arable land. That these intervales were submerged and at a comparatively late period hardly admits of a doubt, as the barriers of these ancient bays can be readily traced above Pawtucket, Amoskeag, Hooksett, Garvin's and Sewall's falls; and upon most of these basins, or intervales, have been found far below their surface, logs, fresh-water shells, and other unmistakable evidences of submersion.

The Merrimack, then, was a succession of bays, from Lake Winnepesaukee to the ocean, a part of which now remain at Sanbornton and Meredith and which add so much of beauty to the scenery of that neighborhood.

These intervales were of very great fertility and of such ready productiveness as to afford an abundant harvest to the scanty husbandry of the Indian. More than two centuries of culture have hardly decreased their fertility.

Then the Merrimack afforded other superior advantages for Indian settlements. Rising in the White Mountains at an altitude of six thousand feet above the level of the ocean, its waters find their way to the Atlantic, through the distance of two hundred and fifty miles; of course there are rapids and falls through most of its entire length. These afforded the most ample fishing grounds to the natives, whereat to spear and take with dip-net and seine, the myriads of alewives, shad, and salmon, that literally crowded the Merrimack during certain seasons of the year. Then the woods upon its banks were filled with moose, deer, and bears—whilst the ponds and lakes, the sources of its tributaries, were teeming with water fowl.

In this beautiful valley of the Merrimack, with all these attractions of fertile planting grounds, an abundance of fish, and hunting grounds of unlimited extent—the first English adventurers found several tribes of Indians occupying localities chosen with Indian taste and with special reference to his comfort and his wants. From its mouth far above its affluents, the Winnepesaukee and Pemegewasset, the shores of this "Silver Stream," were dotted with Indian villages.

It was the very paradise of the Indian imagination. Is it a wonder that the wresting of such a home from "the lords of the soil" should have been accompanied with strife and bloodshed? That the Indian in his ignorance and wildness, when driven from the graves of his fathers at the hands of strangers, should have left the marks of his vengeance behind him, traced with all the horrors of the scalping-knife and tomahawk? It is not strange; nor is it so singular, or so much a matter of reproach, as that a people, fresh from the lash of oppression, laying claim to much of humanity, and ever bearing upon their arm the shield of morality and religion—should have driven the simple hearted natives from their lands without even color of right, except what comes from that precept of barbarism, that might makes right; without even color of title, when title was pretended, except what was purchased for a few blankets, a trucking coat, a few beads and baubles;—or, perhaps still worse—for a runlet of "occupee," or "fire-water"!

These tribes upon the Merrimack were the Agawam, Wamesit, or Pawtucket, Nashua, Souhegan, Namaoskeag, Pennacook, and Winnepesaukee. The Agawam tribe occupied the eastern part of what is now Essex County in Massachusetts, extending from tide-water upon the Merrimack round to Cape Ann. Their territory, skirted upon two sides by the Merrimack and Atlantic, indented by bays, intersected by rivers, and interspersed with ponds, was appropriately called Wonnesquamsauke, meaning literally, the Pleasant Water Place, the word being a compound from *Wonne* (pleasant), *Asquam* (water), and *Auke* (a place). This word was sometimes contracted to Wonnesquam, often to Squam-sauke, and still oftener to Squam, or Asquam.

The deep guttural pronunciation of *asquam* by the Indians sounded to the English like *agawam* and hence the word as applied to the Indians of that locality. Several localities in Essex County are now known by names contracted and derived from this Indian word *Wonnesquamsauke*, as "Squam" the name of a pleasant harbor and village upon the north side of Cape Ann, and "Swamscot" the name of a pleasant village in the eastern part of Lynn.

The Wamesits lived at the forks of the Merrimack and Concord rivers, and upon both sides of the latter river. Wamesit, is derived from *Wame* (all or whole) and *Auke* (a place) with the letter *s* thrown in betwixt the two syllables for the sake of the sound. The Indian village at this place undoubtedly received this name from the fact that it was a *large* village, the *place* where *all* the Indians collected together. This was literally true in the spring and summer, as the Pawtucket Falls, near by, were one of the most noted fishing places in New England, where the Indians from far and near gathered together in April and May to catch and dry their year's stock of shad and salmon. Wamesit was embraced nearly in the present limits of the city of Lowell, in Middlesex County, Massachusetts.

The Indians in this neighborhood were sometimes called Pawtuckets, from the falls in the Merrimack of that name. Pawtucket means "the forks," being derived from the Indian word *Pohchatuk* (a branch). Pawtucket seems, however, to have been applied by the English rather to all the Indians north of the Merrimack than to the particular tribe at the falls of that name.

The Nashuas occupied the lands upon the Nashua and the intervales upon the Merrimack, opposite and below the mouth of that river. Nashua means the "river with a pebbly bottom"—a name said to have been peculiarly appropriate before art had deprived it of this distinctive beauty.

The Souhegans lived upon the Souhegan River, occupying the rich intervales upon both banks of the Merrimack, above and below the mouth of the Souhegan. Souhegan is a contraction of *Souheganash*, an Indian noun in the plural number, meaning "worn-out lands." These Indians were often called Natacooks or Nacooks, from their occupying ground that was free from trees, or "cleared land"—Netecook meaning a "clearing."

The Namaoskeags resided at the falls in the Merrimack, known at present by the name of Amoskeag, in Manchester. This word written variously Namaske, Namaoskeag, Naumkeag, and Naimkeak, means the "fishing place," from *Namaos* (a fish) and *Auke* (a place).

The Pennacooks occupied the rich intervales at Pennacook, now embraced in the towns of Bow, Concord, and Boscawen, in the county of Merrimack. They were thus called, from *Pennaqui* (crooked) and *Auke* (place), the intervales at Concord, which are extensive, being embraced within the folds of the Merrimack, which winds its way along in a very crooked manner.*

The Winnepesaukees occupied the lands in the vicinity of the lake of that name, one of their noted fishing places being at the outlet of the Winnepesaukee, now known as the Weirs, the parts of permanent Indian weirs having remained at that place long after the advent of the

---

It may be that Pennacook means the ground-nut place, *in which case it would be derived from* Penak, *a ground-nut, and* Auke, *a place.*

whites. Winnepesaukee is derived from *Winne* (beautiful), *nipe* (water), *kees* (high), and *Auke* (a place), meaning literally, "the beautiful water of the high place."

Of these several tribes, the Pennacooks were the most powerful, and either from their superiority, arising from a long residence upon a fertile soil, and hence more civilized, or from having been for a long period under the rule of a wise chief—and perhaps from both causes united—had become the head, as it were, of a powerful confederacy.

It is well known that the Winnepesaukee, Amoskeag, Souhegan, and Nashua tribes were completely subservient to the Pennacooks; while the Wamesits were so intermarried with them as to be mainly under their control, acknowledged fealty to Passaconnaway, and finally, with the other tribes upon the Merrimack, became merged with the Pennacooks and ceased to be distinct tribes in fact or name.

The Agawams were also intimately connected with the Pennacooks and acknowledged fealty to them and doubtless were one of the earliest tribes to become merged with them, but still they ceased to exist as a distinct tribe at so early a date that few particulars of their history have been preserved.

Besides the tribes in the valley of the Merrimack, the Pennacooks had control over most of the tribes from the Concord River, in Massachusetts, to the sources of the Connecticut, and from the highlands betwixt the Merrimack and Connecticut, to the Kennebec in Maine. It is known that the Wachusetts, from *Wadchu* (a mountain) and *Auke*, (a place), near Wachusett mountain in Massachusetts; the Coosucks, from *Cooash* (pines), upon the sources of the Connecticut River; the Pequaquaukes from *Pequaquis* (crooked) and *Auke* (a place) upon the sources of the Saco, in Carroll County, in New Hampshire, and Oxford County in Maine; the

Ossipees from *Cooash* (pines) and *Sipe* (a river), upon the Ossipee Lake and River in Carroll County, in New Hampshire, and York County in Maine; the Squamscotts, from *Winne* (beautiful), *Asquam* (water), and *Auke* (a place), upon Exeter River, in Exeter and Stratham, in Rockingham County; the Winnecowetts, from *Winne* (beautiful), *Cooash* (pines), and *Auke* (a place) in the Hamptons in the same county; the Piscataquaukes, from *Pos* (great), *Attuck* (a deer), and *Auke* (a place), upon the Piscataqua River, the boundary betwixt New Hampshire and Maine; the Newichewannocks, from *Nee* (my), *Week* (a contraction of *weekwam*, a house), and *Owannock* (come)—upon one of the upper branches of the same river; the Sacos, from *Sawa* (burnt), *Coo* (pine), and *Auke* (a place), upon the Saco River, in York County, Maine; and the Amariscoggins, from *Namaos* (fish), *kees* (high), and *Auke* (a place), upon the Amariscoggin River, having its source in New Hampshire and emptying its waters into the Kennebec— all acknowledged the power and control of the Pennacooks and were members of the confederacy of which that powerful tribe was the head and Passaconnaway the leading Sagamon or Bashaba.

These Indians from the interior were known and called among the tribes upon the sea shore by the general name of Nipmucks—or Fresh Water Indians. Nipmuck is derived from *Nipe* (still water) and *Auke* (a place), with the letter *m* thrown in for the sake of the euphony. And true to their name, the Nipmucks usually had their residences upon places of still water, the ponds, lakes, and rivers of the interior.

But the Indians in the Merrimack Valley, although properly Nipmucks and living in distinct bands or tribes, were usually called by the English, Pennacooks, from the fact that the tribe at Pennacook was the most powerful one in the valley, and under the rule of Passaconnaway, had become, as has already been seen, the head of a powerful confederacy. This position of that tribe brought its people in contact with the English on all occasions of moment, such as conferences and negotiations, and hence the English, meeting on such occasions Pennacooks almost exclusively, applied the name of Pennacook to the tribes generally inhabiting the upper Merrimack Valley. And in course of time, as the Indians became reduced in numbers by emigration, war, and contact with civilization, the smaller tribes became united with the larger ones, till in 1685, the Pennacooks were the only tribe in, and had exclusive possession of, the Merrimack Valley.

The Merrimack naturally was but a series of falls, rapids, and ripples from the Souhegan to the lower Pennacook Falls (now Garvin's). These afforded the most ample opportunity for fishing, and the name of Namaoskeag was doubtless applied to that section of the river and the adjacent country around; but in course of time, as fish became more limited, the name of Namaoskeag came to be applied to the immediate neighborhood of the principal falls, now known as Amoskeag. The fish at these falls were most abundant, and the facilities for taking them superior to those of any other place upon the Merrimack.

The river below the main fall, in the course of a few miles, is entered by a number of rivers and rivulets having their sources in lakes at no great distance; and of course, at certain seasons, it was filled with alewives, waiting an opportunity to pass up those small streams; thus both in the Merrimack, and in those streams, affording ready opportunity to take them in any quantity.

Then at the same season, the great basin, or eddy, at the foot of Merrill's Falls and at the mouth of the Piscataquog river was literally filled with eels, shad, and salmon, waiting a passage up the falls,

occupied by their earlier or more expert companions, over and among which, the Indian in his canoe could pass and spear or net, at will.

Again, at the foot of the main fall, and upon the western bank of the river, here dividing and passing among and around certain small islands, was, and is at the present time a basin or eddy emptied by a small passage, easily rendered impassable for fish by a weir, and ever filled with fish, in the season of them, from the falls above, the force of the water rushing over the main pitch of the falls, naturally and inevitably driving into this pool those fish, that in the rush did not succeed in passing up the falls. Here they were as secure as in an eel pot, and the Indians could take them at their convenience.

Then, at the main falls, and at the islands below, the river passes amid rocks in narrow channels, and upon these rocks and channels, the Indian could stand through day and night, if he chose, and throw spear and dip-net without missing a fish, or fishes, at each throw. And last, the various fish did not usually arrive at these falls, until after the twentieth of May, when the planting season was over, thus affording the Indians plenty of time to take and cure them, without interruption from their agricultural pursuits, however scanty. Whereas at Pawtucket and the rapids in that neighborhood, the fish arrived usually about the first of May and continued through the busiest time of corn-planting.

These peculiar advantages, pertaining to the fishery at this place, made it *par excellence, the* fishing place, hence as before suggested, the Indian name of Namaoskeag.

These were no ordinary advantages to the Indian, depending as he did for subsistence upon fish, flesh, fowl, and such vegetables as his limited agriculture might produce. Hence we can readily suppose that where fish were so abundant and so readily to be taken, that there the Indians would flock together in vast numbers to supply their future wants, and that the place would be one of great importance. Such was the fact, and Namaoskeag, for a long time, was not only the great point of attraction to all provident Indians, but was the royal residence of the ancient Sagamons of the Merrimack Valley.

At Namaoskeag, upon the bluff immediately east of the falls, was the main village or town occupied by the Indians, as is plainly shown by the abundance of arrow and spear heads and the debris of stones from which they were manufactured, together with pieces of pottery and other unmistakable evidences of an ancient Indian town still to be seen and found, while down the river to the Souhegan, there were smaller settlements wherever were good fishing or planting grounds. In Bedford, opposite Carthagena Island, on land of the Honorable Thomas Chandler and opposite the mouth of Cohos River, such settlements existed, the vestiges of which still exist at the former place and did at the latter, till the hand of improvement swept them away.

But, as before suggested, the main Indian village was at the falls, called by Mr. Eliot, "a great fishing place *Namaske* upon Merimak," and "which," he says, "belongeth to Papassaconnaway."* Here, prior to 1650, Passaconnaway had a principal residence and was so anxious to have the Reverend Mr. Eliot come here and establish

his community of Christian, or "Praying Indians," as his proselytes were called, that he offered to furnish him with any amount of land that he might want for that purpose. The old Sagamon held out such inducements, and the place was of so much importance, that Eliot at one time had serious thoughts of establishing himself here, but the distance was so great to transport supplies, and the natives in Massachusetts were so averse to going farther north, that he thought "the Lord by the Eye of Providence seemed not to look thither,"† and he located himself at Natick.§

There is no doubt that Mr. Eliot afterwards found opportunity to visit this place and to preach and establish a school here, as Gookin in his account of the "Christian Indians" names Naamkeke as one of the "places where they [the Indians] met to worship God and keep the Sabbath; in which places there was at each place a teacher and schools for the youth at most of them."** And as no other man established schools or preaching among the Indians of the interior, save Mr. Eliot, it follows conclusively that he both preached and taught at Namaoskeag. So that our ancient town not only has the honor of having been the scene of the philanthropic efforts and labors of "the apostle Eliot," but also that of having the first "preaching and school" established within its limits, that was established in the state north-west of Exeter, however remiss its white inhabitants may have been in these particulars.

*See Eliot's Letter Mass. His. Coll., Vol. IV., 3d series, ps. 82 and 123.

†See as before Mass. His. Coll., vol IV., 3d series, ps. 123 and 124.

§Natick *means a* clearing, *or place free from trees, from the Indian words* Naa *(*bare*) and* Auke *(*a place*), t being thrown in for the sound. Hence* Neddock *(a cape in York county, Me.) and* Natticook *or* Naacook, *the ancient name of Litchfield, the town upon the east side of the Merrimack, and joining Manchester on the south.*

It would seem from Ralle's vocabulary, that the Norridgewocks had an adjective Nete, *meaning bare or* cleared. *This prefixed to* goo'ike *their noun for* place *or spot of land, forms* Netegoo'ike, *the derivitive noun meaning* cleared land *or a* bare place, *almost similar in formation and sound to* Naa-t-auke *the noun of the same meaning among the Nipmucks or Pennacooks.*

**See Trans. and Coll. Amer. Anti. Society, page 518.

8

Aboriginal Tribes of New Hampshire

Austin J. Coolidge and John B. Mansfield

The native tribes of New Hampshire all belonged to the Abnaki nation but seem to have had a separate government and [to be] independent of those who lived east of the Piscataqua River. They were divided into several tribes. Those living along the Merrimack were the Agawams, the Wamesits or Pawtuckets, the Nashuas, the Souhegans, the Namaoskeags, the Penacooks, and the Winnepesaukees. At the source of the Connecticut River were the Cooash Indians, the only tribe that occupied the banks of the river when discovered by the whites. There is a tradition that a great many tribes besides these had their residence along the banks of this river, but that they had been principally exterminated in the wars with the Mohawks and by the plague of 1616–17. Those that lived in the eastern part of the state were the Pequaquaukes, sometimes called Pequawkets, who inhabited a part of Maine; the Ossipees, the Squamscotts, the Winnecowetts, and the Piscataquas. The population of these tribes, either individually or collectively, is not known; in fact, there is no certainty that an estimate of their numbers was ever made by any authority from the period of the establishment of the first colonial governments.

The most powerful tribe was the Penacooks, who occupied the tract of land known by that name, part of which is now Concord; but in process of time, in consequence of the reduction of the smaller tribes by war, emigration, and the influences of civilization, those who occupied the Merrimack Valley were merged into one tribe and were called indiscriminately Penacooks. Namaoskeag was the site of the principal village, as is evident from the large number of Indian relics there found; and here was the royal residence of the ancient sagamores of the Penacooks. At the mouth of the Piscataquog River was another considerable village, and so again at or near the outlet of Lake Winnepesaukee. There were other and smaller settlements along the Merrimack as far as the Souhegan River; and in Bedford, on Carthagena island, and opposite the mouth of the Coös River, traces of Indian

Source: Austin J. Coolidge and John B. Mansfield, *History and Description of New England: New Hampshire* (Boston: Austin J. Coolidge, 1860), 401–4.

villages were to be seen until recently. The sites of the villages were selected with regard to the fertility of the soil, the sufficiency of game, and the quantity of fish which abounded in the rivers and streams; nor was the beauty of the surrounding scenery lost sight of, as can be seen even at this day; the changes of a century of civilization having left their natural beauties scarcely impaired.

The sagamores of most note among the Penacooks were Passaconaway, Wonnalancet, his son, and Kancamagus, usually called John Hodgkins, his grandson. The first [white settlers] heard of Passaconaway was in 1627 or 1628, perhaps earlier, if the Conway whom Christopher Levett saw in the vicinity of the Piscataqua in 1623 be the same person, as is supposed to be the case from the fact that when Massachusetts desired to arrest him in 1642, directions were given to proceed to Ipswich, Rowley, and Newbury—sufficient evidence that he had a residence at each of those places.* Passaconaway had a great influence over the people who acknowledged his sway. Besides being a powerful warrior, he was an expert necromancer, which of itself, considering the superstitious and untutored minds of the savages, was enough to win for him the highest veneration and the greatest awe. He died prior to 1669; but the exact date is not known. He lived on terms of the greatest intimacy with the English, despite the encroachments they made upon his lands, and his last wish to his people was that they should never make war upon the whites....

Wonnalancet was chief of the tribe in 1669 and lived on terms of the greatest intimacy with the white settlers. He preferred peace to war and seems to have been impressed very strongly with the advice of his father. He appears to have been of a most amiable disposition, to a much greater extent than many of his more civilized neighbors. He was imprisoned by the English in 1642, and, though subjected to many indignities, he never offered retaliation. As a specimen of the goodness of his heart, it may be said that, in 1659, he sold his home to purchase the liberty of his brother Nanamocomuck, who was imprisoned in Boston for debt. He embraced the Christian religion, through the ministrations of Mr. Eliot, in 1674, and is said to have lived up to it strictly. About September 1677, Wonnalancet, finding the lands which the English had granted him taken possession of, retired to the Indian settlement of St. Francis. The last that is heard of him is in 1696, whenhe was placed under the charge of Jonathan Tyng of Tyngsborough. It is probable that subsequently he retired again to St. Francis, where he passed the remainder of his days.

Wonnalancet was succeeded by his nephew Kancamagus about May 15, 1685, shortly after the removal of the former to St. Francis for the first time. This chief was more generally known as John Hodgkins and was the son of Nanamocomuck, Passaconaway's eldest son. He was a polite, brave, and intelligent man, but under his chieftaincy the Penacooks became a formidable foe to the English settlers, which was owing, in a measure, to a want of respect on the part of the provincial authorities; for it is certain, from various letters sent to Governor Cranfield, that Kancamagus desired to retain the friendship of the English. He was the leader of the massacre at Dover, when Major Waldron was so brutally murdered, June 27, 1689, and took part in several other attacks upon the English settlements. His wife and children were taken prisoners by the English in September 1690, and his sister was slain. The

See Winthrop's Journal.

last that is heard of him is in 1691 [1690], when he signed the truce of Sagadahoc, shortly after which, it is supposed, he died.

After the affair at Dover, the Indians, as a general thing, retired from the precincts of New Hampshire, and thus the ancient royal residence of the Penacooks became comparatively deserted. The place at Namaoskeag was occupied as late as 1745 by one Indian, named Christian, who was employed by the English during the Indian wars as a scout and subsequently retired, with others of his tribe, to St. Francis. He was afterwards, however, concerned in some depredations on the English settlements and was one of those who decoyed two negroes from Canterbury, in 1752. The last heard of him was in 1757, when he was at St. Francis, where he probably died. The spot occupied by Christian's wigwam is still shown at Amoskeag Falls, where the relics of his hearthstone, his pipes, arrow-heads, and ornaments, consisting of bears' teeth, together with his tomahawk—have been brought to light.

Thus the aboriginal inhabitants, who held the lands of New Hampshire as their own, have been swept away. Long and valiantly did they contend for the inheritance bequeathed to them by their fathers, but fate had decided against them, and it was all in vain. With bitter feelings of unavailing regret, the Indian looked for the last time upon the happy places where for ages his ancestors had lived and loved, rejoiced and wept, and passed away, to be known no more forever. The wild beasts, who shared with him the forests and were molested only when required to minister to his wants, have also disappeared. The forests have melted away, and the broad intervals, slopes, and uplands, from the Piscataqua to the Connecticut, affording sustenance to a teeming population, attest the change that a century has wrought. The waterfalls, too, have been made to resound with the music of spindles and of wheels, and the streets have become marts of traffic. Civilization has followed the same course here as in all other countries reclaimed from barbarism, by blotting out the original inhabitants and planting another race. The native tribes of New Hampshire fulfilled their mission and passed away. We too shall pass away, and other busy feet will tread upon our graves, as thoughtless of us as we are now of the sleeping dust of the red man.

9

Character of the Penacooks

The Rev. Edward Ballard

Indian depredations occasioned many disasters on the northern frontier of New Hampshire during the French and English wars. They were severely distressing at the time of their occurrence, and their cruelties are even now remembered with a feeling of horror at the thrilling recital. The hardships of the settlers in the towns whose frontier boundary was the unsubdued wilderness were always great from the harshness of the climate in the winter season, and, at all times, from the want of many of the conveniences and comforts, and not unfrequently the necessities, of ordinary life. But to these trials of fortitude and self-denial were added, for a long space of time, the fear of the war-hoop awakening the slumbers of the morning, or the ambush of the enemy to seize or slay the anxious laborer in the corn-field. Thus their life was made a season of perpetual alarm. For mutual defense and security, they were compelled to leave their dwellings and find shelter in the wooden forts which their own hands had reared.

It has been thought that these marauding expeditions were made by the Indians who once inhabited the valley of the Merrimack and its tributaries and whose various dwelling-places are now remembered as Penacook, from which the tribe has received its name, Contoocook, Naticook, Amoskeag, Merrimack, which has given its name to the river; Souhegan, Pawtucket, Wamesit, and other places, where portions of the tribe had their homes, in subjection to the wide-spread sway of Passaconaway, "The Child of the Bear." It has been an opinion that they went forth in armed companies in time of war, to take revenge, because of the ill-treatment received from the hands of white men, in taking their lands at a price which, they lamented too late, was scarcely to be named as a compensation—in cheating them in the traffic for furs—and in acts of personal insult and cruelty, oft times repeated. Unhappily for the memory of the traders and some of the pioneers, these charges were true.

But though these Indians had many provocations to retaliate their injuries, there is sufficient evidence to show that,

Source: The Rev. Edward Ballard, "Character of the Penacooks," in Nathaniel Bouton, ed. *Collections of the New Hampshire Historical Society Containing Province Records and Court Papers from 1680–1692: Notices of Provincial Councilors, and Other Articles Relative to the Early History of the State,* vol. 8 (Concord: McFarland and Jenks, 1866), 428–45.

as a tribe, they were not concerned in these fear-bearing expeditions at all....

Little is known of this tribe [Pennacook] prior to the paternal rule of Passaconaway,* but the indications from tradition and the remains of wigwams still existing on the banks of the Merrimack and its tributaries, with other circumstances, declare that the nation was much larger before it was known to the English than at the date of their first acquaintance, or at any time afterward. The tradition of the attack by the Mohawks on the chief settlement, within the limits of the present city of Concord, shows their original strength to have been greater than ever since known. The loss of their people, occasioned by these ruthless invaders, was never repaired. Their spirits were broken by their defeat in this war of self-defense against the "Men-Eaters" [Mohawk]† of the west, whose name alone was a terror throughout the valley, so that two of the tribe could frighten the people of a village to flee to the wilderness for a refuge. Under this subjected state of feeling they were not prepared to exhibit or ever cherish a warlike spirit against the English.

It is probable, too, that the ravaging disease, which swept off large numbers of the natives on the sea-coast but two or three years before the landing of the Pilgrims on Plymouth Rock, brought a portion of its desolation to this region.§ Indian usages kept up frequent visits between the interior and the sea-board, where the disorder began and prevailed; and as it appears to have been contagious

to the natives, though not to the whites, who were exposed to it in Maine, it was a sufficient cause for the diminution of their numbers and of course their warlike ability.

The debilitated condition of the tribe is further shown by the petition of Passaconaway to the Legislature of Massachusetts (1662) for a grant of land for a residence, as he appeared to have had none that he could call his own. The answer of the government allowed him and his associates a tract "a mile and a half on either side of the Merrimack," about Naticot**— the present Litchfield.

Their peaceful spirit may be also shown from the counsels of this chief in his old age to his assembled people (1660), that they should never quarrel with the English, for though they might do the newcomers much mischief, yet they would in time all be destroyed if they acted in opposition to his advice; that he had tried (probably by his pretended sorceries) to prevent their settlement, but could not effect his purpose. He therefore advised them never to contend with the English, nor to make war with them. He lived to be more than a hundred years old,†† and at his death left his sachemdom and his pacific advice as his legacy to his son Wonnelanset, according to the laws of Indian inheritance. His example had already been in accordance with this advice, for (1632) he had pursued an Indian from the neighborhood of the Mohawks, who had killed an Englishman, and captured the murderer.§§ Thus,

*His name is on the Wheelright Deed of 1629, but this deed may have been a forgery. Farmer on Penacooks, Coll. N. H. Hist. Soc., vol. 1, p. 219.

†Mohawks, from Mo-ho-waugs-uck, the plural form of the noun, derived from the verb Mo-ho, to eat, shortened to Mó-hŏ-waugs in the English pronunciation, and thence to Mó-hawks. Eliot's Key, 209.

§Fox's Dunstable, p. 19.

**Hubbard.

††Gookin's Hist. Praying Indians.

§§Drake 3, p. 94.

both by words and deeds, Wonnelanset was encouraged to imitate the course of his father in the new duties of government.

Before entering on the discharge of his office he had received (1642) a sufficient provocation from the English authorities at Boston to induce his resort to the frequent Indian remedy of revenge on any one of the white race whom he might chance first to meet. On mere suspicion, he was made a prisoner, with a view to disarm the tribe, and on making his escape was shot at by the persons who endeavored to retake him.* For these and other equally censurable actions, the English, fearing the resentment of savage vengeance, sent Cutshamekin to let him know that a portion of the treatment was unauthorized. These "unwarranted proceedings," as they were called even in those early days, produced no retaliation from the natives against whom they were directed....

On the 5th of May, 1674, then about fifty-five years old, Wonnelanset listened to the preaching of Eliot, the missionary, who addressed the natives in his wigwam at Pawtucket. He had previously been opposed to the importunity that urged him to abandon the faith of his fathers. But now he was willing to follow the advice and, in his expressive language, "to leave his old canoe and embark in a new canoe,"† and serve the God of the Christians for the rest of his life. Thus a new motive was added to strengthen the friendly feelings which he had always entertained toward the English, and he never swerved from these relations.

Proof of this fidelity is found in the incidents connected with Philip's war. This wily sachem was capable of large views and jealous of the growing power of the English, whom he saw to be gaining the richest profit from the lands which they had purchased at a small price. He had planned a general rising of all the Indian tribes of New-England for the destruction of the settlers. The people were fearfully alarmed, and in the progress of the strife much cruelty and many deaths followed the barbarous prowess of the invaders. Wonnelanset had heard of the forthcoming conflict, but he had no sympathy with the designs of the sachem of the Wampanoags. Still, he was suspected, and in September 1675, a hundred men, under Captain Moseley, were sent from Massachusetts to ascertain the position of this sachem in regard to war. But when the band arrived at Penacook, they found that all the Indians had withdrawn. They had received notice of the approach of the troops and had concealed themselves in the neighboring woods, where they could easily see the proceedings of the men. The deserted wigwams, containing dried fish and other articles, were burnt in the spirit of wanton mischief, bad enough to have incited the innocent owners to join the forces of Philip. But no act of retaliation followed the loss of their shelters and provisions, though several of the young Indians were impetuous to commence an attack at once on the authors of the ruin. The chief soon afterwards (October 1675) led his followers to the headwaters of the Connecticut, where, in their rude and hastily made wigwams, they spent the winter and supported themselves by hunting.§

After his return the next year, he was allured, at the beginning of autumn, to Dover, with some of his Indians, and there they were made prisoners by stratagem, with others, to the number of about four

*3 Drake, 95.

†Gookin, 2; Drake, 98.

§Hubbard; Drake, III, 96; Gookin, Praying Indians, 2 American Antiquarian Collection, 460–4.

hundred. He was, however, soon set at liberty with his followers and returned to his dwelling on the Merrimack.* ...

Then it appears that he was still on the Merrimack, where (1696–97) he was placed under the care of Jonathan Tyng, of Dunstable, where he probably had his home on or near the island named Wickasaukee, which had been in the possession of the aged Passaconaway. At that time he was nearly eighty years old.

This is the last notice of the ill-treated and gentle Wonnelanset, all whose actions exhibited a peaceful disposition toward the English, though their provocations, with insult and injury, had been frequent and severe. But no ill-treatment could lead him to depart from the peaceful path, marked out for his steps by the counsels of his father and commended to his acceptance by his sincere adoption of the rules of life enjoined in the Christian faith. From this time his name disappears from the history of his tribe, whose pages are sadly marked by the revengeful deeds of Kancamagus, his nephew.

This Indian was the son of Nanamocomuck, the eldest son of Passaconaway. Though not brought under the influence of the religion to which his uncle had yielded, he appears to have had at the first a friendly disposition toward the whites. But the memory of the capture of the four hundred Indians of various tribes, by stratagem, at Dover, still remained in the heart of the natives and rankled in his own. In this capture the Penacooks were included, and some of their kindred in other tribes, who were imprisoned, of whom some were hanged and the rest sold into foreign slavery, to toil in an uncongenial clime

beneath the lash of the task-master. As the stratagem was accomplished by a flagrant breach of hospitality and friendship, it demanded, on their principles of justice, at the proper time a severe retaliation.† ...

One cannot but wonder at this day that they should not have joined in a general war upon the English. They had been treated with neglect or the most flagrant oppression. Their friends had been sold into slavery, hung on trees in Boston, shot down in the streets at noon-day, and burnt in their wigwams by dozens in time of peace. What class or nation of whites, at the present time, would suffer such wrongs to go unavenged? Should we expect more of patience from the rude, untutored red man?§

An assemblage of thirty fighting men in one company, under Kancamagus at Penacook, and its warlike appearance, arrested the attention of the government of Massachusetts.** In a council of these confederated warriors, held before mid-summer 1689 at the home of their leader, it was planned to make an attack on Cochecho, now Dover, and inflict what they deemed a merited punishment on Waldron and the garrison. Intelligence of the intended assault had been borne by friendly Indians to Dunstable, and thence had been sent to warn him of the danger. But the messenger arrived too late. The concerted action of the savages brought them together at Cochecho soon after the agreement was made. No alarm was felt by the aged commander, when he was told that the town was "full of Indians." On the 27th of June an adroit and successful method of gaining entrance within the

---

*Belknap, 78.

†Farmer on the Penacooks.

§"The Last of the Penacooks," by Hon. C. E. Potter, who has rescued many facts from oblivion in his researches.

**Danforth's Let. Farm. Visitor, v. 13, p. 122; 13 Farm. Vis. 133. As early as April 1689, a messenger was sent to Penacook to ascertain the number and intentions of the Indians there.

garrison took him and the unsuspecting inhabitants by surprise, and they became an easy prey to the power and daring of the invaders. Waldron, though at the age of eighty years, leaped from his bed and defended himself with great bravery. But his foes were too numerous. With revolting and torturing barbarity they put him to a lingering death, with insults added to savage cruelty. Twenty-three persons were killed in this attack, and twenty-nine carried into captivity. Houses and mills were set on fire as they started on their retreat, and so rapid had been their movement that they were already beyond danger before the inhabitants of the other parts of the town were aroused to assist the sufferers. They came by the light of the buildings burning in the night to see the havoc which glutted the vengeance that had been nourished for thirteen years. So bitter was the resentment against Waldron that several years after these disasters his treatment of the Indians was remembered in Canada. Actions done fifteen years before these events were recounted as a justification of the war.*

The boldness, skill, and fatal success of this attack struck terror into the colonies. A sentence of outlawry was pronounced on Kancamagus, and a reward offered for his head. Soldiers were sent to Penacook. But the place was forsaken, and the corn found was burnt. The chief part of the Indians hastened with their booty to Canada, and the Penacooks never afterward resided in any numbers in the valley of the Merrimack.

In the month of September, in the next year, Welumbee's [Worumbo's] fort was taken by Captain Church, and the wife, four children, and a brother-in-law of Kancamagus were taken captives in the place where they had probably withdrawn for safety during the expeditions against Cochecho. This loss excited him to enter the war-path again, and on the 21st of the same month he is reported to have united with Welumbee and other Indians in an attack on Casco, in which, after a severe conflict, they were compelled to flee.† It would appear that they were restored, as he was at a meeting of the contending parties at Sagadahoc, in 1691 [1690], without any complaint of his bereavement, and signed an agreement to maintain peace for one year.§

No mention is made of him after this date. His followers of whom a portion were the "Strange Indians," made desperate by Philip's defeat, were afterward scattered among other tribes, and it is thought were principally united with the Pequawkets. ...

It is too late now to lament the policy of the English toward the ignorant and, at first, confiding natives, who were friendly to the discoverers of their country, until they received injury and insult at their hands; and who, in the treatment of their prisoners of war, were as humane as their civilized conquerors.** The policy of the French was different. The first charter, granted to De Monts, provided for their instruction in the Christian religion. To conciliate their good will and interest them in the duties of a better life, their missionaries conformed in many things to their modes and habits and sought to introduce among them the arts and comforts of civilization and domestic enjoyments. Thus they secured their friendship

Belknap, Chap. X.

†*Farm. Visitor, v. 13, 136.*

§*This treaty was made "on the water in canoes, when the wind blew." 3 Drake 122. Magnalia Christ. Amer. B, 7, Act 28, p. 94.*

**Arnold's History R. I., I, p. 418.*

in peace and made them allies to be dreaded in war. But the English pursued a course which produced alienation and hostility, to their own great detriment in life and property. [Samuel] Penhallow, who lived in the midst of the most troublous times and knew the events as they occurred, which have now passed into history, gave a true account of the cause of these wars, when he wrote the following truth-telling sentences:

> God has made them a terrible scourge for the punishment of our sins; and probably that very sin of ours is in neglecting the welfare of their souls, for we have not expressed the like laudable care for them as hath been done in the southern and western parts of the country. But indeed we have rather aimed to advance a private trade than to instruct them in the principles of true religion.*

But while the labors of Eliot are ever to be gratefully remembered, and the generous and untiring efforts of Gookin for their civil welfare were earnest and useful, yet Eliot toiled almost alone, and Gookin received unmerited censure and threats that made him afraid to go along the streets.† A multitude of men, good in the current acceptation of their times, regarded the red man as beyond the reach of human sympathy and consideration, because he was a heathen, an idolater, and a savage, who could not be made industrous, peaceable, or humane. The influence of a better feeling is seen in the power of the preaching of Eliot in the wigwam of Wonnelanset. He was ever after the friend of the English, though he endured vexations greater than those which roused the savage nature of Kancamagus. If the efforts of benevolence instead of cupidity had been put forth and continued, the sufferings of the war-hoop and the tomahawk would have been an unknown on the border towns of the English as they were in settlements of the French. The tribes that were marshaled for battle by Madocawando and other chieftains still have a being, a territory, and a name. But the winds of the Atlantic breathe not on any region where the English came to their early rule, which the red man can call his own. The plow still turns over the fire-colored hearthstones, where the ashes of the cabinfire are even to this day found damp and cold, with the unburnt coals and charred sticks, to show where the smoke of the wigwam rose for the comfort of the little family. All have passed away from the lovely valley.

*Hist. Wars, p. 19; Fox's Dunstable, 34, 75.

†Praying Indians. Transactions Am. Ant. Society, Vol. 2, p. 449.

10

Contributions to the History of Derryfield (Manchester)

William E. Moore

PRELIMINARY OBSERVATIONS

The historian who attempts to draw aside the veil which has for centuries hidden the annals of an obscure people, scant in numbers, low in civilization, destitute even of a written tongue, has before him no easy task, and one rendered still more difficult from the fact that in his first contact with civilization the Indian was surrounded with white men who were themselves illiterate. Only after the passing of the tribe was the effort made to put into some sort of order the scattered records and traditions concerning them, and this was so scantily done that a single paragraph might set forth the story, as who should say: There were Indians; there are no Indians.

NIPMUCKS

There appears to be a general agreement that one or more tribes of Indians inhabited a belt of inland country in Massachusetts and southern New Hampshire, more or less removed from the sea, and that these were known as Nipmucks, signifying by a license of free translation, "freshwater Indians." They seem to have been neither numerous nor warlike and probably held a position of little importance among the stronger and more ambitious tribes surrounding them. It is quite certain they took no prominent part in the bloody drama of the French and Indian Wars, since no Nipmuck name adorns nor deed disfigures the page of history. It is said that the tribe with which we are more immediately concerned was subject to the Penacooks; and this is rendered more plausible from the fact that the headquarters of that tribe, generally made at Penacook, were sometimes transferred to Amoskeag, probably in the height of the fishing season and in virtue of the right of the stronger.

Source: William E. Moore, *Contributions to the History of Derryfield, New Hampshire: Indians and Early Settlements,* pt. 4, printed and published by the author, 1897. A paper read before the Manchester Historic Association. *Manchester Historic Association Collections,* vol. 2, pt. 2, chap. 8 (1900–1901): 75–87.

INDIAN HABITS AND RELICS

From evidence which appears con-clusive we locate the headquarters of the Nipmucks at or near Amoskeag Falls, a place famous for hunting and fishing. Hunting has become a thing of the past, though to this day the search is kept up for any stray fish which may have escaped the Nipmuck nets. The chief village, or more accurately the village of the chief, was situated on the hill-bluff known as "The Willows," now owned by ex-Gover-nor Frederick Smyth. In the steep banks of this bluff and where the soil had been upturned, there was found a great number of broken fragments of rude pottery and other utensils used by the Indians. Nearly everything naturally grouped under the head of Indian relics has been found on the site of this village, including arrow and spear-heads in great variety, stone mor-tars and pestles, stone axes, gouges, clubs, and fish-knives, stone tools for removing fish-scales or scraping skins, bone fish-hooks, needles, hairpins, and numerous other relics, some broken, but many per-fectly preserved. When making an exca-vation on the premises, for the purpose of forming a small artificial pond, there was unearthed a deposit of arrow and spear-heads, knives, etc., of quartz, flint, or chert, which with unfinished specimens and chipped fragments amounted in the whole to several bushels. This was prob-ably one of the workshops or armories of the tribe and undoubtedly the first Amoskeag manufactory. Over the whole section surrounding the falls, on either side, in fact from Goffe's Falls to Martin's Ferry, a great number of the various relics above enumerated have been picked up, several valuable collections having been made, perhaps the most interesting being that of the late Samuel B. Kidder. They were more numerous upon the village-site referred to, on the elevation west of the

P. C. Cheney Company's mills, as well as elsewhere and near by, on the large island below the falls and the level stretch of land immediately below the great eddy. At all these points, as well as in the bed of the river, valuable finds have rewarded the patient relic-hunter. At the mouth of Christian Brook, known also in later times as the "fair-ground brook," and also at the mouth of Ray Brook, there have been found many interesting relics. The bank of the river north of the latter stream is quite steep, and here about twenty years ago the writer found a nest of a dozen or more large chipped slate-stones, wholly unlike the conventional spear-head but yet of undoubted human workmanship, which had been probably used for cleaning fish. They were buried at a considerable depth, having been uncovered by a fall of earth occurring because of high water. There are signs of old fires, pieces of charred wood remaining at a depth of three or more feet. Throughout this entire section similar mementos have been discovered, espe-cially on the sandy margins of lakes and ponds. A symmetrically chipped arrow-head of milk-quartz was found by the writer, when a mere boy, on the beach at Massabesic Lake.

The foregoing facts, even in the absence of other evidence, are ample to establish the presence of Indians here in considerable numbers and for a long period, probably centuries before the advent of the whites. Tradition assigns no spot which we can point out as an Indian burial place. It is said there are several Indian graves near the entrance from the highway to the Devil's Den in Chester. It is also said and has long been currently believed that the site of a number of wig-wams was upon Brown's Island in the Massabesic, and this is altogether likely. The sole indication of a burial place in this immediate vicinity, which has come to our knowledge, was the finding of human bones supposed to be those of Indians in the grading of Penacook Street, about 1875.

The only approach to a permanent settlement was that around the home of the chief. More than forty wigwams were scattered over this picturesque knoll, a fine view of the Merrimack being afforded from the willow palisades surrounding the village. It is quite certain that numerous temporary wigwams were erected at or near the more important points above mentioned, on both sides of the Merrimack, some of which may have been permanent. From the well-known roving character of the Indian it is likely that in the summer months at least they grew like the mushroom in a single night and as soon vanished.

The traditional, dark-red, fawn-like Indian maiden was not of the Nipmucks. She is the creation of a diluted sentimentality, a mere dream of a class of poets too lazy to saw wood but able to invent aboriginal lies by the gross. The bewitching squaw who leaped for love from the top of Rock Rimmon was not after mayflowers; it is much more likely that she was overloaded with muskrats and lost her way. The noble Nipmuck lover was also an invention, patented by [James Fenimore] Cooper. If these romantic types ever existed it was before the era of discovery. In contact with the white man the Indian adopted only his vices; these, superadded to savage traits, could not well produce heroes either in love or war. We have ransacked the records of the past, turned to the testimony of the dead, and listened to the lies of the living but have failed utterly to discover proof of greatness or even the dawn of a progressive and civilizing instinct among either the Nipmucks or Penacooks.

The red man was fond of fishing and hunting, but he killed solely to obtain food, clothing, or materials to give him shelter and was not ennobled by the zest of sportsmanship. In him the instinct of self-preservation scarcely rose above the level of the wild beasts he slew. Our people, however, seem to have a weakness for idols of all colors and stand ready to bow down and serve them. All that is needed is a remote historical episode, recounted by a white Ananias, and an ideal Pocahontas appears. But we soon tire of the old favorites, and one by one the saints, martyrs, and heroes of history are knocked off their perch. Histories are no longer tales agreed upon but begin to be viewed with suspicion. William Tell is a myth, the Scottish Mary was freckled, even King Richard was not a hunchback, and George Washington swore. Soon shall the frivolous generations pass and as they die will fade the memory of men once deemed immortal. Philip, Tecumseh, Logan, Oceola, and Passaconaway have vanished, to be followed by the red drunkard of the reservation.

With as little success we have sought for an aesthetic trait in the Nipmuck character or for some evidence of a moral sense. Surrounded upon the one hand with beauty and upon the other by terrifying aspects of nature, he was blind to the one and by the other affrighted. A seen enemy he attacked and tried to kill; before an unknown danger he cowered and prayed, his so-called acts of worship inspired alone by ignorance and fear.

About him grew myriads of flowering plants and shrubs, in dell or defile, glade or glen, in the natural meadows and over the upland slopes, terraces, and plateaus. When following the chase or crouching in wait for game the moccasined foot could scarcely fall without crushing a blossom. Here the wind-flower and the blue and yellow violet grew, the laurel and the flower de luce; the blue closed gentian and its white-fingered sister, and the great fringed orchis. These do not detain the hunter. He hears not the oration of jack-in-the-pulpit; the wild rose spreads its bloom to him who hastens. To such a woodsman the scarlet robe of the cardinal-flower has no meaning, the sweet-brier no fragrance, the queen of the meadow no style. The red scalp or flaming coat of tanager or wood-tapper may allure him, but the rare blush of Arethusa he passes with indifference. Concerning the world of plant life his thought is, if he has one, can I eat it, or will it cure snake-bite? The wild deer for which he waits will reason as acutely.

The hues of the sky at sunset may suggest to the Indian rain or drowth, but never beauty; and as he looks from his hemlock bed to the crimson light of dawn upon the western summits, in his breast no emotion kindles, as with gutteral accent he says, "This is another day." To a meteor he gives a grunt, to a comet two; and when the Northern Lights begin to flash and in the intermittent gleam the stars grow pale, he sees only a reflection from the campfires of a mightier race of hunters in the far and frozen north.

The wants of the Nipmuck did not make him unhappy, though in this very evil case we find the civilized citizen of to-day. The savage saw neither virtue or sweetness in a useless plant; the average society atom sees no sweetness in character or loveliness in life without a bank-account. We wish to be just—even to an Indian.

The agriculture of the Nipmuck was of a rude sort, the rich soil of natural meadows or intervales being usually selected as planting places, and when these were not available other tracts were reclaimed by fire and the larger trees killed by the process of girdling. The preparation of the ground, planting, hoeing and har-vesting—nearly everything coming under the head of work—was performed by women and children. The men were kind

enough to furnish the raw material for the manufacture of tools, such as the axe, the stone or clam-shell hoe, and other cutting implements, his own time being otherwise fully occupied in making arms and equip-ments for the hunt and allied masculine occupations. So that numerous avenues of employment remained open to the gentler sex, and we are beginning to recognize in our time the wisdom of this arrangement. We now permit our wives and mothers, but more especially the larger class of sis-ters, cousins, and aunts, to whom these relations of life are closed or which have been declined with thanks, to assume some portion of our burdens, at a reduced rate of compensation.

The range of cultivated food-prod-ucts was generally limited to corn, squashes, pumpkins, melons, and kidney-beans. They derived, however, a large part of their winter food-supply from nuts, sweet acorns, dried fish, smoked meats, etc., prepared in various unpalatable ways but capable of supporting life. There were no seasons throughout the year when fresh flesh food, of fish, fowl, or animal, could not be had in abundance, and if there were times of scarcity the cause usually pro-ceeded from indolence or improvidence.

We are unable to give the Nipmuck name of the Indian afterwards known as Christian or Christo. This name is said to have been bestowed upon him soon after his conversion to Christianity by the apos-tle Eliot, but this lacks probability. It is much more likely that he had it from the Jesuits or assumed it for purposes of his own. Like St. Paul he was at times all things to all men—a Nipmuck, an Arosa-gunticook, a Puritan, a convert to Catholi-cism. Christo is first heard of in company with a St. Francis Indian called Plausawa, a not very good pronunciation of Francois. They had sufficient intercourse with the settlers to ascertain that white Christians made slaves of black men and that the profits of the trade were large. Acting upon this hint they stole two negroes in Canterbury and started with them for Canada, one escaping upon the way and the other being sold to a French officer. Christo seems to have had seasons of backsliding and repentance, such as the praying Indians generally enjoyed, and after a series of apocryphal adventures he settled at Amoskeag. His cabin or hut was near the mouth of Christian Brook, which entered the Merrimack immediately west of the Amoskeag Paper Mills. Here he lived in an outward show of peace for some years, professing friendship for the whites, by whom he was distrusted. At length he was suspected of conveying intelligence and giving secret aid to the hostile St. Francis or Arosagunticook Indians, whereupon, during his absence they confiscated his personal belongings and burned his cabin. [Chandler E.] Potter says that Christo subsequently returned and forgave the whites for this cruel injury. Other accounts, more in consonance with the Indian character, say that he openly joined the Arosagunticooks and became an active and implacable foe. This little trout-stream is now hidden beneath the surface by the march of improvement for nearly a mile of its course, and the generation to come will know neither name nor place.

Plausawa had also been an occasional visitor at Amoskeag, accompanied by another drunken brave called Sabbatis, a name representing his baptism to Christianity, literally St. Baptiste. These Indian thieves and murderers, after the commission of a series of outrages in Canterbury, Salisbury, and Warren, as well as in this neighborhood, were finally killed in Boscawen by one Peter Bowen. The full details of this affair are given in Little's *History of Warren.*

Upon the authority of certain early historians we are asked to believe that upon the death of the great chief of the Micmacs or Taratines, a powerful and warlike tribe in the province of Maine, to whom the Penacooks were subject, a war of succession arose, which resulted in the choice of Passaconaway to succeed the dead Bashaba, who had been slain in battle. This war for supremacy became general and involved all the tribes from New Brunswick to the Hudson River and from Massachusetts to Canada. The exact limits were not known and probably can never be determined. The numbers engaged were large, the war continued for years; it is said to have been conducted with great ferocity and to have been especially disastrous to the coast tribes, who were no match for the hardy inland hunters. Many of the names preserved to us are those of chiefs and warriors who had become famous in this great war, which was the most sanguinary and relentless ever waged among the Indians of the east. The great plague, to which nearly all the earlier accounts refer, raged among the Nipmucks towards the close of this war. The origin of this plague has never been satisfactorily accounted for or its nature clearly understood, but we hazard a conjecture that the contagion was communicated by the Indians of New France, who in turn received it from the whites then in Canada in considerable numbers. At all events it was believed the loss by battle and plague literally decimated the ranks of the savages and brought the war to a close before the landing of the Pilgrims at Plymouth. The early accounts must be received with great caution, ample allowance made for the time in which they were written, and due regard had to the sources of information. "Broken English" is scarcely a fit vehicle for the transmission of historical data. The skeletons of those who fell in savage strife or succumbed to plague and famine four centuries ago might as easily be clothed with life as could the details of that distant scene be dug from their oblivion.

Upon this middle ground, between the Plymouth Puritan and the pioneer Jesuit of New France, there was another curious encounter, an episode in the struggle between two forces, whose declaration of war antedated the discovery of America. Whenever and wherever these met in the long centuries, the hostile lines were drawn. And so it came to pass that in a new world, for the soil of which kings contended, the adherents of pope and Protestant, in savage bands, the one inspired by a Mather, the other by a Marquette, each in the name of a common Redeemer, stood opposed in conflict. Thus, upon the virgin soil of New Hampshire, in that first century of its occupation, was shed the blood of religious hatred. Time has fortunately softened these asperities, and in the new dawn of a wiser Christian charity we seem to see the promise of brotherhood and reconciliation.

As the light of the fire-fly is illusive or intermittent, so Indian lore and tradition lead us along a pathway sometimes overcast with darkness and often difficult to follow. The time is distant, the actors are defunct, and the record is becoming more indistinct and uncertain. But we still follow the trail with ardor in an endeavor to enrich our barren annals, and we know that we are on the ground. Some may even thank us for this attempt to restore these fast-fading pictures of the past.

Marriage and Motherhood

It is not certain that the Nipmucks were polygamous, but the line was not far removed. They seldom lived with more than one squaw at the same time, but on the other hand a healthy brave generally contrived to marry from six to nine maid-

ens during an average life of four-score and ten years. The squaw was wedded when quite young, frequently at twelve years of age; but constant drudgery and exposure broke them down early, so that at thirty they became prematurely old and were wrinkled at forty. They endeavored for a time to keep up appearances, just as we observe the old hens of our generation in their efforts to parade with spring chickens. It made little difference to the mother, and none whatever to the pappoose, whether the medicine-man was called in or not. When his services were invoked he commonly made a great powwow in front of the wickyup before entering and more powwow upon emerging, concluding with an invocation or chant addressed apparently to the great Square of Pegasus. In order that the old wife might be supplanted by the new, separation was made easy, and the discarded wife and mother did not complain, afterwards contenting herself with adopting some captive as a son or husband, as the case might be. Some of these captives, thus summarily wedded without ceremony or consent, were white men, and part first of the very pathetic story of Pocahontas rests solely upon this custom.

We have purposely omitted the disgusting details of home-life, suggesting merely that an ample water-supply was not diminished or contaminated, as the Nipmuck squaw never took a bath or any other step toward cleanliness....

Famous Squaws

It is not from choice that we have spoken slightingly of the Nipmuck squaw. She may have filled her place, and there is no doubt that wherever her home it was humble. But she must be put without prejudice in the column of silent factors—passing away without sign. Record, journal, memoir, narrative or history shed little lustre upon her life or character; fiction and poetry have alone befriended her. The eldest daughter of Passaconaway, by her marriage with the great Nobhow, became a queen, but not even her name survives. Her younger sister, the fair Wetamoo, became the bride of a seven-syllabled son of Paugus and has been apotheosized in [John Greenleaf] Whittier's verse. The wedded life of Wetamoo was not a happy one; the youthful pair soon separated, and she went back to the paternal tie-up in Derryfield, where she held court for many years as a grass-widow. These are the facts—the rest is fancy.

After all, it is but a step from the dawn of tradition to our own times; with a stroke of the pen, the turning of a leaf, we pass to the century of baseball and cotton batting.

11

Indians of New Hampshire

Janine A. Carson

The two great Indian tribes east of the Mississippi were the Iroquois and Algonquin families.

The Iroquois were a fierce, warlike people made up of a confederacy of five nations: the Mohawk, Oneida, Onondaga, Cayuga, and Seneca. Their conquests extended from Quebec to the Carolinas, from the western prairies to the forests of Maine.

The Algonquin family extended from Hudson's Bay on the north to the Carolinas on the south, from the Atlantic on the east to the Mississippi on the west. The name *Algonquin* is a family name. The various divisions and subdivisions of the family have many names. The people of eastern Canada, New Hampshire, and Maine had the name Wabenaki or, as more commonly used, Abenaki or Abnaki, which means "peasants" or "people of the east."[1]

ABENAKI

The Abenaki people were fairly distributed over a considerable area of country, which is now represented upon the map of New England as lying within the boundary line of Maine and New Hampshire.[2]

The land occupied by the tribes did not extend far back from the coast inland except upon the larger rivers. It began around the St. John to the eastward and terminated southward, north of the Merrimack River.[3] Because of similarity of customs and traditions, the Etchemin, who occupied eastern Maine and New Brunswick, and the Micmac or Souriquoi, who lived in Nova Scotia, were considered to be one nation with the Abenaki.[4]

Their system of government was practically the same, their movements being directed by one man, who was

Source: Janine A. Carson, "Indians of New Hampshire," *New Hampshire Archeologist* 6 (1950s): 10–16. In this article, the Sokoki are misplaced, a common error in earlier writings. See the section on the Connecticut River valley in the article by Stewart-Smith, below.

According to the *Handbook of the North American Indians* (vol. 15, p. 142), the dates of the various Eastern Abenaki Wars were: Tarrantine War (1607–1615); King Philip's War (1675–1678); King William's War (1688–1699); Queen Anne's War (1702–1713); Dummer's War (1721–1725); King George's War (1745–1748); French and Indian War (1755–1759); and the Revolutionary War (1775–1782).

designated as the sachem, who might have been assisted in his functions of ruling his tribe by councillors or subordinated sachems, who were the heads of subdivisions of the great family. The chief ruler of the Abenaki was known as the *Bashaba*, who was supposed to be the head of the eight tribes known as the Penobscot, Passamaquody, Wawenock, Norridgewock, Anasagunticook, Sokoki, Pennacook, and Malecite. These several tribes had their individual sachems, and as these tribes were divided into families, or clans, these latter were directed in their affairs by a lesser sachem.[5]

Life among the Abenaki

The Abenaki, for the most part, had a fixed habitation. Their wigwams were made of small trees bent and twisted together, covered with mats, barks, or skins. In winter, a fire was made in the center of the wigwam which had an opening at the top for the passage of smoke. There was little furniture, beds being mats or skins placed upon the floor. They sat upon the ground with their elbows on their knees.[6]

Food was dependent upon hunting, fishing, and some primitive agriculture. Fish were taken in weirs, by scooping, or by spearing. They procured animals by traps or pitfalls or shot them, as well as birds, with arrows. To cook their meat, they either broiled it on coals on a wooden grate, roasted it on a forked stick, or boiled it in kettles of stone. The women tended the fields of corn, beans, squash, and pumpkin. Their corn was pounded in mortars of wood with pestles of stone. Their bread was baked either on flat stones set before a fire or in green leaves laid under hot ashes. Clamshells served them for spoons. Their fingers were used for knives and forks[7] The Abenaki squaw was an expert herbal-

ist and could derive cures from many plants.

Their artwork is shown today by specimens of elaborate beading, braiding of grasses and willows, and shell and feather ornaments. The women were the tailors, producing clothes of animal skins. The dress differed according to the age, sex, and occupation of the wearer as well as the occasion.[8]

The canoe, snowshoe, and wigwam were original Indian inventions which could not be improved upon by white settlers.

Canoes were their mainstay of transportation as their traveling took all possible advantage of water carriage. They carried their birch canoes over necks of land which were convenient for the purpose. Dugout canoes were also used and appropriately ornamented.[9]

The snowshoe enabled the Indian to go upon the chase or the warpath when the ground was covered with drifted snow. Thus shod, he could travel like the deer.

The tools used were made of wood, shells, or stone. Hoes were made of sticks with a clamshell fastened to a handle. Axes were of stone with a wooden handle attached to the neck by a withe. Their mortars, pestles, and chisels were also of stone, and they had stone knives sharpened to an edge keen enough to cut their hair.

Their weapons of war were the bow and arrow, the spear, and the tomahawk. The bowstring was commonly made of sinew. The arrows were occasionally the horn of a deer or the claw of an eagle, but most commonly were a sharp stone.[10] A great number of arrowheads have been found, and they are of all sizes from one to two and one half inches in length, pointed and jagged, with a notch on each side of the lower end to bind them to the shaft, the end of which was split to let in the head. Children were early taught the use of the bow and arrow. The tomahawk was merely a stick two or three feet in length headed with a knob or stone. With such simple arrows, the aborigines were able to carry on war in their own fashion, by ambush and cunning surprise which they loved.[11]

The Indian calendar had many feasts and festivals. The young men were trained athletes, fine runners, swimmers, and wrestlers. They had a game which resembled the modern cricket and the game lacrosse is said to have originated with them. Playing ball and pitching quoits were favorite games in which men, women, and children took part.[12]

Dances for joy, war, festivals, or the seasons were held. There was the planting dance, the strawberry feast, the dance of the green corn, and here, when Passaconaway held sway over the region of the Merrimack Valley, there was the eel dance in the season when the eels came up the rivers from the sea in such vast numbers that everybody came to feast on them.[13]

The medicine man, or powwow, was a man of importance. He not only treated diseases, which was believed to be a magical art, but the Indian always associated with it some mystery or charm. Every man carried a charm in a pouch which was regarded as an amulet or protection for him, an object of prayer or worship. The Indian communed with this symbol when alone, he trusted to it for protection on a journey and in every emergency, and he clung to it in the fury of battle.[14]

The position of the sachem was for life. He was elected by the men of his tribe. At his death another election was held, and his successor was chosen with due deliberation. While the office of sachem was not hereditary, the distinction usually descended to the son if he were capable. The inauguration was a round of festivities, which lasted several days,

at which guests from neighboring tribes were entertained with great decorum and lavish hospitality.[15]

The religion was one swathed in legend and traditions. They believed in disembodied spirits, that they exercised a controlling power over human affairs, and they besought them for wisdom and guidance in time of uncertainty, for safety when danger threatened, and for their interference to ward off evil. They said their prayers facing the sunrise. They were a notably moral people and were particularly susceptible to the dogmas of the Jesuits.[16]

The Abenaki were said to have some proficiency in being able to express themselves by picture writing. The common medium of this expression was the bark of the birch and often the flat surface of stones. For a crude pencil or graver's tool, a charred coal, flint, or an arrowhead was used. Upon the rind of the birch tree were inscribed their messages to neighboring tribes. They made their fastest runner their messenger, and answers were returned upon the same material. The Indians inhabiting Maine, Arcadia, and New Hampshire gave the names to most of our mountains, lakes, and rivers which were written down by the French missionaries.[17]

TRIBAL SITUATIONS

Early historians concluded that the Indians who formerly inhabited New Hampshire should be classified under five separate divisions, namely, (1) those tribes residing on the Piscataqua River and its branches; (2) the various tribes on the Merrimack River and its tributary streams; (3) the Ossipee Indians, centering about Ossipee Lake, associated with the savage Pequacket at the head of the Saco River; (4) the Indians on the Connecticut River;

and (5) the Coos Indians in the extreme northern part of the state.[18]

PENNACOOK

Penacook, afterwards Rumford and now Concord, was the especial abode of the Indian tribe bearing that name. It is a historical fact that this tribe was the leading one of all the tribes dwelling along the Merrimack and its tributaries northward to Lake Winnipesaukee and beyond and southward to Pawtucket Falls.[19]

The various bands of this tribe were known from the location where they happened to live, including the Winnipesaukee, the Ossipee, the Amoskeag, the Souhegan, the Nashua, and the Wamesit or Pawtucket. Other sources have included additional tribes in the Pennacook branch of the Abenaki: the Naticook,[20] the Cowasuck (upper Connecticut),[21] the Wachusett on the northern rim of Massachusetts,[22] the Sokoki on the Saco, the Arrosagunticook or Anasagunticook on the Androscoggin, who were divided into numerous branches of which the principal clans were the Ossipee and Pequawket (or Pigwacket), and the Coosuc (junction of Connecticut and Ammonoosuc).[23] Wherever they might live, they were all Pennacook and all under the dominion of Passaconaway, whose chief seat was at Penacook.

Passaconaway's confederation at the beginning of the seventeenth century was estimated at several thousand warriors, but in less than twenty years they had been almost exterminated by famine, pestilence, and pitiless warfare with other Indians.[24]

Passaconaway was not at first a friend of the English who landed on the Atlantic coast. He regarded them as dangerous intruders. He tried his mystic arts against them without success, but finally he accepted his destiny. As time went on, he desired to keep friendship with the English, believing that it would be a protection against the hostile Tarratine of the far east and the Mohawk of the west.

He learned to his sorrow that those whose favor he had sought did not always return his acts of kindness. Thus at one time it was rumored among the English that a conspiracy was forming among the Indians to crush the colonists, and a company of men was sent out by the Massachusetts colony to capture the principal Indian chiefs.

Passaconaway and his tribe were innocent of any hostile intent, but, in spite of proofs of their innocence, Wanolancet, a son of Passaconaway, was taken prisoner with his squaw and little child and most insultingly led to Boston by his captors with a rope around his neck. Wanolancet was kept in prison for some months. At length, the authorities, fearing the results of the act of their agents, sent word to Passaconaway inviting him "to come to Boston and converse with them," together with an apology for their act. The chieftain replied with dignity: "Tell the English, when they restore my son and his squaw, then I will, of my own accord render in the required artillery."

After his son was set at liberty, Passaconaway sent his oldest son to give in the guns which had been demanded. The humiliation of this treatment of his son hurt the pride of the great sachem and no doubt made him regret his alliance with the English more than once.[25]

He did allow the famous Indian apostle, John Eliot, to convert him to Christianity. It is said that he was a sincere believer and never wavered. He tried very hard to persuade Eliot to settle amongst his people but Eliot felt his duty called him to Natick.

Some two or three years later, Passaconaway and his sons put themselves, their people, and their lands under the jurisdiction and protection of Massachusetts, and from this time he was nominally a sort of Puritan magistrate, administering the colonial laws upon his subjects. In 1660, the great sachem, overcome with the burden of his years and weary of honors, abdicated his chieftainship at a solemn assembly of the mountain and river Indians held at Pawtucket Falls (Lowell). His farewell address included these words: "We are few and powerless before them! We must bend before the storm! The wind blows hard! The old oak trembles! Its branches are gone! Its sap is frozen! It bends! It falls! Peace, Peace, with the white men—is the command of the Great Spirit—and the wish—the last wish—of Passaconaway."[26]

According to Indian legend, when 120 years old, Passaconaway retired to a lonely wigwam on the outskirts of the Pennacook domain. One cold winter night the wolves were heard and suddenly a pack dashed through the village harnessed to a hickory sled, carrying a throne covered with beautiful furs. Upon their stopping at Passaconaway's door, the old man came out and was triumphantly borne away amidst the yelps and snarls of his uncanny team. Across Winnipesaukee's frozen waste they sped, and lone hunters, hearing the death chant of the old chief echoing back and forth among the mountain crags, shivered. Faster and faster his team flashed over the trackless waste into the very heart of the great White Hills and finally roared up the steep slopes of Agiochook itself. As the summit of this mighty mountain was reached, the sledge burst into flames and the wolves went howling off into the wilderness, but Passaconaway and his equipage, wrapped in leaping tongues of flame, shot into the sky and vanished amidst the very stars themselves.[27]

Passaconaway's son Wanolancet suc-

ceeded him as chief. He is said to have been "a sober and grave person, of years between fifty and sixty" and to have been "always loving and friendly to the English." He was converted to Christianity by the apostle Eliot and lived a noble life, restraining his warriors from attacking the colonists, even during King Philip's War. Finding it impossible, at a later day, to prevent his people from engaging in open hostilities, he gave up the chieftaincy and with a few families who adhered to him, sought retreat at St. Francis in Canada. He returned to the Merrimack Valley in 1696, but after a short time finally retired again to St. Francis, where he died.[28]

His successor as chieftain, after his abdication in 1677, was his nephew, Passaconaway's grandson Kancamagus. This resolute warrior made several attempts to retain the friendship of the colonists, as is evident from his letters to Governor Crandall [Edward Cranfield], but was unsuccessful and finally yielded, after many slights and much ill treatment, to the solicitations of the warlike and patriotic party in the confederation. He organized and led the terrible attack on Dover in 1689, which was the death throe of the Pennacook. He was present at the signing of the truce of Sagadahoc, but after that disappears from history. He may have retired with the remainder of his people to St. Francis.[29]

Four chiefs of the Sokoki stand out in the memory of the early settlers: Squando, Assacumbit, Paugus, and Chocorua. Squando was a very tall and dignified Indian who, combining a little Christianity with the beliefs of his own people, became a fanatic. He was considered to be a prophet by the Indians and believed to have contact with the invisible spirits. Some sailors caused the near drowning of his baby one day and, as the infant sickened and died shortly afterward, Squando naturally blamed the whites for it. The terrible massacres of 1675 and 1676 by the Indians followed shortly after this.[30]

The Sokoki, the Pennacook's kinsmen, originally occupied lands down the Saco to the sea shore, but the whites drove them from their coastal lands and they early retired to Pegwagget, where Fryeburg, Maine, now is, and kept rather aloof from the whites. They were for a long time the most feared of all the northern Indians. They seem to have been a very powerful people in the days before the whites, as indications have been found of extensive settlements all through the Conways, around Ossipee Lake, and up and down the Saco Valley.[31]

Assacumbit was the most notorious of all the chieftains of the Sokoki as, unlike Squando, he possessed no good qualities. His cruelties to the English made him a great favorite with the French. They valued him so highly as an ally that in 1705 he was taken to France and presented to King Louis XIV, who presented him with a beautiful sword, knighted him, and gave him a pension. When he returned home, he became so insolent and arrogant with his own people that they undoubtedly would have killed him had he not fled to the French for protection. He accompanied the French on their attack on Haverhill, Massachusetts, and is said to have performed feats of valor with the sword the king gave him.[32]

During the year 1724 the Indians had become very bold and had made numerous forays against the settlements, killing and scalping the settlers. The General Court of Massachusetts, aroused by these killings, offered a bounty of one hundred pounds for every Indian scalp taken. This was quite a fortune in those days, so in February of the following year, Captain John Lovewell of Dunstable, with a force of forty men, surprised and killed ten sleeping Indians on the shores of Lovewell's Pond in the present town of Wake-

field, New Hampshire. They found the Indians equipped with extra blankets and snowshoes, evidently intending to raid the settlement and take captives back to Canada. Two months later, he set out again, this time with a force of 46 men, for the Indian village of Pegwagget. Arriving at Ossipee Lake, he built a small fort as a refuge in case of disaster and left a few men to guard it. Marching on with 34 men, he reached Lovewell's Pond in Fryeburg, Maine. The Indians, headed by Paugus, surrounded the company and nearly wiped it out. They fought desperately for a day and a night. Many were left dead, including Paugus, who was killed late in the contest. Only eleven soldiers made their way back to Dunstable after this bloody battle, the only one of its sort in the White Mountains. The Indians, losing their renowned leader, Paugus, became disheartened, and most of them withdrew to the upper waters of the Connecticut and eventually to St. Francis, though a few stragglers remained in the mountains. Thus passed the dreaded Sokoki.[33]

When the Sokoki Indians retreated to Canada, Chocorua refused to leave the ancient home of his people. He became very friendly with an early settler of Tamworth named Campbell. Chocorua had a son, in whom all hopes and love were centered. On one occasion he was obliged to go to Canada to consult with his people at St. Francis, so he left his son in the care of the Campbells until his return. During his absence, the boy unfortunately discovered some poison that Campbell had prepared to kill foxes with and, drinking some of it, died. Chocorua returned to find his boy dead and buried. He blamed Campbell for the killing of the boy and swore vengeance. The settler, upon returning from his work in the field one day, found his wife and children on the floor of the cabin scalped.[34] He tracked Chocorua to the crest of the mountain that now bears his name and commanded him to throw himself over the precipice upon the rocks below. Chocorua replied, "The Great Spirit gave life to Chocorua and Chocorua will not throw it away at the command of the white man." "Then hear the Great Spirit speak in the white man's thunder," said Campbell and, firing on him, wounded him badly. Raising himself on his elbow, Chocorua then delivered his famous curse:

> A curse upon ye white men! May the Great Spirit curse ye when he speaks in the clouds and his words are fire! Chocorua had a son and ye killed him while the sky was bright. Lightning blast your crops! Winds and fire destroy your dwellings! The evil spirit breathe death upon your cattle! Your graves lie in the warpath of the Indians! Panthers howl and wolves fatten upon your bones! Chocorua goes to the Great Spirit. His curse stays with the white man.

This curse did rest on the settlement for many years. The Indians tomahawked and scalped them. The winds blasted down trees on their houses. Their crops failed. Their cattle sickened and died, and at last the remnants of the settlement were glad to move elsewhere. To this day the cattle of this valley are afflicted with a strange disease. Lately, however, scientists have discovered that it is due to a weak solution of muriat of lime in the water, and the remedy prescribed is common soapsuds.[35]

A few remnants of the Pennacook Indians together with a band of St. Francis Indians of Canada made a raid on Haverhill on March 15, 1697, the last year of King William's War. Hannah Dustin, her baby, and her nurse, Mary Neff, were made prisoners of the Indians and were forced to Canada. They stopped at the

island at the joining of the Merrimack and Contoocook rivers. A captured boy, Samuel Leonardson, gained information on how to strike effectively with a tomahawk. That night the three captives killed and scalped ten Indians. A reward of fifty pounds was paid by the General Court of Massachusetts. A granite memorial of Hannah Dustin's exploit was erected in 1784 on the island in the mouth of the Contoocook.[36]

For fifty years the St. Francis Indians had held back the settlement of northern New Hampshire and Vermont. These Indians had great hostility toward the English. Major Rogers in October 1759 led two hundred of his group, Rogers' Rangers, toward St. Francis to rout the Indians. Even though their boats and provisions were taken by the French and Indians, these setbacks did not stop the men. One hundred forty-two Rangers surprised the Indians and the slaughter was terrific. There were other attacks and many details of hardship and starvation before Rogers arrived safely at Fort No. 4 at Crown Point on Lake Champlain.[37]

Though Indian warfare in New Hampshire was practically continuous for nearly a hundred years, early historians divide the record into five separate and distinct wars, namely, Philip's War, beginning in 1675; war with the Indians and their French allies, commonly called King William's War, beginning in 1689; a later war with the French and Indians known as Queen Ann's War, beginning about 1705; Lovewell's three-year war with the French and Indians, beginning about 1717 but continuing as guerrilla warfare with slight cessation; and last, the French and Indian War, beginning about 1754 and continuing for more than fifteen years, terminating in the conquest of Canada while England and France were pitted against each other. [For the historians' dates of the various Indian wars, see the source note at the beginning of this article.] After this the Indians continued guerrilla warfare on their own account until they were finally overcome and driven out of New England.[38]

SETTLEMENTS

Settlements were chosen by the groups in relation to water, fishing, and routes of travel. As it took ten square miles to support one person by hunting and fishing, it was necessary to have great land areas to support themselves.

Manchester

In early colonial times the Manchester region was, at certain periods each year, the home of Passaconaway, head of the Pennacook Confederacy. Not only the Pennacook lived here but other friendly tribes came to Amoskeag Falls at the proper season to take advantage of the excellent fishing.[39] They settled along both sides of the Merrimack, making gardens on the lowland. According to Dr. Harry L. Watson of Manchester, "In ancient times the principal village occupied both banks of the Merrimack extending north and south one quarter to one half mile along the river proper, and one quarter to one half mile back on the highland, or bluffs bordering the falls." Over 10,000 objects were found in this area: knives, war points, broken pottery, and ornaments. There is a widening of the Merrimack with two small islands where, in the narrow outlet of the great basin known as the eddy, was found a weir. Very few burials have been found, perhaps twenty in all. Several caches have been found, along Cohas Brook, Ray Brook, in Auburn, and around Amoskeag Falls. The beaches along Massabesic Lake also show evidence of Indian village sites.[40]

Conway and Ossipee

The Sokoki had their tribal home among the Conway meadows. The villages were located along that stretch of intervale which reaches from the foot of Mt. Kearsarge southward into what is now the town of Fryeburg. The aborigine of this section was known as the Pigwaket or the Pequawket. Still further to the westward were the Ossipee, who are to be taken as a branch of the Sokoki family.[41] On the western shore of Ossipee Lake there is a large burial mound ten feet high and fifty feet in diameter from which several Indian skeletons have been taken, all buried in a sitting position. Tomahawks, relics, and ancient earthenware have been found in the mounds and surrounding meadows. Corn hills are also discernible. Several of these mounds have also been found in Fryeburg, Maine. These groups depended upon their streams for fishing and for highways.[42]

There is much evidence in the Winnipesaukee-Ossipee region that the Red Paint People from Maine infiltrated into this area. These people may have come up the Saco and Ossipee rivers and moved over to the head of the Winnipesaukee or might have come up the Salmon Falls. The Red Paint People painted their bodies with red oxides. Their pottery was of a primitive nature. Burial customs were also primitive, and they buried their dead barely below the ground level. This remote race soon lost contact with the other New Hampshire groups.[43]

Bristol

At Bristol—once called New Chester—the Indians had an abiding place. This is shown from the number of stone implements. Indian arrowheads, spearheads, stone axes, gouges, and pestles have been found on the shores of

Newfound Lake and along the Newfound, Smith, and Pemigewasset rivers. It is said that there is an old Indian burial ground which would seem to indicate that this was a permanent rather than a temporary abode.[44]

Crotchtown

Crotchtown was at the head of the Merrimack where the Winnipesaukee and the Pemigewasset join company on their journey to the sea. The long peninsula between the rivers was a famous Indian resort.[45]

Oxbow Point (Odell Park) is where a sharp S turn occurs in the Winnipesaukee River and is indicated as an Indian village by the extreme number of relics to be found. There is a carry place for portage. The area was cultivated in corn and a weir has been found as an aid to fishing.[46]

Aquadoctan

The Pennacook word for weirs was *aquadoctan*. The natives gathered from far and near to get fish for their winter supply of food. The great stone fish trap was made in the form of a W. The lower points extended quite a distance below the present iron bridge; the walls extended up the river some ten or fifteen rods and touched the shores. Good-sized stones, such as could be picked up in the river and on the shores, were used; the walls were never covered at low water, but at flood times the water overflowed them. The lower points were left open for a few feet for the water and the fish to go through. A short distance below the opening another wall was built in a half circle, and into the spaces were placed wicker-work through which the water could easily flow but which were fine enough to secure fish of good size. The fish were dri-

ven into these traps. That this was the method used by the Indians for ages was shown by the unmistakable age of the great walls. The first white settlers found the weirs in such good condition that they could use them.[47]

East Tilton

At East Tilton, on the Sanbornton side of the Winnipesaukee River extending from Middle Bay of Little Bay, are the remains of an extensive ancient Indian fortress. In 1685 an alliance was made between the Pequawket and the Pennacook in order to defend themselves against the Mohawk. It is probable that this fortress had been prepared as a mutual protection against the enemy. A Mohawk invasion when the fort was entered upon has been recorded and the crossing from the Belmont shore across the stream is called "Mohawk Point."[48]

Concord

The Concord area has been traditionally considered to be the site of three ancient Indian forts and the headquarters of the Pennacook. One is upon the west bank of the river on Fort Eddy Plain; another upon the east bank, opposite, upon the crest of Sugar Ball Bluff; the third is also on the east bank of the Merrimack, near Sewall's Island. The Mohawk were the intruders, and excavations have unearthed many skeletons with skulls clefted by tomahawks.[49]

Notes

1. Mary A. Proctor, *The Indians of the Winnipesaukee and Pemigewasset Valleys*, pp. 1–2.
2. Herbert Milton Sylvester, "The Land of the Abenake" in *Indian Wars of New England*, vol. II, p. 27.
3. *Ibid.*, p. 30.

4. Proctor, p. 27.
5. *Ibid.*, p. 30.
6. *Ibid.*, p. 5.
7. Jeremy Belknap, "Monuments and Relics of the Indians" in *The History of New Hampshire*, vol. III, p. 84.
8. Proctor, p. 6.
9. Belknap, p. 83.
10. Proctor, p. 11.
11. Belknap, p. 86.
12. Proctor, p. 12.
13. *Ibid.*
14. *Ibid.*, p. 13.
15. Sylvester, p. 59.
16. *Ibid.*, p. 60.
17. *Ibid.*, pp. 47, 57.
18. Edgar Harlan Wilcomb, "Ancient Aquadoctan, the Weirs," from *Winnipesaukee Lake Country Gleanings*, p. 7.
19. Proctor, p. 17.
20. Merrimack Valley Region Association of New Hampshire, *Parade of the Merrimack Valley of New Hampshire*, p. 3.
21. Sylvester, p. 42.
22. Proctor, p. 18.
23. Frederick W. Kilbourne, *Chronicles of the White Mountains*, p. 2.
24. *Ibid.*, p. 5.
25. Proctor, p. 21.
26. Kilbourne, p. 6, 7.
27. Ernest E. Bisbee, *The White Mountain Scrapbook*, p. 4.
28. Kilbourne, p. 1.
29. *Ibid.*, p. 2.
30. Bisbee, p. 5.
31. *Ibid.*, p. 5.
32. *Ibid.*, p. 6.
33. *Ibid.*, pp. 6, 7.
34. Kilbourne, p. 11.
35. Bisbee, pp. 7–8.
36. Proctor, pp. 33–35.
37. Bisbee, pp. 11–12.
38. Wilcomb, p. 9.
39. Marshall, "Some Ancient Indian Village Sites to Manchester, New Hampshire," from *American Antiquity*, p. 359.
40. Warren King Moorehead, *The Merrimack Archaeological Survey*, pp. 62–63.
41. Sylvester, p. 41.
42. Bisbee, p. 5.
43. Moorehead, pp. 47, 57.
44. Proctor, pp. 52–53.
45. *Ibid.*, p. 36.
46. Moorehead, p. 47.
47. Proctor, p. 41.
48. Wilcomb, pp. 21–24.
49. *Ibid.*, pp. 39–40.

Bibliography

Belknap, Jeremy. "Monuments and Relics of the Indians," in *The History of New Hampshire*, vol. III. Boston: Belnap and Young, 1792.

Bisbee, Ernest E. *The White Mountain Scrapbook*. Lancaster, NH, 1946.

Drake, Samuel G. "Biography and History of the New England Indians, Continued," in *Biography and History of the Indians of North America from Its First Discovery*. Boston: Benjamin B. Mussey, 1841.

Kilbourne, Frederick W. *Chronicles of the White Mountains*. Boston: Houghton Mifflin, 1916.

Marshall, Harlan A. "The Manners, Customs and Some Historical Facts About the Indians of Northern New England." Compiled by author.

_____. "Some Ancient Indian Village Sites Adjacent to Manchester, New Hampshire," reprinted from *American Antiquity*, vol. 7, no. 4, April 1942.

Merrimack Valley Region Association of New Hampshire, *Parade of the Merrimack Valley of New Hampshire*. Manchester, NH, 1953–54.

Moorehead, Warren King. *The Merrimack Archeological Survey*. Salem, MA: Peabody Museum, 1931.

Proctor, Mary A. *The Indians of the Winnipesaukee and Pemigewasset Valleys*. Franklin, NH: Towne & Robie, 1930.

Sherwin, Reider T. "Tribes Speaking Algonquin Dialects," from *The Viking and the Red Man: The Old Norse Origin of the Algonquin Language*. New York: Funk & Wagnalls, 1940.

State Planning and Development Commission. *Communities, Settlements, and Neighboring Centers in the State of New Hampshire*. Concord, NH, 1937, from Douglas-Lithgow, R. A., *Dictionary of American-IndianPlaces and Proper Names in New England*.

Sylvester, Herbert Milton. "The Land of the Abenake" in *Indian Wars of New England*, vol. II. Boston: W. B. Clarke, 1910.

Wilcomb, Edgar Harlan. "Ancient Aquadoctan, the Weirs," from *Winnipesaukee Lake Country Gleanings*. Booklet F-1, Worcester, MA, 1923.

[The *New Hampshire Archeologist*'s] editor's notes: In the "Indians of New Hampshire" paper by our good authoress, Miss Janine Carson, "Wanolancet ... returned to the Merrimack Valley in 1696, but after a short time finally retired again to St. Francis, where he died." From the records of the Tyng family and the *History of Tyngsboro* plus references in [Charles] Cowley's *History of Lowell*, I believe that Wannalancet returned to the Merrimack Valley in 1692 at the time of King William's War at the urgent request of the settlers of Dunstable and Chelmsford. They remembered his friendship with the whites and believed that they would be safer and more secure if he returned. He did return and spent the last days of a full life in the old Tyng mansion under the protection of his old friend Colonel Jonathan Tyng, who endeavored to repay some of the kindnesses manifested by Wannalancet to the English settlers. Here, the old sachem passed the last four years of his life, dying in 1696. He was buried in the old Tyng Cemetery where lies the Honorable Edward Tyng and his wife, Lady Mary, and their faithful body servants. On a boulder in front of the house where Wannalancet was accustomed to sit in fair weather and gaze out onto the expanse of his beloved Merrimack River, there is a suitably inscribed tablet dedicated to him: "In this place, lived during his last years, and died in 1696, Wannalancet, last Sachem of the Merrimack River Indians; Son of Passaconaway. Like his father, a faithful friend of the early New England Colonists." I have searched historical records, archives, and the burying ground trying to locate his grave. To date, I have not definitely located the grave. Even though the St. Francis Church records contain the names of Indian families that once lived in this valley, Wannalancet's name does not appear in the register of births, baptisms, marriages, and deaths. Until more conclusive evidence is uncovered, I sincerely believe that Wannalancet lies in the Tyng Family Cemetery. J. F. B.

12

The Pennacook Lands and Relations: Family Homelands

David Stewart-Smith

The Pennacook were one of the most prominent, if not the most powerful, tribal forces in central New England. Their unique history and culture distinguish them as a distinct group. During the course of their recorded history, the Pennacook alliance spanned, from west to east, from the Connecticut River to the Androscoggin River, and from north to south, from the Connecticut headwaters to the north shore of Massachusetts. The strength of the Pennacook came from their vast network of alliances and kinship, which literally spanned almost all of New England. Consequently, this ethnographic study focuses on distinct family territories which were probably held for centuries before the settlement of New England by Europeans. The ethnohistory which serves as the basis of my study can only guess at the precontact period. The historical study then confronts the incredible depletion of the native population by repeated diseases, the forced diaspora of many tribes throughout New England due to warfare and cultural crises with English settlement, and lastly, the important role Pennacook played as a gathering place and refuge for Algonquian peoples as the Indian center of New England before their "disappearance."

Our New England European ancestors were not keen on their observations of the New England Indians. Our knowledge of the New England Indians has been eclipsed by two quite distinct forms of cultural myopia: first, the fact that the English settlers of New England had little or no curiosity about native culture; and second, the academic and archaeological proclivity toward other cultures with "greater" material attractions.

The problem which confronts the ethnohistorian researching the north-

Source: David Stewart-Smith, "The Pennacook Indians and the New England Frontier, circa 1604–1733." Ph.D. diss., Union Institute, Cincinnati, OH (Ann Arbor, MI: UMI Dissertation Services, 1999), 15–40. Author no. 9908552. This is an updated and revised version of the article "The Pennacook: Lands and Relations, an Ethnography," *New Hampshire Archeologist* 33–34, no. 1 (1994): 66–80.

eastern New England Indians is also twofold. Added to the prevailing ethnocentrism of the English settlers is the eradication of native culture by disease and warfare. The primary sources for Pennacook ethnology are few and have remained the basis of any study of the tribes of central New England. These early sources include John Smith's account of his exploration of the New England coast (Smith 1833 [1616]), Samuel de Champlain's coastal explorations from 1604 to 1616 (Champlain 1906), William Wood's descriptions of the New England tribes and his observations from the lower Merrimack (Wood 1977 [1634]), and Daniel Gookin's descriptions of the New England tribes (Gookin 1970 [1674]). The best analysis of these primary sources to date with regard to the Pennacook is Sherburne Cook's demographic study, *The Indian Population of New England in the Seventeenth Century*, where he presents a section specifically on the Pennacook (Cook 1976, 13–28).

As my study encompasses a vast area of north-central New England and draws on references from four states, I have had to rely upon the work of many other ethnohistorians. Even though Massachusetts, New Hampshire, and Maine have extensive early history with regard to the early colonization of New England, virtually no recent ethnohistories exist for south-central Maine, New Hampshire, or the north shore of Massachusetts. My study has tried to fill some of that need in the research, as a beginning only.

POPULATION

The initial contact with Europeans on the northern and central shores of New England devastated the Indian population. This culminated in a three-year "plague," by the end of which nearly 90 percent of the Indian population of central New England was dead. The statistics make a strong statement, but in human terms, imagine that a family reunion was held in 1615 where 52 family members attended: grandparents, parents, uncles, aunts, cousins, nieces, nephews, and grandchildren. Upon the return for another reunion in 1618, possibly only five or six people from the entire family would have survived. This is what happened on coastal New England prior to the Plymouth settlement. Many Indian communities were entirely exterminated.

With recent research, the estimate of the pre-epidemic population for the region keeps increasing and, along with it, our realization of the devastation of the epidemic. Colin Calloway, in his article "Green Mountain Diaspora: Indian Population Movements in Vermont, c.1600–1800," mentions the effects of disease among the Abenaki, Pocumtuck, Mahican, and Mohawk in the central interior regions of New England. The Pennacook must have suffered a similar fate. Close relationship to the people along the north shore of Massachusetts would certainly have exposed the Pennacook to an equal, if not greater, extent.

Recent demographic studies approach figures of over 150,000 Indians throughout New England before the epidemic (Thornton 1987, 23–29; Thomas 1990, 25–28, 417–421). Daniel Gookin recorded in 1674 that the Pawtucket consisted of 3,000 *men* in earlier days but that by 1674 the tribe had been reduced to "not above 250 men, *besides* women and children" (Gookin 1970, 12; emphasis mine). If we work with Gookin's figure of 3,000 men for pre-epidemic time, a conservative estimate of Pawtucket population would be 12,000 to 15,000, given that each man represented a household of four or five people.[1] The Pawtucket were one prominent tribal group of several in New England prior to the epidemic (Gookin 1970, 9–12; Calloway 1988, 270).

Interior woodland life centered around the family in village groupings of relatives either by blood or marriage. In Pennacook country, the extent of horticulture was probably quite considerable. Several early accounts refer to cleared lands where winter storage of maize, fish, and game was practiced in the Merrimack Valley. With extensive horticulture and the unsurpassed fishing along the Merrimack, the Pennacook, Pawtucket, and Agawam of the Merrimack Valley were probably a quite prosperous and numerous people.[2] There are no real figures upon which to draw for these groups, but I will hazard an estimate for the Merrimack Valley, the Piscataqua, the lakes region, and the Connecticut Valley of about 15,000 to 22,000 people before the epidemic, accounting for at least three distinct, prosperous groups. In 1631 Thomas Dudley estimated that there were 400 or 500 warriors on the Merrimack as a post-epidemic figure (Young 1846, 306–307). Using standard demographic extrapolation, this would represent a population of between 2,000 and 2,500 people where one warrior is the head of household for five people. Equally, the epidemic survivor figures represent anywhere from 10 percent to 25 percent of the pre-epidemic population, rendering statistics for the Merrimack region in a range from 8,000 to 25,000, with a median around 16,500 for the central area of the Pennacook homeland. This median figure is somewhat more than Cook's figure of 12,000 for the entire homeland (Cook 1976, 27–28). Using Dudley's figure, the 15,000–22,000 range seems reasonable, considering the potential of the Piscataqua, the lakes, and the Connecticut Valley regions to add considerably to the Merrimack Valley figure. This figure would also include

the Maine coastal areas of the homeland, as in Cook's study.

Indian population statistical estimates have been steadily rising over the past several decades with greater archaeological and environmental knowledge of the pre-epidemic climate and resources. Contemporary with Cook's study is Francis Jennings' rendering of a population figure of 72,000 Indians in pre-epidemic New England, using Gookin's demographics (Jennings 1976, 29–30). Cook's figure of 12,000 for the Pennacook/Pawtucket represents about 16 percent of the native pre-epidemic population of New England. An assertion for the relative strength of the Pennacook population comes from Daniel Gookin that the Pawtucket (including the Pennacook) were "a considerable people" in the region (Gookin 1970, 10). Russell Thornton (1987) and Peter Thomas (1990) have both proposed a total pre-epidemic population figure of about 150,000, almost twice that of Jennings. The Pennacook/Pawtucket percentage of 16 percent of this figure is approximately 24,000. Given the Gookin baseline and recent demographic extrapolations, a population range of between 15,000 and 22,000 for the Pennacook/Pawtucket fits the model.

LIFEWAYS

The precontact period picture presents us with a lifestyle and social organization which should not be unfamiliar to most New Englanders. Villages consisted of several families living in a group or band.[3] The Indian life pattern would not have been all that different from that of eighteenth-century Yankee towns where several families located in an area. Within these families, relationships of intermarriage and kinship bound the group through consanguinity and social commerce. The Indians of Merrimack had no less a system of kinship.

There should be no mystery nor anthropological formula necessary to unravel the elements of Merrimack Indian society. Whether eighteenth-century settler or precontact woodland Indian, both groups lived on the land and utilized an area of resources proscribed by natural boundaries. During the frontier settlement in northern New England, the whites' lifestyle and subsistence pattern was probably more akin to an Indian way of life than to an English one. Among the Indians, communal resources were shared, particularly cornfields and fishing grounds. Children were raised by a community of relatives, and each village was a group of extended family members. These relationships extended to neighboring villages through marriage and social commerce (Wood 1977, 88–93; Calloway 1989, 27–29).

At the head of each village was a sagamore,[4] or leader, whose wisdom and sense of community welfare was paramount; often this position was hereditary. At least along the lower Merrimack, leadership was not gender specific. At Naumkeag (Salem, Mass.) and at Pawtucket (Lowell, Mass.), the widow of the sagamore assumed the leadership role as squaw sachem (Wood 1977, 97–99; Bragdon 1996, 140–155). When someone of the village was recognized for his or her healing skills and sense of vision, this person was trained to become the *powwow*, or medicine person for the group (Wood 1977, 100–102; Simmons 1986, 60–64). Herbal medicine was well known and widely used by each household. The powwow, however, had many more spiritual duties to perform than merely prescribing medicines.

Beyond the village was a network of riverways and trails granting wide accessibility throughout the region during the

months without snow (Price 1967). From various contact period sources we know the Indians of the Merrimack gathered at fishing sites in large numbers. The seasonal fish harvest would have greatly contributed to the subsistence of a household for the winter months, possibly their greatest source of protein. Smoking and drying the fish preserved the catch for winter storage (Wood 1977, 107–108; Bragdon 1996, 116–117;Calloway 1989, 17–18). These large gatherings of families along the Merrimack also helped to sustain contact with other groups of families. The seasonal fish runs at the major falls along the rivers were festive occasions where group sports, gaming, and marriage contracts took place.

It is possible that the fifteenth and sixteenth centuries of the precontact period were very important to the political development of the Merrimack Valley Indians. With large centers of population and substantial resources, the potential existed for powerful alliances to secure territory (Cook 1976, 28). It is equally possible that violent contentions for territory also arose at this time (Thomas 1990, 29–30). The pattern we see in the contact period is of strong Pennacook alliances with the Pawtucket and Piscataqua extending along the coast of Maine as far as the Saco River (Grumet 1995, 105–109; Cook 1976, 13–28).

Early explorers noted that the cultivation of maize was practiced from the Saco River southward. The Kennebec Valley Indians apparently had only marginal horticulture (Snow *HNAI* 1978, 138; Salisbury 1982, 67, 76–77; Prins 1992, 56–57). The climate had been getting progressively colder since the middle of the fifteenth century. This "small ice age" (Thomas PC 1993) may have promoted several demographic changes in Indian population during the Late Woodland period. Certainly one area of tremendous fertility and viable climate during this climatic change was the Merrimack Valley (Snow 1980, 333–336).

What we see of tribal organization in the seventeenth century after the ingression of Europeans was only a poor fragment of Indian society. The dramatic devastation of the population after the three-year epidemic was not the only effect. All family households were depleted, and traditional networks of commerce and hereditary location must have changed as a result. In seventeenth-century Indian society in central New England we do see strong leadership figures (A. H. Morrison 1991, 225–245; Eckstorm 1945, 100). It is possible that the social devastation of depopulation accentuated the need for community cohesion with the sagamores gathering ravaged communities together.

LEADERSHIP AND ALLIANCE

Prior to contact, the focus of leadership may have varied with different communities. During the winters throughout the region and in the north country, the villages probably remained quite autonomous, recognizing only a perfunctory political leadership which assisted trade and defense. With the development of greater horticulture in the valleys, the autonomy and isolation of more rural villages may have given way to more centralized towns, sometime at the beginning of the Late Woodland period.[5] Even if we look to the eighteenth-century colonial settlements in northern New England as a model, we have to acknowledge that the geography demands a certain brand of community autonomy.

A contest arose after the ravages of disease had swept the north shore of Massachusetts Bay and the Merrimack Valley. The Tarrantine (Micmac), who had scourged the Eastern Abenaki areas on the Gulf of Maine from 1607 to 1615, succeeded in usurping commerce in the Etchemin area around Penobscot and in the tribal areas along the coast all the way to Agawam (Prins 1996, 108–109). This harrying of the coastline caused many of the groups to move inland, which might explain the strong alliance of the Pigwacket, Amerascoggin, and Saco River Indians.

From Accominta through Piscataqua and Agawam the old Pawtucket lines of alliance held. But in 1619, after the epidemic, the Tarrantine seized the chance to raid the rich lands of the lower Merrimack. Nanepashemet, the sagamore of Pawtucket, was killed at Winnisemet (Malden) on the north bank of the Mystic River (Mourt 1963, 78). His widow became the squaw sachem of Pawtucket. Passaconaway[6] presided in the area when the historical picture began to come into focus around 1629. Nanepashemet's sons were very young when their father died. Two of his sons married two of Passaconaway's daughters, cementing the Pennacook/Pawtucket alliance in a network of kinship (Stewart-Smith 1994, 448–449). These two sons—Montowampate, or James, and Wenepoykin, or George Nobhow—were the sagamores of Saugus and Naumkeag, respectively (Wood 1977, 123). Nanamocomuck, Passaconaway's eldest son, became the sagamore of Wachuset through marriage (Potter 1856, 64). Wonalancet, Passaconaway's second son, is believed to have been married to an Abenaki woman from the St. Francis River area (Gookin 1836, 521). This network of social commerce and marriage wove the Pawtucket and the Pennacook into an inseparable fabric. The Pennacook tribal structure probably has to be looked upon as a heterogeneous confederacy, rather than a homogeneous tribe. Consequently the alliance may have been based more on political and cultural similarities than on tribal ethnicity (Cook 1976, 29). Through the historical record, it is apparent that Passaconaway was recognized as leader throughout Pawtucket, Agawam, and Piscataqua, although each of these areas retained their local sagamores.

The English settlers, for the most part, failed to recognize the deep family systems which placed the sagamores in a role which spoke for community consensus. Instead, the English assumed the sagamores were monarchs with the kind of authority with which they were familiar. Further evidence of English blindness to native and family social systems was subsequently displayed throughout the British Empire in Ireland, Scotland, and Africa, among other tribal peoples. It must also be said that the English *needed* the type of dominion they ascribed to the sagamores in their transactions for vast tracts of territory. The attraction of land ownership in the new English colonies was irresistible, as land ownership in England was proscribed by an elaborate system of inheritance and privilege (Jennings 1976, 128–130). The signature of one sagamore was taken as license to wrest the land from various bands. This satisfied English sensibilities of land ownership but may not have been in harmony with the previous native system of territorial guardianship.

PENNACOOK/ PAWTUCKET HOMELANDS

In his correspondence to the governor of New Hampshire, Passaconaway's grandson, Kancamagus, explained that the lands of his people lay along the Merrimack, which was one river, but that each of the places along the river bore the names of the family territories ("One Rever great Many Names," he wrote in 1685). According to Indian deed testimony in Essex County we know that family homelands were set up with very specific boundaries under the governance of a family leader or sagamore (Perley 1912). The same system carried up the Merrimack. The territories appear to have been permanent areas with established villages, and this arrangement refutes the standard seminomadic anthropological model for the northeastern New England Indians. It would be more appropriate to call the Pennacook semisedentary for they also had established hereditary locations within their tribal homeland.

For the purpose of clarity, we could think of family or band territories as "counties." These areas represented a natural and sufficient division of the geographical resources to support a group of possibly several villages. Larger tribal designations, such as Pennacook, Pawtucket, Massachusett, or Nipmuc, could perhaps be thought of as "states" rather than as nations. These probably represented homogeneous ethnic and cultural groups of families, an aggregate of allied family territories. At one time, most of New England was relatively cohesive as an area of social commerce and consanguinity. Therefore, there are no hard ethnic boundaries between tribes;[7] the range of commerce and relationship ties fluctuated continually. The geographic definition of these tribes conforms to the model in the designation of the Pennacook/Pawtucket family territories. Similar systems existed among the Massachusett and Nipmuc and probably among most of the other New England tribes.

We do not have to be confused by this. In New England, parts of the region are considered under the Boston metropolitan area of influence. Equally, other areas gravitate around local urban zones, and remaining rural areas still have inherent reference to their immediate geography. All of these areas of influence are subject to change and interaction both socially and economically. It was not all that different in tribal New England. Tribal political structures were fluid and predominantly volitional, with a tradition of community interdependence (A. Morrison 1990, 227; K. Morrison 1984, 35–36, 65–66, 106–107).

Pawtucket

As a tribal area, Pawtucket consisted of several territories: Winnisemet, Saugus or Swampscott, Naumkeag, Agawam, Pentucket, and Pawtucket, from the coast going up the Merrimack. Daniel Gookin includes Piscataqua and Accominta in the Pawtucket alliance (Gookin 1970, 10). Early sources such as John Smith and Gookin stress the north shore of Massachusetts Bay and the Gulf of Maine as tribal territories in alliance (Smith 1833 MassHSC, 12). Why the political alliance did not include the Massachusett is a curiosity. Social commerce must have existed between Pawtucket and Massachusett groups, although the early histories consistently draw a demarcation. There was some history of hostility between the Shawmut Massachusett and the Pawtucket (Salwen 1978, 169–170; Salisbury 1982, 121). It appears that the squaw sachem of Pawtucket was from a Massachusett leadership family—a "Massachusets [as in the original] Queen" in her own right—probably from Neponset (Mourt 1832, 57).

Narragansett sources of traditional tribal history mention the link with Pawtucket as the source of their own Pawtuxet. This was due to matrilocal marriages made by Pawtucket men to Narragansett women (Sekatau PC, 4/29/91). I have marked a Narragansett corridor on the map [original maps are not included here but see maps A and B] going up the Blackstone River valley, which shows the link between Narragansett country and Pawtucket Falls on the Merrimack. Pawtucket leaders were allied with the Narragansett against the Pequot in the early 1630s. The tribal name Patuxet is used again around Plymouth Bay but, seemingly, with no connection. The early accounts by Roger Williams and John Eliot stated that the Indians of the Pawtucket territories spoke the same language as the Narragansett and Massachusett Indians (Hodge 1910 2, 225). Williams was the minister at Salem, or Naumkeag, within a Pawtucket territory, before he was banished to Rhode Island. It is impossible to guess at the level of Williams' or Eliot's comprehension of the Algonquian dialects.

Pawtucket Falls

Located properly at Pawtucket Falls and the river confluence at Lowell, this was the seat of Nanepashemet and encompassed Wamesit, part of Chelmsford, and upriver Wickasauke Island, where Wonalancet lived. The confluence with the Concord River was part of the Pawtucket area. The Concord area was called Musketaquid, possibly a Pawtucket-Nipmuc territory (MBR I, 194, 201). Part of Chelmsford along the Concord River and Merrimack drainage was incorporated into the Wamesit reservation by John Eliot in 1653 (Allen 1820, 140–161).

Pennacook Tribal Areas

Resisting terms like *subgroups* or *septs*, I wish to underscore the autonomy of the peoples who came within the Pennacook sphere of influence. The protohistoric map illustrates this area extending to the west bank of Kennebec and as far west as the east bank of Lake Champlain. There can be no inference that this area *belonged* to the Pennacook; it is, rather, a cultural area denoting social commerce and occasional political alliances and consanguinity.

Below the Nashua River inlet, Elmer Hinton, the cartographer for this project, and I have designated two areas: for the Otonic on the east bank of the Merrimack and for the Massapaug on the west bank. The Otonic, according to legend, were located around Hudson. There is an Ottarnic Pond, which may be a remnant name from this group. The Massapaug were their rivals and lived in an area which extended from Dunstable to Salmon Brook in Nashua. There is a Massapaug Pond in Dunstable.[8] Wataunick is given as a name for the village at Nashua where Salmon Brook meets the Merrimack. Simon Willard had a trading post at Wataunick possibly as early as 1653 (Fox 1846, 18).

Central Merrimack

The Souhegan River runs northeast from a three-river plain shared with the Contoocook and the North Nashua. The Souhegan probably utilized the entire Souhegan drainage. Chandler Potter identified them as a group and said they were often called Natacook. In Frederick W. Hodge's *Handbook*, their principal village is listed as Souhegan, now Amherst. (Hodge 1910 2, 617; Potter in Schoolcraft 1860 V, 221–222.)

Passaconaway had his farm at Naticook, and it was here that he spent his last days, petitioning the Boston General Court in 1662 to set his farm aside from further encroachment (Bouton 1856, 25–26; Potter 1856, 61–63). The survey of Naticook to set aside land for Passaconaway was done on March 27, 1663. Naticook was on both banks of the Merrimack and below the inlet of the Souhegan. Passaconaway's land included the islands at Reed's Ferry. This was the epi-

center for the Amoskeag, Naticook, Souhegan, and Nashua territories.

Upriver from Naticook was the famous fishing ground of Amoskeag, now Manchester, New Hampshire. The Pennacook leaders had a residence there on a knoll immediately east of the falls (Potter 1856, 69), possibly now the site of the McIntyre ski area at the head of Sagamore Street. The Smyth archaeological site, just north of the city center on the east bank, is one of the few protohistoric sites in a known Indian town. There are still peripheral areas of this site intact, which should be further protected and investigated (Wesley Stinson PC, 3/20/97; Sargent Museum Archives). The fishing there was also of primary importance to the early pioneers in the region, especially the Scotch Irish of Londonderry (C. W. Wallace 1910 IV, 129–136).

The territory north of Amoskeag is the Soucook and Suncook drainage. The Suncook area extended up these valleys probably as far north as the Suncook Lakes. *Colby's Indian History* sites their main village in Allenstown (Colby 1975, 77–78). When the plantation of Contoocook (Boscawen) was being settled, the overland route to Penacook was from Piscataqua to Gilmanton, then through Canterbury to the Merrimack River. Part of this trail would have gone through Suncook territory.

Penacook

Properly the area of the river at the confluence of the Contoocook and the Merrimack, the Pennacook territory was probably considerably larger than this, extending as far north as the Winnipesaukee River and west past Mt. Kearsarge to the Sunapee watershed. Mt. Kearsarge and the Merrimack River almost certainly had deep spiritual significance to the Pennacook in identifying their homeland. It is impossible to know why the tribal confederation-state became known as Penacook. Of further curiosity, there is almost no evidence of Passaconaway residing at Penacook.[9] Wonalancet succeeded him as sagamore of the Pennacook, but even for Wonalancet, Penacook was not his main residence. Throughout the histories there are sagamores listed for Penacook other than Passaconaway and Wonalancet.

The Indian town of Penacook was maintained as a place of retreat and fortification during the sagamoreships of Wonalancet and Passaconaway. It was a center of refuge after King Philip's War and during the uprisings under Kancamagus. The main fortification was thought to be on the Sugar Ball Bluff somewhere north of the state office park on Hazen Drive. Gordon Day interprets the name to mean "at the falling bank," indicating the obvious bank erosion at this location (Day 1973, 31–37). The locations of the Indian fort and the main town have not yet been established. According to several accounts there were at least three major forts at Penacook: the Sugar Ball Bluff on the east bank, Fort Eddy Plain on the west bank, and most likely toward the north end of Concord near Sewall's Falls. Archaeological evidence has failed so far to reveal these sites. There is reason to believe that the Pennacook also frequented the intervale at the mouth of the Contoocook River, at the present site of Penacook (Coffin 1977, 6–7; Day 1961, 170).

At the head of the Merrimack is the Pemigewasset tributary. I have arbitrarily placed a boundary slightly above the Winnipesaukee River, apportioning the more northern territory as Pemigewasset. Colby mentions the remarkable artifacts of the Proctor Collection from Odell's Park in Franklin in his section on Pemigewasset (Colby 1975, 115–117; Proctor 1930; passim). It is possible that the Pemigewasset bands were beyond a fully viable horticultural range, which would constitute a substantial difference in their subsistence pattern from the Pennacook. It has not been established what kind of interaction the Pemigewasset had with either the Pennacook or the Indians of the lakes region. Because of the mountain passes along the Pemigewasset and Baker rivers, the Pemigewasset may have had more to do with the Cowassuck and groups to the west. As late as 1743 there was a report that four sagamores still held lands in the Pemigewasset territory (NHPP V, 95–96).

Lakes Region

At Lake Winnipesaukee I have designated an area for the Winnepiseogee surrounding the lake. Because of the profuse archaeological evidence along the lake shore and at Lochmere, there can be little doubt that a lake group existed. John Sherman and Jonathan Ince give the names "Aquedahian" for the Lochmere district and "Winnapusseakit" for the lake after their survey in 1652 (NHPP I, 201). The fishing grounds at Lochmere were well known to the Pennacook, indicating that Winnipesaukee could well have been a northern epicenter for the Pennacook, Pemigewasset, Ossipee, and Winnepiseogee Indians during the seasonal fish runs (Silver and Silver 1962, 49–60).

The Ossipee were centered around Lake Ossipee with a known village on the west bank and, more likely, a village site on the northeast side (now under water) (W. T. Silver PC, 1992).[10] The Ossipee River is a tributary to the Saco presenting ready access to their Saco Valley allies. Jeremy Belknap mentions that the remains of Indian stone fishing weirs were found on the Ossipee and Winnipesaukee rivers (Belknap 1973, 67). A trading post was established at Ossipee by

Francis Small of Maine sometime prior to 1662 (YD 2, 116; 3, 16). There are further references for the forts and the mound at Ossipee in Merrill's *History of Carroll County* (Belknap 1973 III, 67; Merrill 1917, 581–582). The Ossipee joined the Pigwacket and Amerascoggin under Kancamagus and Worumbo during the resistance toward the end of the seventeenth century. This group held strong alliances with the Winnepiseogee and the Pigwacket. The Ossipee were part of the Pennacook, or Central Abenakian group.

Saco River Valley

In this area the Pigwacket are perhaps the most illustrious of the interior groups. Samuel Purchas identified in 1602 the country of Mawooshen, which included the upper Saco drainage (Purchas 1905, 1873–1875). Dean Snow places the Pigwacket on the Gulf of Maine as far north as the Presumpscot River which included the area of Aucocisco and into the interior to the White Mountains (Snow 1978, 137–138). The Pigwacket were reputed to have had their own dialect which is designated as one of the four Eastern Abenaki dialects (Frank T. Siebert PC, 5/22/97; Snow 1978, 137). There is not enough linguistic evidence to link this dialect to the unidentified Pennacook dialect, but most of the Pigwacket had strong links to the Pennacook by the eighteenth century. Toward the end of the seventeenth century, the Pennacook chief Kancamagus, son of Nanamocomuck, helped create a powerful alliance among the Pigwacket, Amerascoggin, Piscataqua, Accominta, and other Saco River Indians. Kancamagus joined with the chief of the Amerascoggin, Worumbo, in joint leadership of the Central Abenaki Alliance. It was Worumbo's fort at Amerascoggin (Auburn, Maine) which was attacked by Benjamin Church in 1690 (Church 1829,

85–89). This led to a treaty following Church's abduction of Kancamagus's wife and children. It is in this alliance that we see the strength of the central Abenakian groups.[11]

Piscataqua

This is another fairly complex area consisting of at least three tribal territories: Winnicunnet, Newichawannock, and Piscataqua. Toward the end of the seventeenth century these groups were known as Cocheco Indians. The first historical reference to Passaconaway is as the presiding sagamore over the sagamores of this area.[12] The Winnicunnet, according to early deeds, were located on the coast around the vicinity of the Hamptons. The Newichawannock were located between the Piscataqua River and the Cocheco River on the upper portion of the Piscataqua. The Piscataqua lived on the east bank of the Piscataqua and had complete social confluence with the Newichawannock and Winnicunnet. I have included an area for Washucke, which was west of Great Bay and may have extended as far west as Mt. Pawtuckaway. The name has been interpreted to mean "place on the hill." Pawtuckaway may indicate that this was a Pawtucket location at one time.

Connecticut River Valley

On the upper Connecticut are two groups. In the north, the Cowassuck (Calloway 1986, 210) were at the Wells River and Ammonoosuc outlets and probably farther north. There was a French mission village at Cowass in the vicinity of Newbury, Vermont, before 1713. It is marked on early French maps as an ancient village (Calloway 1990, 46–48). The Ondiake are thought to have been in the vicinity of Lyme, New Hampshire, and probably across the river near the Ompompanoosuc inlet and White River. The Ondiake are mentioned along with the "Pinnekooks and Pacamtekookes" as enemies of the "Maques" for murdering a Mohawk sagamore. Chester Price and Andrea Ohl have located a village, "Ordanakis," in the Lyme area. (NYCD 3, 67–68; Price 1958, map; and Ohl 1991, 33, 69).

There was at one time some confusion as to the location of the Sokoki, placing them on the Saco River in Maine. Not only did the early French sources know the whereabouts of the Sokoki, but there is at least one early map placing them clearly in central New England (Nicolas Sanson's map in HNAI 1978, vol. 15, 414; Day 1965, 237–249). We have located the Sokoki as far north as the Sunapee drainage. The Indians at Sunapee may have been Sokoki. According to Howard Sargent's archaeological work along that lake, the artifacts found there match the Connecticut River area more so than those found in the Merrimack drainage (Sargent PC 1991). I have designated a Sunapee area on the map [not reprinted here]. Their position between the Connecticut and the Merrimack rivers would have been crucial to any movement across the region.

Squakheag is the name given to a location just below the inlet of the Ashuelot River on the Connecticut. Tribally this was a meeting point of at least three groups of Indians: Nipmuc, Pocumtuck, and Sokoki. Gordon Day believes that these bands probably all were "Abenaki language" speakers (Day PC, 1993; Goddard in HNAI 1978 vol. 15, 71). Archaeologically this is an important region with the outstanding Contact period archaeology of Fort Hill (Thomas 1990).

CLOSING

Given an overview of the ethnography, the apparent precontact picture in New Hampshire is that there were four distinct ethnographic areas: the river and estuary of the Merrimack; the coast from the Piscataqua to the Saco River, and probably to the confluence of the Androscoggin with the Kennebec in what was known as Pejypscot; the upper Saco and Androscoggin rivers into the White Mountains, including the lakes region; and the Connecticut Valley from the Deerfield River to the Connecticut Lakes. The cultural epicenters were at Naticook, Cocheco, Pigwacket, Winnipesaukee, and Squakheag, where various events in tribal history were played out.

I have tried to confirm areas through at least three different sources whenever possible. I was struck that several mountains appear to be at "crossroads" of tribal territories. These mountains—Chocorua, Kearsarge, Pawtuckaway, Monadnock, and Wachuset—are all within walking distance of the ranges of several tribal groups. It is hardly surprising that these mountains are sometimes designated as treaty areas, meeting grounds, or sacred places. The geographical cosmography of the Indians of New Hampshire would have been very parochial. The center of their spiritual universe turned on these mountaintops or was born from these lakes and rivers, marking the ancestral homelands for many families.

Recent ethnography has placed most of New Hampshire under the title of Western Abenaki,[13] which is a large aggregate consisting of at least a dozen different groups from central Massachusetts to the headwaters of the Connecticut and beyond. This designation accomplishes the purpose of showing an area of cultural contact and confluence while leaving further tribal-band distinctions rather vague. The term *Abenaki* does not appear in any early English sources pertaining to this region with which I am familiar. It was used originally by Champlain for Indians along the Kennebec Valley. Elsewhere, I have discussed this term in greater detail and argued for a designation of Eastern, Central, and Western Abenaki; the Pennacook and groups described here would come under Central Abenaki.

What the Pennacook history illustrates, in the aftermath of rounds of disease and invasion, was a continuing effort to support refugees from various tribes. Penacook and Cocheco became refuges for the Narragansett and Wampanoag during King Philip's War. Pigwacket became a refuge for Pennacook, Accominta, and Saco Indians. In the long trail away from these homelands, Cowass, Missisquoi, and St. Francis became places of shelter for many displaced people. No matter what the rivalries had been, the hand of hospitality, refuge, and alliance in resistance was given freely throughout the region. The Abenaki word for this region was *Ndakinna*, "our land," conveying a deep spiritual and familial heritage vested in the landscape of New England. (Calloway 1991, 3–7) It is time, perhaps, to honor the ancient tribal legacy of cultural diversity and volition.

Notes

1. This is standard extrapolation for the male warrior supporting four or five dependents. This is a nuclear family model and probably doesn't reflect the extent of the Algonquian extended family system, but for now, it is the best model we have. An extended family model would probably represent a greater number of dependents, factoring in elders, parental siblings, and occasional polygamous marriages.

2. The primary source for early Indian lifeways is William Wood's *New England's Prospect* (1634), Alden Vaughan ed., Amherst: University of Massachusetts Press, 1977, *passim*. Wood witnessed Indian life along the lower Merrimack ca. 1628–1632. It was his

tribal descriptions and observations which were frequently recycled by many other authors. The book was originally written as a handbook for prospective settlers in New England.

3. Band is a very arbitrary term which has been applied to hunting parties, war parties, family groups or just a small group of individuals encountered on the trail or at a location.

4. The term "sagamore" appears to be correct along the Merrimack. There has been some discussion as to whether the term "sachem" refers to a chief overlord. I have tried to avoid any inference of imperial stratification.

5. The archaeological perspective in New Hampshire gives the indication of a culturally dramatic but quite diffuse Middle Woodland demography. However, the Late Woodland and Contact periods are sparsely represented in rural settings. This has led archaeologists to believe that prior to contact, large concentrations of population were centered in the locations of our present cities. [Wesley Stinson, then assistant state archaeologist for New Hampshire, PC (personal communication), May 26, 1993.]

6. Passaconaway signed his name "Papisseconnewa," although there are several forms of his name in the historical documents. The English frequently euphemized Indian words which upset their sensibilities. Hence *Winnecowet* replaced Winnecunnet, and *Winnipesaukee* replaced Winnepiseogee, etc.

7. Ethnographers noticed the tendency of people to think in terms of hard boundaries when dealing with tribal groups, hence the recent fasion of broad designations under larger groupings by language or social commerce which may inadvertently obscure information about specific bands. See Thomas 1990, 421–423 and note 2.

8. *The Nashua Daily Telegraph*, 1896, is cited in Florence C. Shepard's *The Nashua Experience*, Nashua: Nashua Library, Phoenix Publishing, 1978. This reference is somewhat apocryphal but the place names may indicate the existence of these two groups.

9. References to Passaconaway's farm at Sewall's Falls are Chandler E. Potter's *History of Manchester*: Potter 1856, 56, and Amos Hadley, "Scene of the History—Aboriginal Occupation" in *History of Concord NH*, James Lyford, ed. Concord: Rumford Press, 1903, 70,

probably citing Potter. Both of these sources cannot be considered as primary. Richard Waldron was known to have had a trading post in the vicinity.

10. The northeast bank of any lake makes a good winter location due to the sun's winter declination. The northeast side of Ossipee is flooded due to a dam on the lake which has elevated water levels (Richard Boisvert PC, 10/97).

11. The treaty was signed at Sagadahoc on November 29, 1690, by the sagamores of Pennacook, Winnepiseogee, Ossipee, Pigwacket, Ammaroscoggin and Kennebec [*sic*] (cited in Calloway 1988, 285).

12. The first reference to Passaconaway is as Conway, recorded by Christopher Levett ca. 1623 at Piscataqua. *Massachusetts Historical Collections*, 3d series, vol. VIII, 173.

13. Western Abenaki has been associated with the groups of New England Indians who gathered at St. Francis from circa 1660 onward. This is an historic and linguistic designation rather than a cultural or proto-historic definition. There is no doubt that some Pennacook joined the refuge communities of Sillery, St. Francis, and Missisquoi. However, this designation does not answer the question of the Pennacook's close alliance and kinship with the Pawtucket to the south, and Eastern Abenaki groups on the Gulf of Maine.

Bibliography

Allen, Wilkes
1820 "A Memoir of the Pawtuckett Indians," pp. 140–161. *The History of Chelmsford..., 1653–1820*. Haverhill, MA: Green.

Belknap, Jeremy
1973 *Belknap's New Hampshire: An Account of the State in 1792*. Facsimile ed. of vol. III, *The History of New Hampshire*. 1792. G. T. Lord, ed. Hampton, NH: Peter E. Randall.

Boisvert, Richard
NH State Archaeologist, PC (personal communication), 10/97.

Bouton, Nathaniel
1856 *The History of Concord, from Its First Grant in 1725, to the Organization of the City Government in 1853, with a History of the Ancient Penacooks*. Concord, NH: B. W. Sanborn.

Bragdon, Kathleen J.
1996 *Native People of Southern New England, 1500–1650*. Norman: University of Oklahoma Press.

Calloway, Colin G.
1986 "Green Mountain Diaspora: Indian Population Movements in Vermont, c. 1600–1800," pp. 197–228, in *Vermont History*, vol. 54, no. 4.
1988 "Wanalancet and Kancagamus: Indian Strategy and Leadership on the New Hampshire Frontier," in *Historical New Hampshire* 43.
1989 *The Abenaki*. New York: Chelsea House, Indians of North America series.
1990 *The Western Abenakis of Vermont, 1600–1800*. Norman: University of Oklahoma Press.
1991 *Dawnland Encounters: Indians and European in Northern New England*. Hanover NH: University Press of New England.

Champlain, Samuel de
1906 *The Voyages and Exploration of Samuel de Champlain (1604–1616)*. Annie Nettleton Bourne, tr., Edward Gaylord Bourne, ed. New York: A. S. Barnes.

Church, Thomas
1829 *The History of Philip's War, Commonly Called the Great Indian War of 1675 and 1676*. Samuel G. Drake, ed. Exeter NH: J & B Williams. Reprint, Heritage Books, 1989.

Coffin, Charles C.
1977 *The History of Boscawen and Webster, from 1733 to 1878*. 1878. Webster NH: Webster Bicentennial Committee.

Colby, Solon
1975 *Colby's Indian History: Antiquities of the New Hampshire Indians and Their Neighbors*. Exeter NH: Mrs. Solon Colby.

Cook, Sherburne F.
1976 *The Indian Population of New England in the Seventeenth Century*. Berkeley: University of California Press.

Day, Gordon M.
1965 "The Identity of the Sokokis," pp. 237–249, in *Ethnohistory*, vol. 12, no. 3.

1973 "The Problem of Openengos," pp. 31–37, in *Studies in Linguistics* 23.

Day, Gordon
    Western Abenaki scholar, PC (personal communication): 5/25/93.

Eckstorm, Fannie Hardy
    1980 *Old John Neptune and Other Maine Indian Shamans.* 1945. Orono: University of Maine, Marsh Island reprint.

Fox, Charles J.
    1846 *History of the Old Township of Dunstable, etc.* Nashua: Charles T. Gill.

Goddard, Ives
    1978 "Eastern Algonquian Languages," pp. 70–77, in *Handbook of the North American Indians* [HNAI], vol. 15, *Northeast*. Bruce Trigger, ed. Washington, DC: Smithsonian Institution.

Gookin, Daniel
    1836 "An Historical Account of the Doings and Sufferings of Christian Indians in New England, in the Years 1675, 1676, 1677," pp. 423–534, in *Transactions and Collections of the American Antiquarian Society*, vol. II, Cambridge MA: American Antiquarian Society.
    1970 *Historical Collections of the Indians in New England.* 1674. Jeffrey Fishe, ed. N.p.: Towtaid.

Grumet, Robert S.
    1995 *Historic Contact: Indian People and Colonists in Today's Northeastern United States in the Sixteenth through Eighteenth Centuries.* Norman: University of Oklahoma.

Hadley, Amos
    1903 "Scene of the History—Aboriginal Occupation" in *History of Concord, New Hampshire*. James Lyford, ed. Concord, NH: Rumford Press.

Hodge, Frederick W., ed.
    1910 *Handbook of the American Indians North of Mexico*, vol. 1: 1907; vol. 2: 1910. Bureau of Ethnology, Bulletin 30. Washington, DC: Government Printing Office.

Jennings, Francis
    1976 *The Invasion of America: Indians, Colonialism, and the Cant of Conquest.* New York: W. W. Norton.

Lyford, James O., ed.
    1903 *History of Concord.* Concord, NH: Rumford Press.

MassHSC—Massachusetts Historical Society
    Collections of the Massachusetts Historical Society. Boston: MassHS, various years.

MBR Nathaniel B. Shurtleff, ed.
    1854 *Records of the Governor and Company of Mass. Bay in New England*, 5 vols. Boston: Massachusetts State Legislature.

Merrill, Georgia Drew
    1917 *History of Carroll County.* 1889. Somersworth NH: New Hampshire Publishing Co.

Morrison, A.
    1990 "Dawnland Dog Feast: Wabanaki Warfare, c. 1600–1760," pp. 258–278. *Papers of the Twenty-first Algonquian Conference.* William Cowan, ed. Ottawa: Carleton University.
    1991 "Dawnland Directors' Decisions: 17th-Century Encounter Dynamics on the Wabanaki Frontier," pp. 225–245, in *Papers of the Twenty-Second Algonquian Conference.* William Cowan, ed. Ottawa: Carleton University.

Morrison, Kenneth
    1984 *The Embattled Northeast.* Berkeley: University of California Press.

Mourt, G.
    1963 *A Journal of the Pilgrims at Plymouth: Mourt's Relation.* 1662. Pp. 1–77, in MassHSC, vol. IX, 2d series. Boston: MassHS, 1832; New York: Corinth.

NHPP
    Provincial Papers of New Hampshire, vols. 1–7 and 19, 1623–1776. Concord: NH State Legislature, 1867–1891.

NYCD
    Documents Relative to the Colonial History of New York, 15 vols. O'Callaghan, E. B., ed. Albany: Weed, Parsons, 1869–1916.

Ohl, Andrea
    1991 "The Dennis Farm Site: Late and Final Woodland Utilization of an Upland Location on the Connecticut River Drainage." *New Hampshire Archeologist*, vol. 32, no. 1.

Perley, Sidney
1912 *Indian Land Titles of Essex County, Mass.* Salem: Essex Book and Print Club.

Potter, Chandler E.
1856 *History of Manchester, New Hampshire.* Manchester, NH: C. E. Potter.
1860 "The Pennacook," pp. 221–222, in vol. V of Henry Schoolcraft's *Indian Tribes of the United States*, 6 vols. Philadelphia: J. B. Lippincott.

Price, Chester B.
1958 Historic Indian Trails of New Hampshire, map.
1967 Historic Indian Trails of New Hampshire, text.

Prins, Harald E. L.
1992 "Cornfields at Meductic: Ethnic and Territorial Reconfigurations in Colonial Acadia," pp. 55–72, in *Man in the Northeast*, no. 44.
1996 *The Mi'kmaq: Resistance, Accommodation, and Cultural Survival.* New York: Harcourt Brace.

Proctor, Mary
1930 *Indians of the Winnepesauke and the Pemigewasset.* Franklin NH: Towne & Robie.

Purchas, Samuel
1905 *Description of the Countrey of Mawooshen, discovered by the English in the Yeere 1602 ... and etc.* 1625, vol. 4, pp. 1873–1875, in *Hakluytus Posthumus, or Purchas His Pilgrimes.* Glasgow Scot.: J. MacLehose & Sons, 1905–1907; London: H. Fetherstone, 1625.

Salisbury, Neal
1982 *Manitou and Providence: Indians, Europeans, and the Making of New England 1500–1643.* New York: Oxford University Press.

Salwen, Bert
1978 "Indians of Southern New England and Long Island: Early Period," pp. 160–176, in *Handbook of the North American Indians* [HNAI], vol. 15, *Northeast*, Bruce Trigger, ed. Washington, DC: Smithsonian Institution.

Sanson, Nicolas
1650 Map, pp. 414, in *Handbook of the North American Indians* [HNAI], vol. 15, *Northeast*, Bruce Trigger, ed. Washington, DC: Smithsonian Institution, 1978.

Sargent, Howard
Professor of Anthropology, PC (personal communications): 1991–92.

Sargent Museum Archives, Georges Mills and Concord, NH.

Sekatau, Ella
Ethnohistorian for the Narragansett Tribe, PC (personal communication): 1991–92.

Shepard, Florence C.
1978 *The Nashua Experience.* Nashua: Nashua Library, Phoenix Publishing.

Siebert, Frank T.
Eastern Abenaki scholar, PC (personal communication): 5/22/97.

Silver, Walter T., and Helenette Silver
1962 "The Indian 'Fort' at Lochmere," pp. 49–60, in *Historical New Hampshire*, vol. XVII, June.

Silver, Walter Theo
NH frontier historian, PC (personal communications): 1992–1995.

Simmons, William
1986 *Spirit of New England Indians: Indian History and Folklore 1620–1984.* Hanover, NH: University Press of New England.

Smith, Capt. John
1833 *General History of Virginia, New England and the Summer Isles. Sixth Booke: the General Historie of New England.* 1624, in MassHSC, 3d ser., vol. 3. Boston: MassHS.

Snow, Dean R.
1978 "Eastern Abenaki," pp. 137–147, in *Handbook of the North American Indians* [HNAI], vol. 15, *Northeast*, Bruce Trigger, ed. Washington, DC: Smithsonian Institution.
1980 *Archaeology of New England.* New York: Academic Press.

Stewart-Smith, David
1994a "The Pennacook: Lands and Relations, an Ethnography," pp. 66–80, in *New Hampshire Archaeologist*, vol. 33–34, no. 1.
1994b "Pennacook-Pawtucket Relations: The Cycles of Family Alliance on the Merrimack River in the 17th Century," pp. 445–468, in *Actes du Vingt-Cinquième Congrès des Algonquinistes.* William Cowan, ed. Ottawa: Carleton University.

Stinson, Wesley
  Assistant NH state archaeologist, PC (personal communication): May 26, 1993.
  President of Sargent Museum of Archaeology, PC: March 1998.

Thomas, Peter.
  1990 *In the Maelstrom of Change: The Indian Trade and Cultural Process in the Middle Connecticut Valley, 1635–1665.* Published Ph.D. dissertation, Univeristy of Massachusetts, 1979. New York: Garland Press.

Thomas, Peter
  Archaeologist, PC (personal communication): May 18, 1993.

Thornton, Russell
  1987 *American Indian Holocaust and Survival: American Indian Population Since 1492.* Norman: University of Oklahoma Press.

Wallace, The Rev. C. W.
  1910 "Amoskeag in Early Pioneer Days," pp. 129–136, in *Manchester Historic Association Collections*, vol. IV: 1908–1910. Manchester: MHA. Reprint, Heritage Books, Bowie MD, 1992.

Wood, William
  1977 *New England's Prospect.* 1634. Alden T. Vaughan, ed. Amherst: University of Massachusetts Press.

YD
  1887 *York Deeds.* Portland ME: John T. Hull.

Young, Alexander, ed.
  1846 *The First Planters of the Colony of Massachusetts Bay, from 1623 to 1636.* Boston: Charles C. Little and James Brown.

PART III

COLLECTIONS, SITES, TRAILS, NAMES

13

Provenience of Artifacts by New Hampshire Towns

Patricia Hume and Donald Foster

Codes

BHS Boscawan Historical Society

CHS Canaan Historical Society

DCM Dartmouth College Museum (Hood)

DHA Durham Historical Association

DHR Division of Historical Resources, Archaeology Division

DHSM Derry Historical Society Museum

EHS Exeter Historical Society

FPL Franklin Public Library

GML Gale Memorial Library, Laconia

HHS Hancock Historical Society; Hinsdale Historical Society

HS New Hampshire Historical Society

LHS Londonderry Historical Society

LHSM Littleton Historical Society Museum

MHA Manchester Historic Association

NHAS-SL-FI New Hampshire Archeological Society Slide Files

NHS Nashua Historical Society

P Personal Collection

PA Portsmouth Athenaeum

PEA Phillips Exeter Academy

PHS Plaistow Historical Society

PMHU Peabody Museum, Harvard University

PPL Portsmouth Public Library

SB Strawberry Banke

SHS Swanzey Historical Society

SHSM Sandown Historical Society Museum

UNH University of New Hampshire, Anthropology Department

WHS Wolfeboro Historical Society

WIM Woodman Institute Museum, Dover

WTH Wilton Town Hall

Sources: Patricia Hume and Donald Foster, "A Guide to New Hampshire Sites and Collections," *New Hampshire Archeologist* 33–34, no. 1 (1994): 121–23. This article consists of several parts: "New Hampshire Collections Housed and/or Listed in the Files at PEA"; "Personal, Institutional, and Survey Collections"; "Provenience of Artifacts by Towns"; "Sites Described in NHAS Bulletin since 1980 by Towns Where Sites Are Located"; and "New Hampshire Collections Housed at Private and Public Institutions." Included also is information on "Historical and Antiquarian Societies, Libraries, Museums, and Archeological Sites with Museums."

LOCATIONS
AND COLLECTIONS

The following is a list of towns where artifacts were originally found along with the current location of the collections containing these artifacts.

Allenstown: C. Berry Collection (MHA)

Amherst: C. Berry Collection (MHA)

Auburn: C. Berry Collection (MHA); D. Hardy Collection (PEA); P. Holmes Collection (PEA); Magnuson Collection

Bedford: C. Berry Collection (MHA)

Belmont: Drake Site (Lochmere Archeological Site) (DHR)

Berlin: Magnuson Collection, Mt. Jasper; R. Boisvert (DHR)

Boscawen: L. Adams Collection (BHS); First Fort Site (DHR); C. Folsom Collection (BHS); Theo Silver Collection (P)

Bow: C. Berry Collection (MHA)

Brentwood: Smith Farm Site

Canaan: C. Berry Collection (MHA); Historical Society Collection (CHS)

Canterbury: Canterbury Shaker Village (on site)

Claremont: Hunter Site (H. Sargent)

Concord: C. Berry Collection (MHA); L. Corliss Collection (P); Garvins Falls Site (PEA, NHAS-SL-FI, DHR); Hart Collection (St. Paul's School); Hazeltine Pottery Site (DHR); Sewall's Falls Area (4 sites; DHR)

Conway: Chapman Collection

Deerfield: C. Berry Collection (MHA)

Derry: W. Brown Collection (P); Historical Society Collection (DHSM); M. Proctor Collection (DCM)

Dover: Museum Collection (WIM)

Durham: Adams Point Site (PEA, UNH); P. Davis Collection (P); Historical Association Collection (DHA)

Epsom: M. Yeaton Site (PEA)

Exeter: A. Cote Site; B. Dix Collection (P); Fort Rock Site (PEA); Historical Society Collection (EHS); Oaklands Site; Pickpocket Falls Site (PEA, NHAS-SL-FI); Powder House Point Site (PEA); Stanley Site (PEA); W. White Collection (PEA on loan); J. Williams Oaklands Site Collection (PEA, NHAS-SL-FI)

Farmington: S. Parker Collection (Goodwin Library, Farmington)

Fitzwilliam: Meadow Pond Site (PEA, Sportman's Pond)

Franklin: C. Goodhue Collection; M. Proctor Collection (DCM); Public Library Collection (FPL)

Georges Mills: Russell's Inn Site (Sunapee Historical Society)

Goffstown: C. Berry Collection (MHA)

Greenland: R. Mori Collection (P); NH40-5 Site (NHAS-SL-FI)

Hampton Falls: W. White Collection (PEA on loan; NHAS-SL-FI)

Hancock: Historical Society Collection (HHS)

Henniker: Huntoon Collection

Hinsdale: J. H. Smith Collection (HHS)

Hooksett: C. Berry Collection (MHA); B. Seavey (P)

Hudson: C. Berry Collection (MHA); Musquash Pond Site (P. Hume); Reitan Collection (P)

Kensington: Batchelder Collection; W. White Collection (PEA, on loan; NHAS-SL-FI)

Kingston: Brox Site (PEA); D. Hardy Collection (PEA)

Laconia: Weirs Beach Site; H. Winchester Collection (NHAS-SL-FI); Gale Memorial Library Collection (GML)

Lee: Wadleigh Falls Site (UNH); Wadleigh Farm Site (PEA)

Litchfield: C. Berry Collection (MHA); Campbell Site (DHR); Litchfield Site; Rodonis Farm Site (DHR); Smolt Site (DHR); K. Thebodeau Collection (P)

Littleton: Historical Society Collection (LHSM)

Lochmere: Prindle Collection (PEA, NHAS-SL-FI)

Londonderry: C. Berry Collection (MHA); E. Kostigan (P); Nisula Collection (P); Parmenter Farm Collection (LHS); Webster/Beckley Collection (LHS); Viner Collection (P)

Lyme: Dennis Farm Site (PEA, V. Pushee); B. Mayo Site Collection (P)

Lyndeboro: D. Hardy (glass factory) (PEA)

Madison: West Branch Brook Site (DHR)

Manchester: Belanger Collection (PEA); C. Berry Collection (MHA, PEA); Eddy Site (PEA); F. Edwards Collection (P); D. Hardy Collection (PEA); J. House Collection; H. Marshall Collection (MHA); Neville Site (NH38-5) (PMHU); G. Nicholas (Cohas Brook area, PEA); K. Rhodes Collection (PEA); Smyth Site (NH38-4) (PEA, H. Sargent); H. Stevens Collection (NHAS-SL-FI)

Meredith: C. Berry Collection (MHA)

Merrimack: C. Berry Collection (MHA); Camp Naticook Site (DHR); Hume Site (DHR); Sargent Road (DHR)

Milford: Contract near bridge and other sites (DHR); E. Fitch Collection (P); G. Fitch Collection (P); H. Holt Collection (?)

Nashua: C. Berry Collection (MHA); several sites (DHR); C. Lund Collection (NH52-1) (NHS); Mine Falls Site (PEA); F. Robinson Collection (P)

New Boston: J. Dodge Collection (NH37-12) (P); V. B. Parsons Collection (P)

Newfields: L. Crosbie Collection (PEA); H. Folger Collection; White and Finch (Stetson Farm Site) (PEA, NHAS-SL-FI)

New Hampton: C. Berry Collection (MHA)

Newmarket: Wiswall Falls Site (PEA)

Newton Junction: Harvey Mitchell Site (NH46-12); P. Holmes Collection (PEA, PHS)

Northfield: Lisbon Collection (PEA)

Northwood: Northwood site (NHAS-SL-FI)

Ossipee: R. Boisvert Field School Sites (DHR); D. Hardy Collection (PEA)

Pelham: C. Berry Collection (MHA)

Pembroke: C. Berry Collection (MHA); M. Blaisdell Collection (P); G. Ferguson Collection (William Fisher); Mason Site (DHR)

Pittsfield: Lisbon Collection (PEA)

Plaistow: Brox Site (PEA); P. Holmes Collection (PEA); F. Lombardi Collection; Plaistow Dump Site (PEA)

Plymouth: R. Boyd Collection; NH19-2 Site (NHAS-SL-FI)

Portsmouth: Athenaeum Collection (PA); Strawbery Banke Collections (SB); Public Library Collection (PPL)

Raymond: Raymond Site (NHAS-SL-FI)

Rye: Wentworth Golf Course Site (DHR, PEA)

Salem: Mystery Hill Site (on site)

Sandown: Sandown Historical Society Collection (SHSM)

Seabrook: Rocks Road Site (NH47-21) (UNH, NHAS-SL-FI)

Shelburne: Stevens Brook Site (PEA)

South Hampton: South Hampton near Aspen Hill Collection (PEA, NHAS-SL-FI)

Stratham: Wiggin Site (DHR)

Swanzey: A. Whipple Collection (P); Whipple Site; Historical Society Collection (SHS); Antiquarian Society of the Mount Caesar Union Library (library may be in Keene)

Tamworth: Argillite Workshop Sites (NH20-1, NH20-2) (UNH)

Temple: New England Glassworks (DHR, Temple Historical Society)

Thornton's Ferry: Proctor Collection (DCM); Thornton's Ferry Site (DHR)

Tilton: C. Berry Collection (MHA); E. Lisbon Collection (PEA); C. Virgin Collection (P)

Walpole: L. Chapin Collection (?)

Wilmot: Historical Society Collection (WHS)

Wilton: Town of Wilton Collection (WTH)

Winchester: Broad Brook Site (NH41-17) (Colony House in Keene)

Windham: R. Barlow Collection (P); R. Thorndike Collection (P)

Wolfeboro: Historical Society Collection (WHS); H. Libby Collection (Libby Museum, Wolfeboro); J. Wentworth Plantation Site (NH27-2) (DHR)

14

Indian Sites in the Manchester-Auburn, New Hampshire, Area

Thaddeus Piotrowski

Because of the ever-present danger of site disturbance and even vandalism by contemporary Indian relic hunters, the following section is limited only to those sites which now have been almost completely destroyed by "progress," and about which information has been already published. Dozens of other active sites could be easily added to this list. The latter sites and those yet to be discovered should be assiduously preserved for future investigation. They are already protected by federal mandate and the "right to know" law does not apply to them.

AMOSKEAG SITES

According to Potter (1856, 27, 29), the designation "Namaoskeag" (written variously as Naimkeak, Namaske, Namaskeag, Namaskik, Naumkeag, Amokeag, and finally Amoskeag) was initially applied to the series of falls, rapids and ripples as well as to the adjacent land extending from the Souhegan River by the town of Merrimack to Garvins Falls in Concord. Eventually its use was limited to the immediate neighborhood of the principal falls, now known as Amoskeag. Both the Smyth and the Neville sites are located

Sources: Clyde Berry's maps and field journal located in the Manchester Historic Association; Eugene D. Finch, "Cartagena Island," *New Hampshire Archeologist* 12 (1963): 1–5; Victoria Bunker Kenyon, "Middle Woodland Pottery of the Central Merrimack Valley in New Hampshire," *New Hampshire Archeologist* 23 (1982): 103–18; Harlan A. Marshall, "Description of Ancient Indian Village Sites Situated on Little Massabesic Brook, Auburn, New Hampshire," a 1944 manuscript in the Manchester City Library, New Hampshire Room files; Harlan A. Marshall, "Some Ancient Indian Village Sites Adjacent to Manchester, New Hampshire," *American Antiquity* 7, no. 4 (April 1942): 359–63; George Peter Nicholas II, "The Cohas Brook Site (NH45-24), Manchester, New Hampshire: A Preliminary Report," *New Hampshire Archeologist* 20 (1978–79): 1–30; and Harry L. Watson, "Indians and Indian Relics of the Merrimack Valley," a talk given at the Manchester Institute on April 8, 1927, in the Manchester Historic Association files.

on the east side of the river at the falls (Map C, 2).

Before the spindles of Manchester's textile mills were turned by the power of the Merrimack, Amoskeag was considered to be one of the best fishing places in New Hampshire. The peculiar configuration of the falls and the great basin or eddy below produced a natural weir and facilitated great caches of salmon, shad, and eels during the spring run. But fishing was still good at Amoskeag even after the coming of the mills. The white settlers, it seems, especially relished eels, which ran twice a year. This predilection is reflected in the following words of William Stark, a "scholar, poet, and naturalist," read at the Manchester centennial celebration on October 22, 1851:

> I suppose we have no idea of the immense number of fish with which this river once abounded. My father has seen the shad so thick as to crowd each other in their passage up the falls, to gain the smooth water above; so that you could not put in your hand, without touching some of them; and yet there were more alewives than shad, and more eels than both. It is no wonder that eels were called "Derryfield beef" [Derryfield is the former name of Manchester], for I have heard those say, who would be good judges in the matter, that eels enough were salted down in a single year, to be equal to three hundred head of cattle [Gordon and Marston, 4–5].

Stark's lengthy poem composed for the centennial contains a delightful and often-quoted section on "Derryfield beef" (Stark 1–20; Potter 1856, 29–47).

Before the days of the plague, the Indian settlement at Amoskeag was fairly large, extending one quarter to one half mile along both banks of the Merrimack. The 1616–19 epidemic, however, had swept away so many natives that eventually the Namaoskeag ceased to exist as a distinct group. Thereafter the site was visited periodically by neighboring tribes or bands; after the fishing season, they would return to their own villages.

We know that the Pennacook often transferred their headquarters to Amoskeag and that prior to 1650 this was Passaconaway's principal residence, "the royal residence of the ancient Sagamons of the Merrimack Valley" (Potter 1856, 30). "Here," Potter continues, "without a doubt, he sat in royal state, held his council fires, determined upon his war paths, gave royal feasts, and performed those feats that held his wondering followers as with the spell of enchantment" (ibid., 56).

John Eliot's letters indicate that Passaconaway greatly desired to have him come and preach the gospel at Amoskeag and that he offered the apostle friendship and all the land he wanted (ibid., 58–59, and Eliot's letters in Marshall, "The Manners"). Yet, in spite of the known facts that he did speak with Passaconaway at Pawtucket, that a friend of Eliot had written of his going to Wamesit "with Mr. Flint, Captain Willard of Concord, and sundry others, towards Merrimath River unto that Indian Sachim Passaconnaway" (Potter 1856, 31; Marshall, "The Manners"), that the Indians of Amoskeag did meet to "worship God and keep the Sabbath," and that a school was established there for the young, Eliot probably never visited Amoskeag.

In addition to the main village at the falls themselves (the Smyth-Neville complex), there were several other Indian villages located in the area, one of them existed above the falls at the confluence of Ray Brook and the Merrimack River (Map C, 1). The many stone artifacts found there indicate that this may have been a large campground.

The two small islands in the eddy just

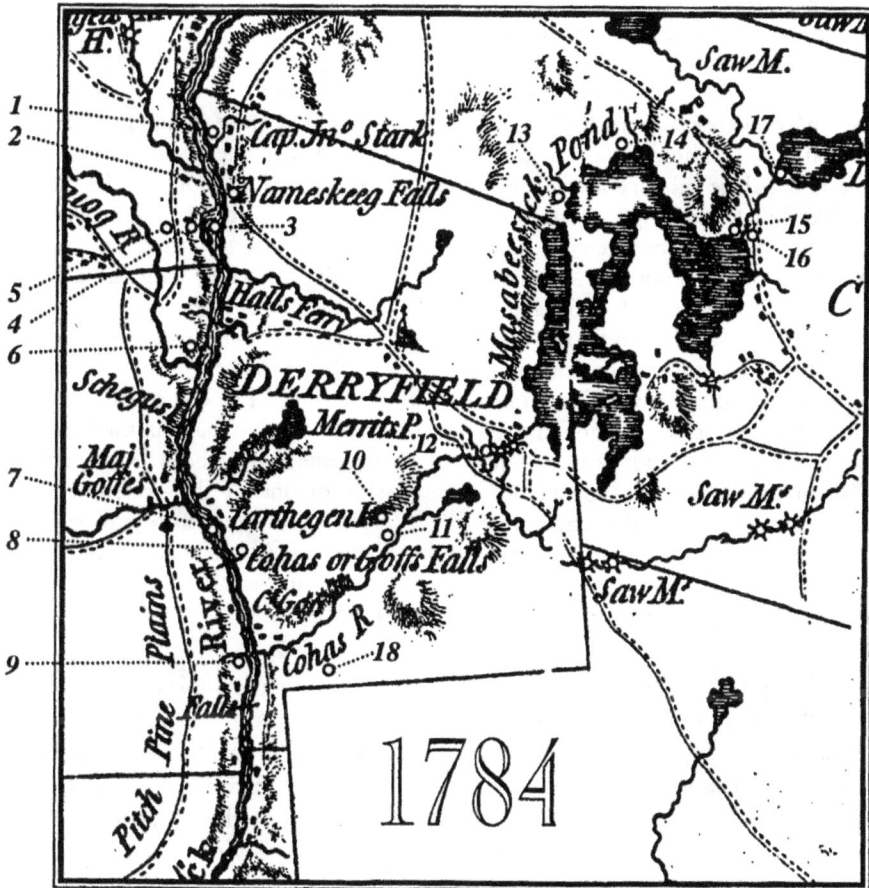

Map C

SITES: *1* Ray Brook; *2* Smyth and Neville; *3* Eddy Islands; *4* Eddy; *5* Table Land; *6* Piscataquog River; *7* Carthagina Island; *8* Short Falls; *9* Goffs Falls; *10* Cohas Brook; *11* Cohas Brook Swamp; *12* Dickey Plain; *13* Massabesic Circle Beach; *14* Severance Beach; *15* Preston Beach; *16* Auburn Village; *17* Little Massebesic Brook; *18* Manchester Airport

Indian sites in the Manchester-Auburn, N.H., area. This map segment comes from Samuel Holland's *A Topographical Map of the State of New Hampshire*, a wall map printed in England in 1784 for William Faden, Geographer to the King. Derryfield was the former name of Manchester. Base map courtesy of David Allen, *Old Maps*, West Chesterfield, N.H. Sites and date have been added.

below the falls were both occupied over long periods of time (Map C, 3). According to George Calvin Carter:

> The island in the Merrimack River just below Amoskeag Falls was, for many years, the most prolific single source of Indian artifacts in this state. There seemed to be no end of the things that could be found each year, especially after the spring freshets. The waters of the Merrimack would seem each year to replace in number any items that had been taken from the island the previous summer and fall, but, in the spring of 1936, Manchester suffered a flood, the like of which the city had never experienced before. There had been floods at this location as far back as New Hampshire history had been recorded, but the damage was not as great as that of 1936 because civilization had built structures along both sides of the river and erected two 10,000-gallon oil tanks on the island. This flood lifted the oil tanks and spilled the contents on the surface of the river. The tanks went down against the bridge. In the meantime, the rushing waters furrowed the island like the farmer's plow before the planting season, and the remaining Indian artifacts were sent down the river, buried in mud or covered with gravel and rocks [Carter 1948, 72–73].

The Eddy site (NH38-6) is located on the west bank of the Merrimack below the falls along the eddy (Map C, 4). A weir constructed of large rocks and brush was located at the southern end of the basin. The recovered stone artifacts and potsherds indicate that this Indian village extended for a quarter of a mile along the river bank and up to the high bluff on the west side of the city. A radiocarbon date of 7,900 B.P. has been established for this site.

The Table Land site (NH38-9) is located on the bluff west of the Eddy site and covers about 100 acres (Map C, 5).

According to Potter, it was here and at Amoskeag that the Indians gathered for their assemblies and ceremonies. One campsite was discovered on the east side of this site; another, at its northernmost end directly west of the falls themselves. Around 1936 a group of collectors dug up the southern end and found numerous large stone tools and also potsherds. In 1937 the five graves excavated on the plateau just west of the eddy gave rise to the notion that this may have been an Indian burial ground. According to Harlan Marshall:

> Two graves contained the remains of adults and the third, the skeleton of a child. The three skeletons were flexed. Included in the graves, some actually among the hand bones of the skeletons, were some of the ceremonial stones.... Two additional graves were found closely associated with these but two feet deeper, or seven feet below the surface. The latter burials were in poorer condition than the former and possibly were older. The rest of the ceremonial stones ... were found in these two burials, [one] having been found on the left side of one of the skeletons. Arrow points ... were also found with these skeletons. A large quantity of red ochre was found in all the burials [Marshall 1942, 361].

One final Amoskeag site deserves a special mention: the site where the last known Indian in the area made his humble abode. On the old city maps the site was located at the junction of Christian Brook and the Merrimack on the east side of the river directly opposite the islands in the eddy. (Christian Brook, which once ran toward the back of the armory property, is no more.)

Christian (or Christo or Christi), as he was renamed, was one of those "praying Indians" who was on friendly terms with the white settlers. (Christian Brook, however, was perhaps not named after Christian the Indian, but rather after the Scotch-Irish wife of John McNeil, one of the first settlers of Manchester; she also bore the name "Christian.") One day Christian (the Indian) "was accused at length of rendering assistance to his brethren in time of war, but with how much truth we are not able to state, as this charge was usually brought against the 'praying Indians' by certain prejudiced persons, whether they were guilty or not" [Potter 1856, 98; *see also* "Contributions to the History of Derryfield (Manchester)"].

Tradition has it that because of this accusation some whites came from Dunstable and Haverhill intending to take his life, but not finding him at home they burned his wigwam instead. That the charge of conspiracy against Christian was unjust is substantiated by the fact that after the accusation he was in the employ of the English as a scout in several Indian wars. He was even on the payroll of the legislature as late as 1745. Thereafter he left for the Jesuit-Abenaki St. Francis refuge in Quebec.

Somewhere along the way Christian must have had a change of heart, for in 1747 he supposedly assisted in the raid on Mr. McCoy's house in Epsom and in the capture of his wife. He may have also been a member of the party that sometime later attacked Suncook and Rumford, killing cattle as well as a certain Mr. Estabrook. And again, in 1752, we hear that Christian together with Sabbatis and Plausawa kidnapped two black slaves in Canterbury and carried them off. The last news of Christian comes from 1757, when Moses Jackman, an Indian captive from Canterbury, recognized him at or near St. Francis. Chandler Potter, on whose account this story is by and large based, ends his narrative with the following words:

> The spot occupied by Christo's wigwam at Amoskeag Falls, is now shown, where the ashes of his hearth stone, his pipes,

arrow heads, and ornaments consisting of bears' teeth, together with his tomahawk, have been ploughed up within the memory of the present generation. And his tomahawk, an iron one, with an eye like that of a hoe, and without any head, is still in possession of the former proprietors of the soil [Potter 1856, 100].

PISCATAQUOG RIVER SITE (MAP C, 6)

Located on the west side of the Merrimack, this site lies just north of the confluence of the two rivers after which it is named.

CARTHAGINA ISLAND SITE (MAP C, 7)

Carthagina Island is located in the Merrimack River north of Short Falls and north of where the combined NH-101 and the beltway (I-293) cross the river. Although no Indian artifacts have been found on the island in recent years, A. J. Coolidge and J. B. Mansfield reported in 1860 that "on Carthagena island, and opposite the mouth of the Coos river [Cohas Brook], traces of Indian villages were to be seen until recently" (see "Aboriginal Tribes of New Hampshire").

SHORT FALLS SITE (Map C, 8)

Located in the Goffs Falls area where NH-101 and I-293 cross the Merrimack, this site lies on the east bank of the river south of Carthagina Island and overlooks Short Falls.

GOFFS FALLS SITE (MAP C, 9)

The mouth of Cohas Brook where it meets the Merrimack, known as the Goffs

Falls area, was another famed place for spring fishing. Vast quantities of fish were taken there well into the nineteenth century. The west side of the river in that location may have been another Indian burial ground; several skeletons were found there.

COHAS BROOK SITE
(NH45-24) (MAP C, 10)

This site is located north of Cohas Brook below Huse Road and Claire Street on an old shoreline terrace of Great Cohas Swamp.

COHAS BROOK SWAMP SITE
(NH45-27) (MAP C, 11)

The swamp site lies just south of the Cohas Brook site on a low terrace within the swamp itself. It has been recently damaged by the introduction of a logging road. Both Cohas Brook sites served as short-term camps during the entire Archaic period.

DICKEY PLAIN
SITE (Map C, 12)

This half-mile–long site lies on the north bank of Cohas Brook at its junction with Cohas Avenue. In addition to being a source of fish, the brook was also an important waterway trail between the river and the lake. It is small wonder, therefore, that the banks of the Cohas are strewn with Indian artifacts.

MASSABESIC LAKE SITES

Massabesic Lake is a relatively large body of water so constricted in the middle as to give it the appearance of two separate ponds. Its entire shoreline was no doubt dotted with Indian villages. Some of the more important sites on the front (or east) pond are: Massabesic Circle Beach (Map C, 13), Severance Beach (Map C, 14), and Preston Beach (Map C, 15). Another site is located in Auburn village near the mouth of Griffin Brook at Raymond, Hooksett, and Chester roads (Map C, 16). Griffin Brook has been called Penacook River (perhaps because the First Path Penacook Trail paralleled it) as well as Oswego Brook, Clark Brook, and Auburn Brook.

LITTLE MASSABESIC
BROOK SITE (MAP C, 17)

This site is situated on the north bank of Little Massabesic Brook (the outlet of Little Massabesic Lake) near Griffin Brook into which it empties. Griffin Brook, in turn, empties into Massabesic Lake about a mile downstream. In the past, these brooks were considered good fishing places and were used as waterway trails by the Indians. The Indian village itself was situated on a circular knoll about twelve feet high with a diameter of about 200 feet. The approximately 300 artifacts recovered there strongly indicate that this was a permanent Indian site and not a seasonal one. About 200 of the above-mentioned artifacts were collected by Sebastian S. Griffin and are displayed at the Griffin Museum in Auburn.

MANCHESTER AIRPORT
SITE (Map C, 18)

An Indian village stood in the area now occupied by the Manchester Airport. This half-mile site was located on a sandy elevated plain along a pond and wetland that drained Cohas Brook.

15

Cartagena Island

Eugene D. Finch

The graves of Pasaconaway and Wannalancet are marked by no monument on the bank of their native river.
—Thoreau, *A Week on the Concord and Merrimack Rivers*

Cartagena Island lies in the Merrimack between Manchester and Goffs Falls, just north of the new beltline bridge. Long, narrow, heavily wooded, it extends nearly 500 yards alongside the eastern shore of the river, a little far to swim, but within easy hailing distance.

Extensive as it is, most geographers have ignored it. It does not appear on the maps of G. Mitchell (1737), Langdon and Sawyer (1784), Belknap (1791), Lewis (1804), Carrigain (1814), Wallace (1823), Robinson (1849), Colton (1859), Coolidge (1859), Guernsey (1874), Hurd (1885), Rand Avery (1891), Sweetser (1891), Walker (1892), Walling (1892), or Rand McNally (1893). The U.S. Geological Survey map (1944) shows the island but does not affix a name to it. Samuel Holland's map of 1784 shows the island and calls it "Carthegen I," a name which becomes "Chartegen I" in the German edition of 1796. On the map in the *History of Bedford* (1851), the island figures as "Carthagen I^d." The same island is "Passaconnaway Island" on the map in J. W. Meader's *The Merrimack River* (1869).

This is the island that Thoreau noted in 1839. Of it he wrote:

> We passed a large and densely wooded island this forenoon between Short's and Griffith's Falls, the fairest which we had met with, with a handsome grove of elms at its head. If it had been evening, we should have been glad to camp there. Not long after, one or two more were passed. The boatmen told us that the current had recently made important changes here.[1]

Cartagena led him on to several pages of erudition and the pleasure his imagination took in islands.

Another nineteenth-century observer of the island was Pliny Steele Boyd of Amesbury, Massachusetts. In chapter 9,

Source: Eugene D. Finch, "Cartagena Island," *New Hampshire Archeologist* 12 (1963): 1–5.

"Passaconaway Island," of his *Up and Down the Merrimac: A Vacation Trip* (1879), he tells of his five-day stay on "one of the loveliest and yet wildest of all the islands in the Merrimac." Although he compares in a poetic mood his discovery of this island, "the home of the eagle," with the discovery of San Salvador by Columbus, he still supplies some specific detail; he calls it a wooded island and comments on the groves of pine ("some ancient and ambitious"), hemlock, elm, oak, birch, and maple, with intervals of grass. The island was, he says, "nearly a quarter of a mile long, and wide enough for a fine building lot."[2] He thought it covered six to eight acres. There was no dwelling place on it.

George Woodbury (whose family owned Cartagena for about two hundred years), in the Manchester *Sunday News* of October 2, 1960, stated that the island was "the last home of the Indian Chief Passaconaway and perhaps the first Indian reservation ever set aside in the New World." The documents, however, do not bear out this statement.

In 1662, Passaconaway petitioned the General Court of Massachusetts in the following terms:

> To the honerd John Endecot esq[r] Go[v]nr together with the rest of the honerd Generall Court Now Assembled in Boston the petition of papisseconewa in the behalfe of him Selfe as also of many other Indians whoe were for a longe time o[r] Selves and o[r] progenators Seated Upon a tract of Land Called Naticot and is Now in the possetion of m[r] William Brenton of Rhode Island marshaule; and is confirmed to the saide m[r] Brenton to him' his heires and assignes ac'ordinge to the Lawes of this Jurisdiction (by reason of which tracte of Land beinge taken up as aforesaide) and thereby y[r] pore petition[r] with many others in an Unsetled Condition

and must be forced in a short time to remove to sum' other place; The Humble request of y[r] pore petition[r] is that this honrd Courte wolde please to grante Unto Us a parsell of Land for o[r] com'fortable ciutation; to be stated for o[r] Injoyment: as also for the comfort of o[r]s after Us; as also that this honrd Court wolde please to take into y[r] Serious and pious considration the condition and also the request of y[r] pore Supliante and to apoynte two or three persons as a comitte to Assiste sum'e one or two indians to Vew and determ'in of sum' place and to Lay out the sam'e.

> Not furder to trouble this hon[r]d Assem'bly hm'bly Craveinge an expected Answer this present Sections I shall Still remain y[r] Humble Servante Wherein y[u] Shall commande.

Boston: 9: 3[mo] 1662:   Papisseconewa[3]

On May 9, 1662, the petition was favorably acted upon, the magistrates granting "unto papisseconeway & his men or Associates about Natticott above mr Brentons lands where it is free a mile & a halfe on either side merremack River in breadth a 3 miles on either side in length."[4]

John Parker and Jonathan Danforth, surveyors, laid out the grant and reported:

> According to order of Honord General Court there is laid out unto the Indians Passaconneway and his associats the inhabitances of Naticott, three miles square, or so much (eather) as containes it in the figure of a romboides upon Merrimack River; beginning at the head of Mr. Brenton's Lands at Naticott, on the east side of the River, and then it joineth to his line, which line runs half a point North West of the east, it lyeth one mile and a halfe wide on side of ye river and somewhat better, and runnes three miles up the River, the Northern line on the east side of the river, is bounded by a brook (called by the Indians) Suskayquetuck,

right against the falls in the River called Pokechuous, the end line on both sides of the River are parallels: the side line on the east side of the River runes halfe a point eastward of the No: No: east and the side line on the west side of the river runes Northeast and by North all which is sufficiently bounded and marked with I, also there is two small islands in the River, part of which the lower end line crosses. One of them Papisseconeway had lived upon and planted a long time, a small patch of intervaile Land on the West side of the River anent and a little below ye Islands by estimation about forty acres, which joineth their land to Souhegan River, which the Indians have planted (much of it) a long time, and considering there is very little good land in that which is now laid out unto them, the Indians do earnestly request this Honerd Court, to grant these two small Islands and ye patch of intervaile as it is bounded by the Hills.

This land was laid out 27, 3rd mo. 1663 By John Parker and Jonathan Danforth, surveyors.[5]

If there were a map of this tract "bounded and marked with I," it has disappeared. At least inquiry at the Massachusetts Archives has elicited nothing. But the report alone makes it sufficiently clear that Cartagena Island could not have been one of the islands in the grant to Passaconaway. The "two small islands" can only be Reed's Islands. The lower end line crosses them. They are a little above a patch of intervale, which joins their land to the Souhegan River.[6]

Moreover, the surveyors state that the east line runs three miles up the river and that the northern line on the east side of the river is bounded by a brook called by the Indians Suskayquetuck, right against the falls in the river called Pokechuous. Potter identifies the Suskayquetuck as Great Cohas Brook, and therefore

Pokechuous Falls are Goffs Falls.[7] Yet Great Cohas Brook is approximately three and three quarters miles from the northernmost tip of Reed's Islands. Furthermore, if one runs the south line across the northernmost tip of Reed's Island "half a point North West of the east," following magnetic north rather than true north, and runs the east line three miles up the river, "halfe a point of the No: No: east," the north line would cross the Merrimack about five hundred feet north of Little Cohas. Either the surveying or the identifications must be faulty. But even if we assume that the northernmost limit of the plat was the true one, Great Cohas Brook, Cartagena Island would have been a good mile and three-eighths farther north, well outside the area three miles square granted to Passaconaway.

If Cartagena was not included in the grant, it seems doubtful that the island was Passaconaway's "last home." There is the suggestive fact, however, that it is called Passaconaway Island by Meader and by Steele. But conclusive evidence I have not found. Hurd says flatly, "One of the residences of Passaconaway, and his last in this section, was upon Reed's Island, which he called 'my beautiful island of Natticook.'"[8] Blood does not mention Cartagena but merely says that Passaconaway occupied Sewall's Island, north of Concord, and that his permanent residence was the bluff east of Amoskeag falls.[9]

There is a romantic misapprehension that Passaconaway may have been buried on Cartagena Island. Here is George Woodbury's account:

Dr. Peter P. Woodbury and Dr. Freeman Riddle, both of Bedford, in exploring this former haunt [Cartagena Island] of Passaconaway in the summer of 1821, excavated an Indian burial in a remarkable state of preservation. There were three bodies placed in a seated position, facing downstream. Within [*sic*] them lay complete equipment for their journey into the next world, clothing, utensils, weapons, and tools. There were two males buried and one female. Both doctors felt that one of the male bodies was that of Passaconaway himself.

There was at that time no museum in the country interested in archaeological material such as this. Dr. Woodbury sent the three bodies and material found with them to the Museum of Natural History in Paris, France. Inquiry in 1928 showed on the acquisition files of the venerable French museum that they were still there and that they had been given by Dr. Woodbury of Bedford, and were Indian remains, perhaps Passaconaway's.

Peter Woodbury told the story of this exhumation twice—in 1824 in "A Topographical and Historical Sketch of Bedford, in the County of Hillsborough" by A. Foster and P. P. Woodbury, in the first volume of *Collections of the New Hampshire Historical Society*, and in 1851 in the *History of Bedford*, the work of a publishing committee of three, one of whom was Dr. Peter P. Woodbury. Both accounts specifically state that the burial was on the west bank of the Merrimack, opposite Goffs Falls. No mention is made of Cartagena Island. No mention is made of Passaconaway. Indeed the 1824 account says, "These bones undoubtedly belonged to some of the aborigines."[10] The 1851 account says also, "The skeletons were sent to Paris, by Dr. Woodbury, for anatomical investigation." There is no proof, then, that Cartagena was a part of an early Indian reservation, that it was Passaconaway's last home, or that it was the site of his grave.

Reliable records of the island are few. The earliest dates from 1736. Captain

William Tyng's soldiers had petitioned the Massachusetts House for a grant of land in reward for their services. In 1736, the surveyor, Samuel Cumings, presented a plat of a tract on Piscataquog River "with a small Island Containing Twelve Acres Lying in Merrimack River between Crosby's Brook and Short falls so Called."[11] There is only one island between Crosby's Brook (the modern Bowman's Brook) and Short Falls, and that is Cartagena. Note that the surveyor said it contained twelve acres.

On March 29, 1754, the proprietors of the province of New Hampshire recorded in Portsmouth:

Whereas John Goffe Esqu[r]y[e] 23d Instant Represented to this Propriety that in that Tract of Land called Rands farm there is about eight Acres of land which lyes between a Tract of land granted to James Walker and himselfe and the forty Acres granted to the Widow Secomb, which said Eight Acres is not yet granted or appropriated by Said Proprietors,—and also that there is a Small Island called Carthagene & Sukuos Island, one containing about four Acres the other about half an Acre—which said tract of land about eight Acres and the Said Islands the Said John Goffe also Prayeth the said Proprietors would Grant to him in Consideration of what Services he hath done for Said Proprietors—

In Consideration thereof—Therefore Voted That there be and hereby is granted unto the Said John Goffe esqu[r] all the Right Title and Interest of the said Proprietors of in and to the abovesaid Tract of about eight Acres of Land and to the abovesaid two Islands to have & to hold to him his heirs and assigns for ever.[12]

Sukuos Island? Holland's 1784 map puts a Schegus Island in the Merrimack halfway between the Piscataquog River and Crosby River, hence about a mile north of Cartagena, but no island is there now. Potter mentions—he is writing of the fishing in the Merrimack in the eighteenth century—the Baker seine at Musquito Island, between Piscataquog and Griffins Falls.[13] Matthew Patten of Bedford records on July 7, 1761, catching "2 at Scheeroos brook," and on July 28, 1767, he records, "we catched 4 Salmon at pattersons Brook one at cold brook and 4 at Sceekos brook." Sukuos, Schegus, Sceekos, Scheeroos, Musquito—are these variant forms of one name for a vanished island? Does the disappearance of the island fit in with the reduction of Cartagena from twelve acres to four in eighteen years?

Regardless of its size, Cartagena must have been a valuable fishing property when John Goffe acquired it in 1754. About 1762, according to the *History of Bedford*:

[A]t the Carthagenian seine, drawn on the east side of Carthagenian island, and opposite Thomas Chandler, Esq., 1500 shad were taken at one haul of the net. There was also Caratunk seine at the head, and Sky seine at the foot, of Walker's falls, on the west side. Quantities of fish were taken by fly-nets during the Summer and after. Shad and salmon were scooped up by the scoop-net. This was carried on at the head of the above named island.[14]

One would suppose that the Indians had used the island as a fishing place for centuries before the white man. Coolidge and Mansfield in 1860 wrote, "and in Bedford, on Carthagena island, and opposite the mouth of the Coos river, traces of Indian villages were to be seen until recently."[15] Potter (1856) says, "In Bedford, opposite Carthagena Island, on land of Hon. Thomas Chandler, and opposite the mouth of Cohos river, such settlements [Indian villages] existed, the ves-tiges of which still exist at the former place, and did at the latter, till the hand of improvement swept them away."[16]

The Manchester Historic Association, the Peabody Museum in Cambridge, and the Dartmouth College Museum have no artifacts known to have come from Cartagena Island.

Limited surveying of the island by the New Hampshire Archeological Society has not revealed any trace of Indian occupation. Some dozen test pits revealed that the island had been flooded at various times. Quite possibly the island has been both eaten away and built up. Certainly it is not the twelve acres of 1736, nor the four acres of 1754, nor the six to eight acres of 1879. It would appear now to be in the neighborhood of three acres. It does not have the shape of the island as portrayed in the map in the *History of Bedford*. There it is shown as approximately 137 yards by 53 yards, not its present approximately 500 yards by 25 yards. Neither does it have the same alignment. The Bedford map shows its main axis almost at a 45° angle with the flow of the river. The island today parallels the east bank. The question rises, of course, whether the present island represents any part of the island as the Indians knew it. Probably it does, and the important changes of which Thoreau was told did not include the washing away of the entire island and the building up of another. Under layers of silt lie layers of humus that could hardly have been built up in the last 360 years. There is some further evidence of the antiquity of the island in the fact that it was heavily wooded in 1839 and in 1879 and is heavily wooded now. If we can find evidence of Indian occupation, the layers of silt left behind by floods may clearly mark different periods of Indian culture. Certainly further research on the island should be made.

Notes

1. H. D. Thoreau, *A Week on the Concord and Merrimack Rivers*, p. 320 (Riverside edition, 1894).

2. Pliny Steele Boyd, *Up and down the Merrimac: A Vacation Trip*, p. 87 (Boston, 1879).

3. *Massachusetts Archives*, vol. 30, p. 110a.

4. *Ibid.*, p. 120a.

5. *Ibid.*

6. *Ibid.*

7. C. E. Potter, *The History of Manchester*, p. 63 (Manchester, 1856).

8. D. Hamilton Hurd, *History of Hillsborough County, New Hampshire*, p. 489 (Philadelphia, 1885).

9. Grace Holbrook Blood, *Manchester on the Merrimack*, p. 19 (Manchester, 1948).

10. A. Foster, and P. P. Woodbury, "A Topographical and Historical Sketch of Bedford, in the County of Hillsborough." *Collections f the New Hampshire Historical Society*, vol. 1, p. 295.

11. *State Papers, New Hampshire*, vol. 24, p. 183.

12. *Ibid.*, vol. 29, p. 466.

13. C. E. Potter, *op. cit.*, p. 649.

14. *History of Bedford*, p. 205 (Boston, 1851).

15. A. J. Coolidge, and J. B. Mansfield, *History and Description of New England. New Hampshire*, pp. 401–2 (Boston, 1860).

16. C. E. Potter, *op. cit.*, p. 30.

Bibliography

Belknap, Jeremy. *The History of New Hampshire*. Dover, 1831.

Blood, Grace Holbrook. *Manchester on the Merrimack*. Manchester, 1948.

Bouton, Nathaniel. *The History of Concord*. Concord, 1856.

Boyd, Pliny Steele. *Up and Down the Merrimac. A Vacation Trip*. Boston, 1879.

Browne, George Waldo. *The Amoskeag Manufacturing Company*. Manchester, 1915.

Browne, George Waldo. *The River of Broken Waters—The Merrimack*. Manchester, 1918.

Clarke, John B. *History of Manchester, New Hampshire*. 1875.

Coolidge, A. J., and J. B. Mansfield. *History and Description of New England: New Hampshire*. Boston, 1860.

Eastman, Herbert W. *Semi Centennial of the City of Manchester*. Manchester, 1897.

Fogg, Alonzo J. *Statistical Gazetteer of New Hampshire*. Concord, 1874.

Fox, Charles J. *History of the Old Township of Dunstable*. Nashua, 1846.

Holden, Raymond P. *The Merrimack*. New York, 1958.

Hurd, D. Hamilton. *History of Hillsborough County, New Hampshire*. Philadelphia, 1885.

Manchester Historic Association. *Collections*, vol. 8. "Early Records of Derryfield, New Hampshire, 1751–1782." 1905.

Mann, Moses Whitcher. "The Middlesex Canal." *The Bostonian Society Publications*, vol. 6 (Boston, 1910), pp. 67–88.

Marshall, Harlan A. "Some Ancient Indian Village Sites Adjacent to Manchester, N. H." *American Antiquity*, vol. 7, no. 4, April 1942.

Marston, Philip, and Myron Gordon. "Notes on Fish and Early Fishing in the Merrimack River System." New Hampshire Fish and Game Department. *Biological Survey of the Merrimack Watershed* (Concord, 1938), pp. 186–198.

Meader, J. W. *The Merrimack River: Its Source and Its Boundaries*. Boston, 1872.

Moore, William E. *Contributions to the History of Derryfield, N. H.* Printed and published by the author, 1896–7.

New Hampshire. *State Papers*.

Patten, Matthew. *Diary of Matthew Patten of Bedford, N. H.* Concord, 1903.

Piper, Bertha L. *Navagation of the Merrimack*. Durham, 1943, a Master's essay.

Poor, A. *Historical and Genealogical Researches … of the Merrimack Valley*. Haverhill, 1857–8.

Potter, C. E. *History of Manchester*. Manchester, 1856.

Prescott, William. "Report on the Alterations in the Channel of Merrimack River." *Collections of the New Hampshire Historical Society*, pp. 433–442. Concord, 1863.

Proctor, Mary A. *The Indians of the Winnipesaukee and Pemigewasset Valleys*. Franklin, 1930.

Thoreau, Henry David. *A Week on the Concord and Merrimack Rivers*. Boston, 1894.

Town and City Atlas of the State of New Hampshire. Boston, 1892.

Walker, Joseph B. "The Valley of the Merrimack." *Collections of the New Hampshire Historical Society*, pp. 414–432.

Walling, H. F. *Atlas of the State of New Hampshire.* New York, 1877.

Woodbury, George. *John Goffe's Legacy.* New York, 1955.

Woodbury, George, in Manchester *Sunday News*, October 2, 1960.

Woodbury, Peter P., Thomas Savage and William Patten. *History of Bedford, New Hampshire, Being Statistics, Compiled on the Occasion of the One Hundredth Anniversary of the Incorporation of the Town, May 19th, 1850.* Boston, 1851.

16

Historic Indian Trails of New Hampshire

Chester B. Price

To describe the important Indian trails of New Hampshire has involved me in the study of much source material—old maps, old books, and manuscripts—and in the attempt to retrace on foot some of the well-known trails.

The first English colonists were greatly indebted to the Indians for the use of their trails. In a listing of the contributions of the American Indians to humanity as a whole, historians seldom mention the fact that, thanks to the Indians, the early New Englanders inherited a vast network of trails which not only covered the New England states, but extended as far west as the Rocky Mountains. Several of the more famous of these trails were the Mohawk Trail; the Kennebec Trail, which during the American Revolution became the Arnold Trail; the Cumberland Trail; the Sante Fe Trail; the Oregon Trail; and the Sauk (Sac) Trail.

In our immediate vicinity, no such trail has been immortalized. Nevertheless, the trails were here, well trodden by usage over countless years. The first settlers would have found the going much more arduous had there not been these footpaths, crude as they were, showing the shortest possible route between two points, with due consideration to natural barriers and personal safety.

The Indians of New Hampshire left no markers on their trails, and their highways were but paths through the primeval forests accompanied in places by an occasional slash on a tree trunk made with a *temahigan*, better known as a tomahawk. Trained from childhood, they could make their way along these paths with the help of *kisos* (the sun), *pogwas* (the moon), and *alakwsak* (the stars) in the direction of *Sowanaki* (the South), *Pebonkik* (the North), *Wajinahilot* (the East), and *Alinkihlot* (the West), as they chose to travel. They also observed closely the formation of the bark of the trees and the accumulation of moss which grew on the tree trunks, for guidance during storms and cloudy weather. Certain rocks, fallen trees, and particularly water courses also served as landmarks for the traveling aborigine.

Source: Chester B. Price, "Historic Indian Trails of New Hampshire," *The New Hampshire Archeologist* 14 (1967): 1–12.

154

Of course some Indians had more knowledge of the trails than others. Blind Will, sagamore of the Newichwannock tribe, boasted that he knew every trail in New Hampshire. Major Waldron of Dover availed himself of this knowledge and often entrusted Blind Will with messages to the sachems of distant tribes. Unwittingly, Major Waldron sent Blind Will to his death when he directed him to locate some strange Indians who had been seen to the west of Dover. Accompanied by several tribesmen, Blind Will took the trail which led to what is now Barrington, where his little force was ambushed by a band of bloodthirsty Mohawk Indians from New York, mortal foes of the Pennacook and Abenaki tribes. Blind Will, forced to retreat, was overtaken and slain at the confluence of the Isinglass and Cocheco rivers.

On the previous day, March 22, 1677, Wonalancet's son had been hunting in the woods on the banks of the Merrimack and had discovered fifteen Mohawk near Souhegan. They shot at him several times, but he escaped, fled home to Chelmsford, and notified Captain Hinchman.

At the beginning of King Philip's War, Wonalancet heeded the advice of his father to keep peace with the English and withdrew with his people into the woods near Sewall's Falls, near Penacook. They then retired farther into the wilderness and passed the winter of 1675–6 near the headwaters of the Connecticut. They did not return until after the war was over and then went into Dover, where a treaty was signed on July 3, 1676. Wonalancet was alive in 1697, but died soon after. He is thought to have been buried in the family lot of Jonathan Tyng, who cared for him in his old age.

Many of the more important Indian trails later became the roads used by the English colonists who first used them for bridle paths and later widened them for ox teams. Today many of New Hampshire's highways follow, in many places, the route of the ancient Indian trails.

The first Indian trail used for a bridle path and later widened for ox teams led from Winnichahannet (Winn-i-kchi-han-ek), Dover Point, to the Cocheco River at what later became known as Dover Landing. This road was then relocated to nearly its present course.

Some time later the Winnicoek (Winn-i-co-ek) Trail, often referred to as the Abenaki Trail—which led from the Merrimack River through Winnicoek, now Hampton, along the seashore to the Piscataqua River at Strawberry Bank, now Portsmouth—was used by the colonists as a bridle path.

The words *level*, *dry*, and *air line* give us the key to the aspects of most of the Indian trails. There were exceptions, such as trails following a waterway, but even those kept to the terraces above the swamps and lands that often flooded. There were also many hunters' trails which led to the hills and the mountains. *Nolka*, deer, usually stayed on the ridges and hills, but ventured into the swamps during a part of the season. *Mos*, moose, usually chose the localities about ponds, lakes, and streams where they fed on the tender shoots and roots of the water lilies. *Awassos*, bear, roamed everywhere but usually denned in the hills and mountains, as did *molsem*, the wolf. The hunters' trails, unlike the regular Indian trails, usually led along ridges and mountain elevations from which the hunters could observe the deer, moose, and caribou (*magallibu*) feeding in the lowlands. Such a location was Moosilaukee (Mos-wil-aki) Mountain: "very good moose place."

The locations of the many Indian villages played an important part in the routes chosen for the early Indian trails. During the severe epidemic that swept through New England in 1616, 1617, and

1618 many Indian villages were abandoned. Captain Richard Vines and the ship's crew spent the winter of 1616 near the Saco River and reported that the terrible scourge had nearly depopulated the entire countryside. Among the abandoned villages were Namasawilok (Ashuelot) at what is now Swanzey; a Nipmuck village near Richmond; the Senkek (Suncook) village which was located near what is now Gilmanton Ironworks; Kchitegu, sometimes referred to as Chateguay, now Conway; and Pisgatoek near Somersworth. A nearby Maine village, which was charted as "Quack" by the explorer Martin Pring and which was known to the Indians as K'goak ("Their Marshes"), was abandoned due to the pestilence. K'goak was located at the mouth of the Agamenticus River, in what is now York, Maine.

It was not possible for the Indian traveler always to keep dry his *mkezenal*, better known as moccasins, for at some points marshy lands had to be crossed and rivers and brooks had to be forded, although when possible the Indians would fell large trees across the streams and use the trunks as bridges, affording a one-lane passage from either side. Often driftwood would lodge against these bridges necessitating a *w'nigan* (portage) for those who, in their canoes, used the waterway to reach their objective. Beaver dams also often made portages necessary.

Although the primary intent of the writer is to describe and delineate the overland trails, one should not slight the fact that the Indians used the rivers for waterway trails. In their bark canoes and log dugouts the [Indians] traveled from one point to another over the lakes, ponds, and rivers of New Hampshire until the waters froze. Chief among the river waterways were the following:

Ammonoosuc River (Omanosek: "at the narrow fishing river")

Androscoggin River (Namas-ek-goaggon: "to the fish spearing place")

Ashuelot River (either Namas-a-wil-ok: "to the good fishing place" or Joss-a-wil-ok: "to the place of the beautiful mountains")

Asquamchumaukee River (Msquamchumaki: "salmon spawning place")

Bellamy River (Pisga-iss-ek, Piscasset: "to the place of the little dark river")

Cocheco River (Ko-kchi-kook: "at the place of the great pine trees," although the first falls of the Cocheco, in the heart of the city of Dover, were called Chochichok: "fast [water]")

Connecticut River (Quanni-teg-ok: "long river")

Contoocook River (Kon-wan-teg-ok: "the pine river from the place of many little falls")

Exeter River (Squamscott, Msquam-s-kook: "at the salmon place")

Magallo River, northeast branch of the Bellamy (Magallibu: "caribou river")

Magalloway River (Magallibu-aki: "place of the caribou")

Merrimack River (Molou-mak: "deep waters")

Minnewawa River ("berries among the poplars")

Ossipee River (Awoss-sebi: "the river on the other side." The main village of the Ossipee tribe was on the western shore of Ossipee Lake, where they had a fort, and they referred to the Ossipee River as the "river on the other side." The Housatonic River in Connecticut actually was Awoss-aden-ek: "to the place the other side of the high mountain." Another interpretation of "Ossipee" has been Joss-sebi: "mountain river.")

Otter River (Winigegwok: "place of the otter")

Oyster River (Shaw-unk-hassik: "winding [river], more or less sandy")

Pemigewasset River (Pen-i-joss-ek: "bear's grease river")

Pine River (Koa-tegwa: "pine river"), flowing into Lake Ossipee

Piscataqua River (Pisga-tegwa: "the river, it is dark")

Piscataquog River (Pisga-tegu-ok: "at the place of the dark river")

Powwow River, where an Indian consultation was held on Powwow Hill

Saco River (So-kook: "at the southern place")

Salmon Falls River (Newichwannock [New-ij-wan-ok]: "to many little falls in the long distance")

Souhegan River (Sowa-nigan: "jutting or difficult portage")

Sugar River (Askutegnik: "at the end of the river fork")

Suncook River (Sen-kek: "stony [water] place")

Winnicott River (Winn-i-co-ek: "at the place in the pines where the water flows in." The word has also been written as Winn-i-cum-ek, and as *cum* is an ancient Abenaki word meaning "narrow," this would alter the phrase to: "at the narrow place where the water flows in.")

This list of New Hampshire Indian trails would be incomplete without the waterway trails of the ponds and lakes. The largest lake, Winnipesaukee, lies in the central part of the state and formed the longest lake waterway. In the northeast lived the Ossipee tribe of the Sokoki nation, and in the south and southwest were villages of the Pennacook Confederacy. A small island south of Moultonborough Neck was where the Pennacook and the Sokoki met to trade.

Winnipesaukee comes from Wiwininebesaki ("the lake in the vicinity of which there are other lakes and ponds") or perhaps better "lakes region," from *wiwini* (around, in the vicinity), *nebes* (lakes or ponds), and *aki* (region or territory).

One of the first white men to visit the lake, and probably the first to circumnavigate it, was Gabriel Druillettes, a Jesuit missionary who visited the Indian villages and camps in the autumn of 1650, afterward proceeding to Pequaket, and later to the Kennebec River, where he was stationed.

Lake Sunapee (Sen-nippi Wobagilmak: "stony waters of the wild goose"), another large New Hampshire lake set in scenic splendor, was also a waterway for the Sunapee tribe of the Pennacook Indians.

Umbagog Lake (Wombagwog: "white clear lake") was a waterway much used by members of the Aroosagunticook tribe on their way to the present Rangeley Lakes in Maine.

Ossipee Lake and Silver Lake were waterways for both the Ossipee and Pequaket Indians. There was a large village of the Ossipee located on the western shore of Lake Ossipee. The Sokoki Indians used the chain of ponds extending from Conway Lake to Ossipee Lake as a waterway, with several portages.

Newfound Lake was known to the Indians as Passaquaney (Pass-agua-nik: "landing place at the sand bar on the fork of the river").

Lake Winnisquam, Squam Lake (Msquam-nebis: "salmon lake"), Contoocook Lake (Monomanak), Massabesic Lake (located on the Indian trail from Pentucket, or Haverhill, Massachusetts, to the Merrimack River at Namaskik, hence its name: "to the place of the great river"), Long Pond (Quinnibaug, now Highland Lake), and many other smaller lakes and ponds were waterways for the New Hampshire Indians. Lake Kanasatka (Kanos-as-aki: "place of the willows") was much frequented by the Ossipee tribe. It is interesting to note that the state of Kansas takes its name from the Indian *kanosas* (willows).

The largest village of the Piscataqua tribe is believed to have been at what is now Greenland, on Great Bay, another large body of water forming a much traveled waterway.

IMPORTANT INDIAN TRAILS

1. Merrimack-Winnipesaukee Trail

The Mouro-mak–Win-nebis-aki Trail began at Pawtucket Falls (Pontegwa: "river falls"), a locality near what is now Lowell, Massachusetts, and following the Merrimack River, led past Watanic, now Nashua, past the Indian village at Cohas Brook (Ko-iss: "small pine trees"), and thence on to what is now Manchester and Amoskeag Falls (Namas-kik: "the fishing place"), which was a gathering place for hundreds of Indians during the spring run of the salmon, shad, and sturgeon that ascended the river from the sea—the salmon and shad on their way to the lakes and to their spawning grounds in the northern ponds and rivers. Some of the [Indians] came in canoes and dugouts, others over the Indian trails. The word *Mouromak* is ancient Abenaki; the modern Indian word is *Moulomak*.

Several historians have stated that the venerable John Eliot, often called "Apostle to the Indians," visited Namaskik; others assert that he stayed at Pawtucket Falls.

From the number of artifacts, including pottery, which have been found on an island at the mouth of Cohas Brook and on the river banks nearby by Harlan Marshall of the Manchester Historical Society, it seems quite obvious that there was an ancient Indian village on or near Cohas Brook.

A continuance of this trail led along both sides of the river to the Indian village of Penacook ("at the crooked place"), now Concord. Passaconaway, the grand sachem of the Pennacook tribe, divided his time between Penacook, Amoskeag, and Pawtucket Falls.

Penacook was the scene of several legendary battles between the Pennacook Indians and their traditional enemy, the Mohawk of the Iroquois nation, who came by way of the Mohawk, Pocumtuk, and Konwantegok trails. To the Pennacook Indians the Mohawk were the Maquas, or Man-Eaters. According to the historian J. P. A. Maurault in his *Histoire des Abenakis*, during King Philip's War so many Massachusetts Indians fled to New Hampshire and pretended to be Pennacooks that they were called *Patsuikets*, "the people who lived by deception."

One history reads, "The Pennacook fortified the eastern heights beside the Merrimack River and, in one battle with the Mohawk, suffered fearful losses but repulsed the enemy...."

The Merrimack Trail terminated at what is now Franklin, where there was a junction of two trails, the Pemigewasset Trail and the Winnipesaukee Trail. At Franklin, on a peninsula in the Winnipesaukee River, now Odell Park, there have been located many Indian artifacts, indicating the site of an ancient village.

At what has been known as Lochmere, on the Winnipesaukee River, was located the only colonial fort ever built in the lakes region. It was built in 1746 by colonial militia under Colonel Atkinson of Portsmouth and was occupied for a year by several hundred soldiers. The stone walls of this fort were used to build a dam for a nearby mill. Atkinson's Fort has often been called an Indian fort, and many flowery Indian legends have been fabricated on this supposition, but the Indians of New Hampshire never built forts of stone.

The Winnipesaukee Trail led past

Lake Winnisquam (Winn-i-msquam: "where the salmon waters flow out"). The Indian word for salmon was *msquamagwa*, usually shortened to *squam*, and the eminent Indianologist Father Jeremiah O'Brien, who spent several months at the Indian reservations studying the Abenaki language, defines *winn* as "outlet," which may be expressed: "where the water flows out."

The trail also passed a small body of water which was known as Round Bay, and later as Lake Opechee. *Opechee* is a word taken from the Sioux language and means "robin."

At Canterbury, a fort was erected at the beginning of the first so-called French and Indian War in 1744 and called Fort Clough. Fort Clough was not used in the last French and Indian War (1754–61).

The Winnipesaukee Trail reached what is now the Weirs where, during the shad run, the Indians had nets strung across the narrow place in the river. There must have been a portage, and Aquadoctan, which Johnson and Willard, the surveyors, termed Aquedohcan, may have been Agua-dak-'gan, which means "a landing for portage" (*agua-dak*, a landing, and *'gan* short for *wnigan*, portage). Aguadakguangonok, a locality near Bath, Maine, is interpreted as "a landing at the spearing place," and Aguahassikdak, on Merrymeeting Bay in Maine, is listed as meaning "where the canoes are pulled up at the sandy [*hassik*] place." An Indian village of the Winnipesaukee tribe of the Pennacook nation was located at Aguadakgan, since called Aquadoctan, and now the Weirs.

The Winnipesaukee Trail continued to Wicwas Pond (Wequash: "head of the bay"). Another Wequash was located at the head of Merrymeeting Bay in Maine. The trail passed what is now Meredith Neck and Little Neck and continued along the shore of the lake, terminating at Chenayok (Kchi-nayok: "great point"), now Moultonborough Neck, at the location of a village of the Winnipesaukee tribe.

2. Connecticut Trail

The Quanna-teg-ok ("at the place of the long river") Trail actually began where the river flows into Long Island Sound and extended along the banks of the river, terminating at the Connecticut Lakes. But that part in which we are most interested began at Msquamkik ("the salmon place"), now East Northfield, Massachusetts, and, pursuing a northerly course passed the ancient Squakheag village, which was located at what is now Hinsdale. Here the Indians erected a large fort which proved inadequate, as the Mohawk burned the village and destroyed the fort, and the locality was abandoned by the survivors. Up the river, the trail led past a mountain which derived its name from a river which flows into the Connecticut River from Vermont, opposite the mountain. Now known as West River, this stream was known to the Indians as Wanaskwtegek (*askw*, at the end; *teg*, abbreviation for *tegu*, river; *ek*, from the place; and *wan*, many little falls, the whole phrase meaning: "at the end of the river from the place of many little falls"). The trail passed Cold River, which the Indians called Tibeksek, and near Cold River was a pool of running water known as Ticopeesok, now called Abenaki Spring.

On this trail, at Chesterfield, was located the English Fort No. 1; at Westmoreland was Fort No. 2; at what is now Walpole was Fort No. 3. Pierce Island in Lake Spofford was a favorite camping place of the Indians, and many artifacts have been found there.

Another important historical location along this trail was Kchipontegu ("great river falls"), a famous fishing place opposite Walpole. At what is now Charlestown was Fort No. 4, erected by the English as a protection against the St. Francis Indians. This site was the scene of many battles between the colonists and the combined forces of the French and Indians, who either came down the river in canoes or marched along the overland trails. The tale of the Johnson family, captives of the Indians, is well known, and was given prominence in *Histoire des Abenakis* by Maurault. The gallant defense of Fort No. 4 by its garrison against the onslaughts of superior forces is a highlight in American history. But for this blocking of the river and trail which led to Massachusetts and Connecticut, colonial history would have had many more dark pages, and the contributions of these fighting colonists to the saving of a nation cannot be too fully praised or emphasized.

The trail continued northerly through the Coos country. The word Co-os has been interpreted to mean "small pine trees." It is also possible that it may have been Ko-joss: "pine mountains." The letter *j* in the Abenaki language often had the sound of *z*; thus *joss* was pronounced *zoss*.

The Abenaki word for "high mountain" is *aden*, as in Kek-aden, now called Katahdin ("at the place of the high mountain"), in Mon-aden-ok ("to the place of the bare high mountain"), and in Woban-aden-ok ("to the place of the high white mountains"). *Joss* is a middle-sized mountain, as in Mass-a-joss-ek ("to the smaller of the great mountains"), the Blue Hills, now Massachusetts. The word for "hill" or "small mountain" was *wajo* or *wajoss*, and sometimes *aga*, as in Wajos-ik, Wachusett ("small mountain"), and as in Aga-wam ("village on the hill").

At what is now Newbury, Vermont, on the western side of the Connecticut River was the Indian village of Coosuck ("people of the pine mountains"). Although French historians called them Loups (Wolves) indicating a Mohegan origin, it is believed that they were members of the Coosuck tribe. There was a camping place, possibly an ancient village, at East Barnet, Vermont, and on the New Hampshire side of the river there is much evidence that there was an ancient Indian village at Lyme, on land used as a farm in the eighteenth century and now owned by Bartlett Mayo. Many stone artifacts and fragments of pottery have been found here.

After Major Rogers and his Rangers had raided and burned St. Francis, the Abenaki stronghold in Quebec, they retreated by way of Lake Memphremagog to the Connecticut River and the Indian trail. In a starving condition, some headed into the Coos country near what is now Lancaster and passed into oblivion. Most of the surviving rangers followed the Connecticut Trail to the lower Ammonoosuc, where they gathered until food was brought to them from Fort No. 4 at Charlestown.

3. Newichwannock-Sokoki Trail

The Newij-wan-ok ("to the place of many little falls in the long distance") Trail began at tidewater below Kwam-pi-gon ("many tall trees") and Newichwannock—both villages being located in what is now South Berwick, Maine. This part of the trail was on the east side of the river and passed through what is now Berwick, Maine, and on to Toba-wan, a phrase taken from Toba-woz-wan ("seven little falls"). This Indian camping ground was located in what is now South Lebanon, Maine, and the local name is now Stairs Falls. At this point the trail passed into what is now Rochester, New Hampshire. After a French force under Seigneur Hertel de Rouville, accompanied by a small Sokoki force under Wahowa, better known as Hope Hood, had ravaged and burned Salmon Falls, New Hampshire, and Berwick, Maine (now South Berwick), they retreated over this trail. A force of nearly 150 colonists pursued the raiders and in the late afternoon of March 27, 1690, caught up with them at a brook called Wooster's River. After three hours of exchanging shots from behind trees, the colonists ran out of ammunition, and the French and Indian force retreated to Tobawan, where they camped overnight. About 15 on both sides were killed or wounded. Early the next morning the French and Indians crossed the river into New Hampshire and passed northwesterly over the Chenayok Trail to Lake Winnipesaukee.

In the summer of 1955 Berwick highway employees engaged in loading gravel at Tobawan found a skull and bones which were examined by an anthropologist and adjudged to be those of a white woman who had been buried more than a century ago. There is little doubt that the bones were of an ill-fated captive of the Sokoki.

Tobawan was the terminus of the K'sen-nebi-ok (Kennebunk) Trail often used by the eastern Maine Abenaki Indians in their raids on the English colonial towns, as their seacoast trail was blocked by the settlements and garrison houses at Wells and York. The most famous of the Penobscot Indians, the Kchi Sogmo (or great sachem) Madockawando, camped several times at Tobawan.

The Newichwannock Trail led northward to Nasbaug, now Milton, New Hampshire, and continued to Newichwanimak Lake (now Great East Lake) in Wakefield. From this lake the trail passed overland to Koa-tegwa, now Pine River, and thence along the banks of Pine River to what is now Lake Ossipee. Following the east bank of the lake, this trail—which had now become the Sokoki Trail—continued northward following a line of small

ponds to Conway Lake, and from thence to the ancient Indian village site at Kchitegu, now Conway, New Hampshire. Following the Saco River eastward it reached the Sokoki village at Pequaket, now Fryeburg, Maine. From Pequaket, the Sokoki Trail continued along the river bank, reaching the sea at what is now Saco.

In 1655, before King Philip's War when the Mohawk made a number of raids into New Hampshire, the sachem of the Ossipee tribe journeyed to Dover where, with the promise of many beaver skins, he induced two Dover carpenters to go to Ossipee Lake to build a large fort of planks and palisades on the site of the tribe's main village. This fort was burned by the militia in November 1676 and completely destroyed.

Nearly fifty years later, Captain John Lovewell and his men stopped at the site of the old fort and built a small shelter for several of the militiamen who had been taken ill and had to be left there. Following the battle of Pequaket, in which the commander and many of his men were slain, the survivors retreated along the Sokoki Trail to the shelter, which they found deserted. From Ossipee they continued over the Newichwannock Trail to Rochester.

The Sokoki tribe made many excursions over these trails when they raided Rochester, Dover, Oyster River (now Durham), and many other New England towns.

It was over the Sokoki Trail that in 1632 Darby Field, accompanied by two Cocheco Indians, made an exploratory journey to the White Mountains. They were joined at the Saco River by several Pequaket Indians, and all reached the base of Mt. Washington. Over the vigorous objections of the Pequaket Indians, who insisted that Maji Neo-waska (Bad Spirit) lived on the mountain, Field and one of the Cocheco Indians reached the summit. Field was the first white man to climb the mountain. A month later he paid another visit to the mountains accompanied by two other white men, Jocelyn and Neal.

In 1668 an enterprising English colonist loaded a canoe with goods and entering the Saco River at Saco, Maine, continued up that river to its confluence with the Ossipee River. Proceeding up the latter river, he reached the place now known as Effingham Falls, where he set up a trading post. This was a strategic spot, as it commanded the Ossipee Trail to the west and the Sokoki Trail to the north. At the outbreak of hostilities the trader decamped, leaving most of his goods. In later years, during a time of peace, other traders opened a post here.

4. Androscoggin Trail

The Namas-ek-guagon ("fish spearing place") Trail actually started at Merrymeeting Bay in Maine and followed in many places the Androscoggin River to its source at Wombagwog (Umbagog: "the white [water] lake") Lake. It also led to "up Magallibu way," now the Magalloway. *Magallibu* is the Indian word for caribou. The trail led past Mt. Aziscoos in Maine, to the hunters' trail beyond that mountain. Aziscoos was formerly the Indian Awass-iss-ko-oss ("to the other side of the mountain of the little pine trees").

The northern section of New Hampshire and the Magalloway of Maine were much frequented by hunters of the Aroosagunticook tribe. The Sokoki often joined them in their expeditions.

5. Ammonoosuc Trail

The Omanosek began at the upper reaches of the Saco River and passed through Crawford Notch and onward to the Ammonoosuc River. It did not always follow the curves of the river, but reached it here and there. This trail was often used by the Sokoki to and from the Connecticut River.

From the top of Cherry Mountain, Timothy Nash, a famous hunter in the Coos country, observed the notch in the mountains. Imparting this information to another hunter named Sawyer, he agreed to make the trip with him through the pass. When they got through, they proceeded to Portsmouth and reported to Governor Wentworth, who granted them a tract of land known as the "Nash and Sawyer's Location." Some historians have stated that they were the first white men to negotiate this pass. This statement is obviously not true, as the Sokoki Indians of Pequaket took many white men (captives from the seacoast villages) through the pass on their way to Canada. When Pequaket was abandoned later by the Indians, they migrated along this trail on their way to the Abenaki reservation at St. Francis. In the spring of 1755, at what is now Northumberland, Captain Robert Rogers and his men erected a log fort near the junction of the Connecticut River and the Upper Ammonoosuc. It was called Fort Wentworth on Holland's map; the area was surveyed by Grant in 1772.

6. Pemigewasset Trail

The Pemigewasset ("bear's grease river") Trail began at what is now Franklin and followed the Pemigewasset River to its source near Profile Lake in the Franconia Notch. The Woban-aden-ek ("to the place of the high white mountains") Trail led beyond, one branch going to Littleton and the other going to the region of Mt. Washington.

From the Pemigewasset Trail the Indians must have seen that natural wonder, the "Great Stone Face."

7. *Asquamchumaukee Trail*

The Msquam-chum-aki ("salmon spawning place") Trail led from Lake Winnipesaukee at what is now Meredith Neck northwestward to the southern shore of Msquam-nebis ("salmon lake," shown in Father Aubry's [Joseph Aubéry's] 1715 map as "Msquam-nebis"), now Squam Lake, thence along the northern shore of Little Squam Lake, and thence to the Pemigewasset Indian village at what is now Plymouth. From this point the trail led along the banks of the Asquamchumaukee River, now the Baker River, to what is now Wentworth, where it turned northward along the branch river to what is now Glencliff. Thence through the Oliverian Notch to a point north of the present Haverhill, where it crossed the Connecticut River to the Coosuck village at what is now Newbury, Vermont. In the seventeenth century, the Pemigewasset Indians were nearly exterminated either by an epidemic or by a victorious force of the Mohawk. Although the latter reason may be legendary, it is given credence by several historians.

It was over this trail that several French and Indian expeditions against the New England colonists made their way to and from Montreal and St. Francis; Seigneur Hertel made three such round trips. Hundreds of English colonists—men, women, and children captives of the Indians—traveled northward along this trail on their way to Canada to be either adopted or held for ransom.

The name of the Asquamchumaukee River was changed to Baker River in honor of Captain Baker, who led a detachment of militia to this region in search of Indians. They surprised and killed nearly an entire band of Indians from Canada who were hunting and trapping in this locality. Historians record that the furs collected by the Indians were taken to Haverhill, Massachusetts, where they fetched a good price.

Another fish-spawning place was a small river flowing into the St. Croix River near the New Brunswick border. This river was called Cham-kook ("spawning place").

8. *Ossipee Trail*

The Awoss-sebi Trail led from Chenayok (Kchi-nayok: "great point"), now called Moultonborough Neck, northward through what is now Moultonborough and Sandwich. At this point it turned eastward along what is now the Bearcamp River (Awasso-kik) to Ossipee Lake, thence along the southern shore of the lake to the Ossipee River, thence along the banks of the river, terminating at the confluence of the Ossipee and the Saco rivers in Maine, where it merged into the Sokoki Trail.

The Winnipesaukee Indians traversed this trail to visit their friends and neighbors at Ossipee Lake. Near Ossipee was located the so-called Indian Mound, about which many flowery tales have been written. In 1950 the New Hampshire Archeological Society excavated this mound under the direction of Lawrence M. Crosbie and found it to be of glacial, not Indian, origin.

The Pequaket Indians reached Lake Winnipesaukee via a short trail from what is now Purity Pond in East Madison, passing along the northern shores of Monamak (Mour-a-mak: "deep water"), now Silver Lake, and then along the Ossipee Trail.

9. *Chenayok or Sobagwa Trail*

This trail, as the words indicate, was the Kchinayok ("great point") or the Sobagway ("ocean") Trail. It started at Moultonborough Neck. The Indians crossed the bay by canoe to the outlet of the Melvin River at what is now Melvin Village. The trail then continued past Mirror Lake, where an Indian village was located on the land in the rear of the present post office, past what is now the Libby Museum, on to what is now Wolfeboro Falls, and thence to South Wolfeboro at what is now Rust Pond, called Win-nebos-e-kek ("at the place where the water flows out of the pond"), an Indian camping place. Then it passed on to what is now Shaw's Pond and along the north base of Mt. Jesse to what is now Middleton, thence to what is now West Milton, then to the Chestnut Hill section of Rochester. From this point one branch joined the Cocheco Trail at Chemung, now Farmington, while the main trail continued to East Rochester and, crossing the Salmon Falls River, arrived at the famous camping ground at Tobawan, South Lebanon, Maine. From this settlement the [Indians] using this trail could reach the ocean either via the Kennebunk Trail or by going south on the Newichwannock Trail.

This trail was one of the most historic in New Hampshire. After camping overnight at Tobawan, the forces of Hertel and Hope Hood retreated along this trail, having ravaged Salmon Falls the previous day. With them there were over sixty captives. One prisoner, Robert Rogers of Salmon Falls, attempted to escape but was recaptured. At Chestnut Hill, on the present Henderson farm, the Indians halted and held a powwow, after which they burned Robert Rogers at the stake. Chief Hope Hood with a dozen warriors remained in the neighborhood and afterward raided Exeter, Hampton, and Newington. Then they crossed the Piscataqua River, joined forces with other Indians, and attacked Portland, Maine, then known as Casco. Hertel and his force, with the remaining Sokoki Indians, then

retraced their steps over the Chenayok Trail and went on to Montreal with their closely guarded prisoners.

Eighteen years later the same Hertel, accompanied by Deschaillons with a French force, and Nescambuit, with 100 Indians from St. Francis, came down over this trail and met scouts of a Penobscot Indian band at Lake Winnipesaukee. Proceeding to Tobawan, they were joined at that spot by the Penobscot band and a small force from Pequaket. The Hertel-Deschaillons-Nescambuit force, reinforced by the Penobscot and Sokoki, had planned to attack Portsmouth, but their scouts reported the presence of a large force of militia. Their plans were necessarily changed, and they attacked Haverhill, Massachusetts, instead of Portsmouth.

Some words should be written about Nescambuit, who the English termed "Assacambuit." The French historians record him as a Sokoki, but as the Ossipee tribe was regarded as Sokoki, and practically the entire tribe removed to Canada previous to 1690, whereas very few of the tribe at Pequaket removed to Canada until nearly seventy years later, there seems to be a basis for the belief that Nescambuit was of the Pequaket tribe. It will be noted that Nescambuit guided the expedition to the rendezvous at Tobawan by way of Chenayok because it was much nearer than by way of Aquadoctan and Quannippi (Alton Bay). The Indians had abandoned Aquadoctan in 1696 and had gone to Pequaket.

Nescambuit was a savage, ruthless killer. But to the French and especially to the Indian tribes, he was a hero. He was taken to France, where he was knighted by King Louis XIV and presented a gold-handled sword and an annuity. He boasted to the king that he had scalped 139 of the king's enemies. At Haverhill, Massachusetts, he added nine more to his gory list.

Captain John Lovewell, accompanied by nearly fifty militiamen, made his second expedition to Lake Winnipesaukee over this historic trail, camping the first night near Middleton. The next day, the force reached Rust Pond and Lake Winnipesaukee, where they found three empty wigwams. Proceeding along the lakeshore to what is now Wolfeboro, they failed to locate any Indians. Finally they turned eastward and reached Tumble-Down-Dick Mountain, from the summit of which Captain Lovewell observed the smoke of a campfire farther toward the east. A forced march in the darkness through what is now Brookfield brought them to the shore of what is now called Lovell Lake at Sanbornville, where on an island in the pond they discovered ten Indians sleeping by their campfires. A volley from the militiamen's rifles ended the lives of these [Indians], who were found to have extra blankets and snowshoes with them in anticipation of taking captives to Canada. The company was later paid a large bounty at Boston for the Indians' scalps.

When the colonial Governor Wentworth decided to build a summer home beside the lake which bears his name, he ordered that a highway should be built from Rochester to Lake Wentworth. With the help of the militia and many ox teams hired at Rochester and Dover, the road was completed. It followed, between Rochester and Middleton, the ancient Chenayok Trail of the Ossipee Indians. The colonists called it the "Governor's Road." It was completed through what is now Brookfield. The "King's Highway," which followed in places the ancient Indian trail, led from Middleton to South Wolfeboro, Wolfeboro, and Melvin Village.

It was on this trail at Melvin Village that the late Harold Ley, Sr., placed in 1955 a granite marker to commemorate

the spot where in 1817 the bones of a gigantic Winnipesaukee Indian had been uncovered in the churchyard beside the Melvin River. This discovery was made famous later in the century by John Greenleaf Whittier's poem "The Grave by the Lake." Edwin A. Charlton, in his *New Hampshire as It Is* (Claremont, 1856, 3d ed.), wrote:

> About the year 1817, on the north line of the town, near the mouth of Melvin River, a gigantic skeleton, apparently that of a man seven feet in height, was found buried in the sand. The Ossipee tribe once lived in this region; and several years ago a tree was standing, on which was carved in hieroglyphics a history of their deeds and expeditions.

10. Contoocook Trail

The Kon-wan-teg-ok ("the pine river from the place of many little falls") Trail took its name from the fact that the Contoocook Valley was once heavily wooded with pine trees. Between Henniker and Hillsboro, and especially at Jaffrey, there were long series of little water falls.

This important Indian path led from a junction with the Pocumtuck Trail, which crossed northern Massachusetts eastward from Greenfield, Massachusetts. It led northward from what is now Winchendon to Lake Monomonac, past Contoocook Lake, and followed the banks of the Contoocook River to its confluence with the Merrimack River.

At the mouth of the Contoocook River is a small island which was the scene of the heroic deeds of Hannah Dustin, who, with the help of Mary Neff and young Samuel Leonardson, exterminated their sleeping captors and, taking one of their canoes, made their way down the Merrimack River to Haverhill, Massachusetts, where they were warmly welcomed. About two weeks previously the Indians had ended the life of Mrs. Dustin's infant daughter, a possible hindrance in their planned trip to Canada.

Over the Mohawk, Pocumtuck, and Konwantegok trails the Mohawk, a tribe of Iroquois Indians from upper New York state, made several invasions of New Hampshire and Maine.

11. Souhegan Trail

The Sowa-nigan ("jutting or difficult portage") Trail began at the confluence of the Souhegan and Merrimack rivers and followed the banks of the Souhegan to Pratt's Pond. A high waterfall and jutting rocks made a difficult portage near Greenville. The trail continued to Contoocook Lake near Rindge.

The Nashua (Niswa-ok: "place of two [rivers]") tribe of Indians, whose main village was at what is now Lancaster, Massachusetts, also maintained a small village called Watanic at what is now Nashua and utilized the fertile meadows of the Souhegan Valley for their cornfields. Wa-ta-nic is a corruption of Askwa-teg-nik ("at the end of the river fork"), where the Nashua River flows into the Merrimack.

In 1667 a trading post was opened at Watanic by Major Simon Willard, and another trading post was opened at Pennichuck (Pen-i-kchi-ok: "at the place of the great rapids") by John Burroughs. These trading posts thrived until the outbreak of King Philip's War. Several English settlers came to this vicinity and called the place Dunstable.

On a branch trail along the Sebossen-ek ("to the place of the stony brook") at what is now Greenfield, New Hampshire, was a much-used camping ground of the Nashua tribe.

The last invasion of New Hampshire by the Mohawk came over the Souhegan Trail from the Contoocook Trail. Reaching the Merrimack River they crossed into Litchfield and Hudson, where they were first seen. They then continued on to what is now Epping, where they burned several wigwams.

12. Coos or Penacook Trail

The Ko-iss ("small pine trees") Trail began at Oyster River, now Durham, and followed a line of ponds—consisting of Mendum's Pond, North River Pond, Bow Lake, and Wild Goose Pond—to what is now Barnstead Parade, and then followed the Suncook River to its source. At Gilmanton it connected with the Penacook Trail through Loudon to the Indian village at Penacook. The Coos Trail crossed the Winnipesaukee River south of Laconia and eventually became a part of the Asquamchumaukee Trail. This trail continued to what is now Woodsville, and from that point followed the Ammonoosuc Trail to what is now Littleton. Several exploratory expeditions passed over this trail, including that of Captain Peter Bowers, who journeyed to the Coos country to ascertain if the French and Indians had constructed fortifications in that region.

At the head of North River at North River Pond in Nottingham was an ancient Indian village whose warriors during King Philip's War committed many depredations against Oyster River. They were finally driven from their village by the New Hampshire militia.

In 1689 a colonial force left Dover on a punitive expedition following this trail to what is now Barnstead, where the forces were divided. One company, under Captain Noyes, proceeded to Penacook, where they destroyed the Indians' corn; the rest, under Captain Wincol, proceeded to Lake Winnipesaukee, where they also destroyed growing corn.

13. Ashuelot Trail

The Namasawilok Trail began at what is now Hinsdale and in general followed the banks of the Ashuelot River to Ashuelot Pond in Washington, and thence to Lake Sunapee.

At the base of Mt. Caesar in Swanzey there was an ancient Squakheag village at a point on the eastern side of the river. Here there is still evidence of an ancient fish weir. Whether this village was abandoned following the epidemic of 1616 or whether it was destroyed by the Mohawk at the same time as they destroyed the Indian villages at Hinsdale and Richmond is not known.

When the English colonists settled at what is now Keene, they called it Upper Ashuelot. There they built a fort as a defense against the attacks of the St. Francis Indians. A fort was also constructed at Swanzey. At Hinsdale, the colonists' fortifications were called Hinsdale's Fort, Shattuck's Fort, and Bridgman's Fort. Across the Connecticut, near what is now Brattleboro, Vermont, was Fort Dummer.

From the Indian village at Swanzey branched out three minor trails: the Winigegwok ("place of the otter") Trail, which led to East Sullivan, Center Pond, and Island Pond in Stoddard; the Minnewawa ("berries among the poplars") Trail, which led to Lake Nubanusit and to what is now Greenfield and Peterborough; and the Monadenok Trail, which led to what is now Jaffrey.

Captain John Lovewell and a small force left Dunstable and passed through the Monadnock region in search of a band of Indians who had been raiding the Ashuelot River region. They reached Ashuelot Pond and later climbed a mountain in Washington in their unsuccessful search. Finally they proceeded to Fort No. 4 at Charlestown. It is believed that the Indians covered their tracks and escaped in the direction of the Stoddard ponds. The mountain in Washington, from the summit of which the colonial force scanned the countryside for the smoke of an Indian campfire, has since been named Lovewell's Mountain.

14. Piscataquog Trail

The Pisga-tegu-ok ("to the place of the dark river," from *ok*, to the place; *pisga*, it is dark; and *tegu*, river) Trail started at the confluence of the Piscataquog and Merrimack rivers, and followed the former to its source at Pleasant Pond. It then continued through what is now Deering, making a junction with the Contoocook Trail near Hillsboro. A branch trail led from what is now Goffstown to East Weare and Weare. The trail passed to the north of Mount Uncanoonuc, which is believed to be Uncanoonucks ("maiden's breasts").

On this trail at New Boston lived a famous Indian, Joe English, a former member of the Agawam Indian tribe at what is now Ipswich, Massachusetts. Joe English was a staunch friend of the English settlers and lost his life in their defense.

15. Mascoma-Aquadoctan Trail

The Mas-kam-ok–Agua-dak-gan ("from the place of the great trees" to "the landing place") Trail led from a junction of the Connecticut Trail and the Mascoma River at what is now West Lebanon, New Hampshire. Then it paralleled the Mascoma River and Mascoma Lake, continued to Crystal Lake, Grafton Pond, and Halfmoon Pond to Smith River, and continued along that river to Bristol, thence to Pemigewasset and Wickwas ponds, terminating at what is now the Weirs. During the shad run at the fish weirs, the Coosuck and other Connecticut River

Indians came over this trail to join the Winnipesaukee Indians in the netting of the shad.

A fork of the river at Bristol led to a body of water now known as Newfound Lake, but to the Indians it was known as Passaquaney (Pass-agua-nik: "landing place at the sandbar on the fork of the river," from *agua*, landing; *pass*, river-bottom rising, a sandbar; and *nik*, fork of the river). The word *nik* was often used in New England, as in Taconic (Tegu-nik: "river fork"), Connecticut, and Nicatous (Nik-a-tegwa), Maine.

The Mascoma-Aquadoctan Trail was one of the most important hunters' trails of the Winnipesaukee tribe.

16. *Quannippi Trail*

This trail began at Win-nebos-e-kek ("at the place where the water flows out of the pond"), now called Rust Pond at South Wolfeboro. It followed the eastern shore of Lake Winnipesaukee and the body of water now known as Alton Bay to the southern tip of the lake where the village of Alton Bay is now situated.

There was an Indian camping place at Clay Point, near the present Camp Kabeyun (a summer camp for boys). A half mile south of the camp buildings is the so-called Fort Point. As early as 1722 the Provincial Assembly voted to build a fort on this site and cut a road from Dover to supply it. But the money to do this was never appropriated, and the first road to Alton was not built until the end of the French and Indian Wars and the Treaty of Paris in 1763.

The trail name and the ancient name of the bay, Quan-nippi, means "long water."

17. *Pentucket Trails*

The Pen-teg-ek ("at the place of the river rapids") Trails were two of New

Hampshire's most historic Indian paths. The southern Pentucket Trail led from Pentucket, now Haverhill, Massachusetts, to Massapaug ("Great Pond") near Kingston, and from that point to Pakwa-kek ("at the place of the arrows"), where stones suitable for points were found. This place was near what is now known as Pickpocket Falls. The trail then led to Msquam-skook ("at the place of the salmon") called Squamscott by the colonists, and now Exeter. From Exeter the trail led to the Shaw-unk-hassik, a river which the settlers called Shankhasset (*shaw*, taken from *shwazwa*, winding; *unk*, from *unka*, more or less; and *hassik*, soft sand, the whole phrase meaning "winding [river] more or less sandy"). The Shawinigan of Shawinigan Falls in the province of Quebec means in Abenaki "winding portage." The colonists renamed the Shankhasset as Oyster River. The trail led from Durham to Cochichok and the river falls at Dover, and a continuation of the trail led past Quamphegan, Maine, to Agamenticus, now York, Maine. This trail was abandoned by the Indians when English settlements were made at Wells (Woball-ek: "the white [water] place"), Ogunquit (Negona-kik: "the ancient place"), York, Newichwannock, Dover, Durham, and Exeter.

The northern Pentucket Trail also led from Pentucket to Great Pond, and from that point to what are now Epping, Lee, Barrington, Gonic, Rochester, and Tobawan, now South Lebanon, Maine. After the southern route was blocked by the colonists the Indians used the northern trail in their raids on the New England settlements of New Hampshire and Massachusetts.

There was at one time a small Indian village beside the river at Atkinson. The sachems Passaquo and Saggahew, with the consent of Passaconaway, sold this village and lands for a distance of over twenty miles each way to settlers of Pentucket (Haverhill) for goods valued at less than five English pounds. Many artifacts have been found at Great Pond, including old French coins, indicative of the spot where a French and Indian force once camped.

At one point on this trail the colonial militia and a band of Kennebec Indians fought the battle of Wheelwright's Pond in which Captain Wiswall and 15 of his men were killed.

On the Pentucket Trail, at Wadley's Falls on the Lamprey River, was an ancient village called Washucke (Waj-ok: "place on the hill"). In 1659 Wadononamin, sagamore of Washucke, sold this village and all of the land between the Lamprey and Bellamy rivers to the English.

One Indian force came from the east over this trail to attack Oyster River, now Durham, and was seen by a colonist who hastened to give the alarm to a small body of militia stationed at the village. This force met, gave battle to the Indians, and routed them, killing their leader, who they found to be a half-breed, probably of a prominent French family as was evident by his reddish blond hair, his silken shirt, and other indications of nobility found on his body, as well as a written list of Indians under his command. Around his headgear were strung a dozen little bells, so that as he tramped over the trails his followers would know of his exact whereabouts. At first it was thought that he was the son of the baron de Castine, who had married the great chief Madockawando's daughter, but this belief proved wrong and history has never revealed his true identity.

It was over this trail that in 1694—coming by way of the Abenaki, Kennebunk, and Pentucket trails—the combined forces of General Villieu and the aged Madockawando from the Penobscot region of Maine, numbering about 250 men, attacked Oyster River. The colonists' casualties in this battle were in excess of ninety men, women, and children killed, wounded, or made captive. Of 12 small forts, called garrison houses, five were destroyed and seven successfully defended.

In 1676 the "Unholy Three"—Simon, Andrew, and Peter—Newichwannock Indians attacked a farmhouse at Bradford, Massachusetts, killed Thomas Kimball, and captured his family, although within six weeks they restored voluntarily the woman and five children. As boys, these three Indians had been converted by the minister of a Dover church, who, when they were presented for baptism, scanned the list of Indian names and, finding them unpronounceable, tore up the paper and baptized them Simon, Andrew, and Peter. Later, because of an alleged wrong done unto them, these Indians became renegades and were hated and feared for their cruelty.

During King Philip's War, Simon, Andrew, and Peter were the scourge of the countryside from Haverhill, Massachusetts, to Casco, Maine. Nevertheless, thanks either to their Christian baptism or to some survival of cruder Indian morality, they had their moments of grace. For example, when they attacked a farmhouse near Dover they recognized the colonist as the one who had found Andrew's mother in the woods with a broken hip and had taken her to the farmhouse where she was nursed back to health. Out of gratitude they immediately ceased the attack, and during the many years of war to follow the farmhouse and its occupants were never again molested.

It was over this trail that a force of 100 friendly Natick Indians from Massachusetts marched to assist the garrisons at Dover, Salmon Falls, and Berwick in their struggle with the French and the Abenaki Indians.

18. Squamanagonek Trail

This trail began at Msquam-a-na-guan-a-gon-ek ("at the narrow salmon spearing place")—shortened by early colonial writers to Squamanagonic and finally condensed to Gonic—and led westward through what is now the Meaderboro section of Rochester and Farmington. The route continued through the southern part of Farmington and New Durham, through the valley north of Blue Job Mountain, to Halfmoon Pond in Barnstead, from thence to Suncook Lake, and then turned to the north, terminating at what is now Alton Bay. An Indian mortar was recently located on this trail near Halfmoon Pond.

It was over this trail, after their invasion during which they had slain Chief Blind Will, that the Mohawk proceeded to Alton Bay, where they surprised and slaughtered two Ossipee Indian fishermen. An Indian boy escaped by diving from the canoe into the lake and swimming underwater. This boy later brought the news of the attack to Major Waldron at Dover.

19. Cocheco-Winninanebiskek Trail

The Ko-kchi-kook ("at the place of the great pine trees") or, as another interpretation reads, Co-chich-ok ("at the place of the fast water") Trail actually began at Winnichahannet (Winn-i-kchi-han-ek: "at the place surrounded by the great waters flowing out"), now Dover Point. From Dover Point the trail followed along the shore of the Piscataqua to what is now called Dover Landing at the outlet of the Cocheco River. Continuing alongside the Cocheco River at times, the trail reached what are now Gonic and Rochester. The present highway from Rochester to Farmington follows in many places the old Indian trail.

The new Spaulding Turnpike, after passing through what were the ancient Indian cornfields west of Dover, follows in many places the Cocheco Indian Trail. About two miles east of Farmington the trail turned toward the river.

At a point north of the present Wagonwheel Ranch was a famous camping place of the Indians. It was at this spot that they built many of the birch bark canoes that they used on the Cocheco River, hence its name, Chemung (Chemun-ek: "canoe place"). *Chemun* is an Algonquin word for canoe. The bark for the canoes was said to have been taken from the *maskwa* (birch trees) which grew on the present Chemung farm in Farmington.

Continuing northwest from Farmington the trail followed the Ela River to New Durham, became a direct path through the woods, crossed Merrymeeting River near Jones Pond, crossed over the hill past the Bennett farm, reached the river again at Alton, and continued to Alton Bay until it reached the junction of six Indian trails. There is ever-increasing evidence that there was once an Indian village near Alton Bay, located on the eastern shore of the Merrymeeting River. This village, probably of the Winnipesaukee tribe, was believed to have been located on land now used for a garden by Perley Barr of Alton. Many artifacts have been found here, and it has been reported that several years ago an amateur archaeologist, following a plow over the field, retrieved enough artifacts to fill a good-sized pail. The strip of level meadowland in the rear of the village site was undoubtedly an Indian cornfield, as stone artifacts used as garden tools were found here.

Beyond Alton Bay, and extending to the Indian fish weirs at the outlet of Lake Winnipesaukee, the trail became the Winninanebiskek ("at the narrow place where the water flows out of the lake") Trail.

Over these two trails, on March 26, 1690, the combined forces of Hertel and Hope Hood (Wahowah) passed eastward bent on the destruction of Salmon Falls. They camped overnight at Chemung (Farmington). Over these trails too Captain John Lovewell with a small company of militia made his first expedition to Lake Winnipesaukee. Proceeding to Loon Cove, they found a solitary Indian fisherman, and they left his body buried in the sands at that spot.

The earliest historical reference to the Cocheco Trail is the following: "On May 4, 1657, 200 acres of land on the west side of the Cocheco River, bounded by the Indian path, was set aside for Mr. Edward Rawson" (*New Hampshire Provincial Papers*, vol. 1, p. 229). The late Mary P. Thompson of Durham, author of *Landmarks in Ancient Dover*, asserts that this tract of land was the Indian cornfield. Later, the "Indian path" was widened for ox teams which were used to haul the masts from the primeval forest to be used on ships in the king's navy. Thereafter, the colonists called this Indian trail "the great mast path." Later, it was cut through to Rochester and still later, to Farmington. The tall trees marked for masts are aptly described in the Indian phrase Ko-kchi-kook (Cocheco): "at the place of the great pine trees."

20. Abenaki Trail

The word *Abenaki* is taken from Wobanaki, which literally means "white land," but which the Indians assert means: "land where the sun first bathes the earth in light." This famous trail began at Agawam ("hill village"), now Ipswich, Massachusetts, crossed the Merrimack River near what is now Newburyport, and continued inland to what is now Hamp-

ton Falls and the Indian village of Winn-i-co-ek near the junction of Taylor River and Hampton Falls River.

Continuing, the Abenaki Trail followed the beaches at Hampton and Rye, crossed the Piscataqua River at Portsmouth, led easterly along the seashore, and eventually reached the Penobscot (Pen-apskw-kek: "where the rapids flow over the ledges") River and the village at what is now Indian Island, Oldtown, Maine.

It was over this trail that Squanto and Samoset often traveled between Maine and Massachusetts. While with the Pilgrims, Squanto died of Indian fever in 1621. The trail which they used was by way of Naumkeag (Namas-kik: "fishing place"), now Salem; Msquamscott (Msquam-s-kek), now Swampscott; Winnisimmet (Winn-i-siwan-ek: "where the salt waters flow out"), now Chelsea; Mich-a-wam ("great village"), now Charlestown; Shawmut (Shaw-mak: "winding waters"), now the Charles River at Boston; Unkataquisset, another name for the Charles River at what is now Milton, Massachusetts; Quonahasset (Quann-a-hassik: "long sands"); and Matta-ki-s-ek (*matta* meaning "farthest" and the entire phrase meaning "to the farthest places," indicating a trail leading west from Duxbury, Massachusetts).

Squando was a sachem of the Saco Indians and was a staunch friend of the English until two sailors, venturing from their ship in a dory on the Saco River, reached into a canoe containing Squando's squaw and papoose, seized the baby, and threw it into the water to see if it could swim. The squaw saved the papoose from drowning, but it soon died from pneumonia, and the outraged Squando became a sworn foe of the English.

Squando died by his own hand more than fifty years after the death of Squanto (Tisquantum).

21. Suncook Trail

The Sen-kek, or Sen-kook ("stony [water] place") Trail led from Namaskik (Amoskeag, now Manchester) along the east bank of the Merrimack River to the Suncook River, followed the banks of that stream through the Suncook Valley to the ancient village north of Suncook Lake, and turning northward, reached another Indian village on the Merrymeeting River at Alton Bay. The regions of Suncook, Gossville, Chichester, Pittsfield, and Barnstead were much frequented by the ancient Indian tribes, as attested by the great numbers of very old artifacts found at those places. In a short history of the region, published in 1855, is the statement: "The farmers of the Suncook Valley are constantly ploughing up stone tools of the Indians." The Suncook Valley, including Gilmanton, was an Indian hunting ground, especially for moose, which frequented the many ponds of the area.

22. Misaden or Waumbek Trail

The Misaden ("great high mountain") or W'ombek ("to the white place") Trail led from the Androscoggin River near what is now Gorham, New Hampshire, and following a brook at the base of the White Mountain range, led over the hill to the Israel River, and along that river to what is now Lancaster. This trail was much used to and from the upper Coos country by the Aroosagunticook and Sokoki tribes.

There was an Indian portage near what is now Wni-gan-ok ("to the southern portage"). The word has evolved into Siwooganock. After the Treaty of Paris in 1763, some Indian families returned to northern New Hampshire, where they hunted, fished, trapped, and traded with the early settlers in that vicinity. During the Revolutionary War some of them

fought on the side of the colonists against the British. The Indians of Canada fought on the side of the British and made raids as far south as Royalton in Vermont and Bethel in Maine. They committed several depredations against the settlers there but were finally driven back to Canada.

23. Sunapee Trail

The Sen-nippi ("stony water") or, as it was sometimes called, Sen-nippi Wo-bagilmak ("stony waters of the wild goose") Trail began at a junction with the Connecticut Trail at the mouth of a stream now known as Sugar River. On the Vermont side is a mountain which may have taken its name from the Indian name of Sugar River, where it flows into the Connecticut River from New Hampshire. The word *askwa*, or *asku*, is much used in Maine Indian place names and means "at the end"; *teg* is short for *tegu* (river); and *nik* means "a fork or branch." The whole phrase Asku-teg-nik, means "at the end of the river fork" and has become Ascutney. Sebasticook (Seb-askw-kook), a branch of the Kennebec River, means "the place at the end of the river fork," at Winslow, Maine. Winslow was also called Taconnet (Tegu-nik: "river fork").

Eastman, a Connecticut trapper, risked his life in 1752 when he ventured alone along the Sugar River, where beaver, mink, and otter were plentiful. His remains, with a crushed skull, were later found in a wild spot on the river.

The Sunapee Trail followed the banks of the Sugar River to the western shore of Lake Sunapee. Another trail followed the southern branch of the river to Rand's Pond, and thence to the southern part of the lake. From this point the trail led to Todd's Pond and the Warner River. A branch trail led to Lake Massasecum. As *cum* means "narrow," Massasecum could be rendered as "great narrow lake," or it may be Massaguigum: "great duck lake." Continuing, the trail led along the banks of the Warner River to what is now Contoocook village, where it connected with the Contoocook Trail. Crossing this river, one trail led to present-day Hopkinton and Dunbarton, and the other trail to Penacook, now Concord.

When Colonel Joseph D. Blanchard's regiment, including Captain and later Major Robert Rogers and his Rangers, left Dunbarton and Hopkinton on their way to Fort No. 4 at Charlestown, they journeyed over the ancient Sunapee Indian Trail from a point near what is now Contoocook, along the banks of the Warner River, past Todd's Pond to what is now Newbury. About three miles west of Newbury, they took the *sowanaki* (southern) branch of the Sunapee Indian Trail, past Rand Pond, and through what are now Goshen and Unity, to what is now Crescent Lake, and continued along the northern bank of Little Sugar River to the present North Charlestown. From this point they proceeded southward to Fort No. 4, later crossing southern Vermont to the scene of active warfare at Lake George and Lake Champlain. Some time previous to Colonel Blanchard's leaving Dunbarton for Fort No. 4, he had authorized John Scott of Canterbury to widen the Indian trails from Fort Clough through to Fort No. 4 so that several cannon could be transported over them. After the power of the French and Indians at Lake Champlain had been broken, Rogers and the Rangers made their historic march to the Abenaki village at St. Francis, which they devastated.

A branch trail led from the main trail at what is now Bradford and heading northward reached Lake Winnipocket (Winn-i-baak-ek: "to the place where the water flows out of the pond"). Crossing the Blackwater River, the trail continued to Walker's Pond and from there to the Merrimack River trails.

Another trail led from the present Sunapee village northward along the western shore of Lake Sunapee, to Otter Pond, Star Lake, and Lake Kolelimook (Ko-wal-a-mak: "lake of the pine trees, shallow in places," from *ko*, pine trees; *wala*, shallow; and *mak*, pond, lake, or waters). This trail led on to George Pond, Crystal Lake, and Lake Mascoma (Mas-kwam-ok: "at the place of the great woods or trees"). The local name for Lake Sunapee at Newbury was Quascacanaquen (O'quass-kikon-a-quan: "region of the long trout," from *o'quass*, an ancient Abenaki word for trout; *kikon*, a fish field or region; and *quan*, long). Oquossoc (O'quass-ok) at the Rangeley Lakes of Maine means "at the place of the trout." A village of Indians of the Pennacook tribe was located near Newbury, and there were many camping places about the lake. Many Mohegan Indians from Massachusetts and Connecticut visited Lake Sunapee, coming by way of the Connecticut and Sugar rivers.

24. Massabesic Trail

The Mass-sebis-ek ("to the place of the great river") Trail was just what the interpretation implied. Beginning at Pentucket (Haverhill, Mass.), the trail led to Angle Pond, and through what are now Chester and Sandown, reaching Lake Massabesic at what is now Auburn, and continuing along its northern shore and along the Cohas Brook, terminating at the Indian settlement on the Merrimack River.

There was a small Indian village at what is now Sandown, and on an island in Lake Massabesic was another small village. It is recorded that when the white settlers arrived in this vicinity, there were a dozen wigwams on the island.

When King Philip began his war

against the English colonists, he sent emissaries to nearly all of the Pennacook and Sokoki villages seeking their help in a common cause. One historian states that the first villages reached by these messengers were at Watanic, now Nashua, and at Sandown.

The Massabesic Trail was actually a continuation of the Merrimack Trail, which began at Salisbury, Massachusetts, reached Lake Attitash at what is now Merrimacport, and connected with the Massabesic Trail at Pentucket.

The foregoing is a list of the more important Indian trails of New Hampshire. There were many minor trails scattered throughout the state.

It will be observed that an attempt has been made to show the actual Indian place names based on the actual words as published in the Abenaki language books and based on research by leading Indianologists. Attention is called to the fact that early writers and cartographers changed the suffixes of many Indian words. Many place names now ending in *et* should actually end in *ik*, *ek*, or *ok* locative words, all of them meaning "at," "to," "from," or "of" as is appropriate. If you were there, they would mean "at the place"; if you were headed there, or noted a trail or waterway leading there, they would mean "to the place"; and if you had been there, or noted a trail or waterway leading from that direction, they would mean "from the place." The suffixes "ket," "cott," and "cook" are actually the Indian *kek* or *kook*, usually meaning "at the place." The words "keag," the Indian *kik*; "aukee," the Indian *aki*; and *ki*, pronounced *kee*—all mean "earth, land, or place."

17

Ancient Indian Places

Chester B. Price

ANCIENT INDIAN VILLAGES

Anasagunticook, near Bethel, ME
Aquadoctan (Aguadek'gan), the Weirs, NH
Aroosabaug, Mirror Lake, NH
Ashuelot, Swanzey, NH
Atkinson River, Atkinson, NH
Chemung, Farmington, NH
Chenayok (Kchi Nayok), Moultonborough Neck, NH
Chetegway, (Chateguay, Kchi-tegu), Conway, NH
Cocheco, Dover, NH
Cohas, Cohas Brook, Manchester, NH
Coosuck, Newbury, VT
Massabesic Island, Massabesic Lake, Auburn, NH
Massapaug, Great Pond, Kingston, NH
Msquamkeag, Northfield, MA
Namaskik (Namaskeag), Manchester, NH
Nipmuk, Richmond, NH
North River Pond, Nottingham, NH
Odell Park, Franklin, NH
O'quasskikonaquan, Newbury, NH
Ordanakis, Lyme, NH
Ossipee, Ossipee Lake, NH
Pasaguaney (Passaguanik), Bristol, NH

Passumsic, East Barnet, VT
Pemigewasset, Plymouth, NH
Penacook, Concord, NH
Pentucket (Pentegok), Chelmsford, MA
Pequaket, Fryeburg, ME
Phillips Pond, Sandown, NH
Pisgatoek, Somersworth, NH
Quamphegan, South Berwick, ME
Quannippi, Alton Bay, NH
Senikok, Gilmanton Ironworks, NH
Sowcook, Litchfield, NH
Squakheag, Hinsdale, NH
Squakheag, Vernon, VT
Squamanagonic, Gonic, NH
Squamscott, Exeter, NH
Wamesit, near Lowell, MA
Washucke, Wadley's Falls, Lee, NH
Watanic (Niswaog), Nashua, NH
Winnicut, Great Bay, Greenland, NH

Note: Most of these villages were abandoned prior to 1685.

INDIAN TRADING POSTS

Merrimack, at Merrimack, NH, 1665-Cromwell's

Source: Chester B. Price, "Historic Indian Trails of New Hampshire," a map originally published by the New Hampshire Archeological Society in 1967 and reprinted in 1974. A few corrections and additions have been made, and the entries have been alphabetized.

Ossipee, at Effingham Falls, NH
Penacook, at East Concord, NH, on
    east bank of the Merrimack River,
    1667–68-Waldron's
Quamphegan, at South Berwick, ME
Sowcook, at Litchfield, NH
Watanic, at Nashua, NH

INDIAN FORTS

East Concord (east of Merrimack River),
    Concord, NH
Ossipee Lake, Ossipee, NH
Squakheag, Hinsdale, NH

ENGLISH FORTS
(EXCLUDING GARRISON HOUSES)

Atkinson's Fort, Lochmere, NH
Clough's Fort, Canterbury, NH, 1744–48
Contoocook, now Boscawen, NH
Fort Dummer, Brattleboro, VT
Fort No. 1, Chesterfield, NH
Fort No. 2, Westmoreland, NH
Fort No. 3, Walpole, NH
Fort No. 4, Charlestown, NH
Fort Wentworth, Northumberland, NH
Great Island, Newcastle, NH
Hinsdale Fort, Hinsdale, NH
Lovewell's Fort, Ossipee Lake, NH
Lower Ashuelot, Swanzey, NH
Upper Ashuelot, Keene, NH

INDIAN MISSIONS (ALL
TEMPORARY, NO STRUCTURES)

Jesuit mission at Coosuck, Newbury, VT
Jesuit mission at Pequaket, Fryeburg, ME
Protestant mission at Quamphegan, South
    Berwick, ME, maintained by a Dover
    minister
The Rev. Gabriel Druillettes' Jesuit mis-
    sion at the Weirs, NH, 1650
The Rev. John Eliot's mission at Paw-
    tucket Falls, Lowell, MA

INDIAN CAMPING GROUNDS

Baker Pond, Wentworth, NH
Bald Peak Colony Club, Moultonbor-
    ough, NH
Bear Pond, Sandwich, NH
Big Island, Lovell Lake, Sanbornville,
    NH
Camp Baycroft, Tuftonboro, NH
Camp Kabeyun, Clay Point, Alton, NH
Halfmoon Pond, North Barnstead, NH
Hooksek, Hooksett, NH
Kolelimook, Lake Kolelemook, Spring-
    field, NH
Konwantegok, Contoocook Lake,
    Jaffrey, NH
Lancaster, NH, near the Connecticut
    River
Maskwamok, Lake Mascoma, Enfield,
    NH
Massasecum, Bradford, NH
Melvin River, Melvin Village, NH
Meredith Point, Meredith, NH
Mononomak, now Lake Monomonac,
    Rindge, NH
Nasbowk, Milton, NH
Newichwanamak, Great East Lake,
    Wakefield, NH
Nidetheman, Lake Tarleton, NH
North Conway, NH, near railroad bridge
Pickpocket Falls, Exeter River, Exeter,
    NH
Piscasset (Pisgaissek), Great Bay, near
    Newmarket, NH
Pontook (Pontegwok), Milan, NH
Pottery Point, Nineteen Mile Bay,
    Tuftonboro, NH
Province Lake, Effingham, NH
Quinipaug, Highland Lake, Stoddard,
    NH
Robert's Cove, Alton, NH
Sandwich Notch, Sandwich, NH
Sebasenek, near Crotched Mountain,
    Greenfield, NH
Seminenal, Piscataqua River, Eliot, ME
Squam Lake (Msquamnebis), near Hold-
    erness, NH

Stinson Lake, Rumney, NH

Sunapee and several other camping spots, Sunapee Lake, NH

Suncook River, Chichester, NH

Tobawan, Salmon Falls River, South Lebanon, ME

Umbagog (Wombagwog), Umbagog Lake, near Errol, NH

Wahowa's camp, Chestnut Hill, Farmington, NH

Winneboaseket, Rust Pond, South Wolfeboro, NH

Winnichahannet, Dover Point, NH

Winnisquam, at outlet of Lake Winnisquam, Laconia, NH

Woodstock, NH, at Pemigewasset River

18

Indian Names
in New Hampshire

Thaddeus Piotrowski

In this listing of Indian names only the more common variations are included; Winnipesaukee, for example, is spelled 132 different ways (see Douglas-Lithgow, 86–87), and Penacook admits of at least two dozen variations. Substantively different meanings of words may be accounted for either by translations from different Indian dialects or languages, or by different roots within the same dialect or language—although a few of the entries surely are the product of a given researcher's poetic soul. The asterisk next to a name signifies that the term appears in the official *New Hampshire Highway Map*.

Sources: Edward Ballard, "Indian Modes of Applying Names" and "Indian Names" in Nathaniel Bouton, ed., *Collections of the New Hampshire Historical Society Containing Province Records and Court Papers from 1680–1692: Notices of Provincial Councilors, and Other Articles Relative to the Early History of the State*, vol. 8 (Concord: McFarland and Jenks, 1866), 446–52; Percy S. Brown, "Indian Names in New Hampshire," *New Hampshire Archeologist* 7 (1954): 11–21; George Calvin Carter, "Indian Names in New Hampshire," May 12, 1968, a typewritten manuscript in the New Hampshire Room files of the Manchester City Library; F. Parkman Coffin, "Indian Names on the Piscataqua River, Great Bay, and Its Tributary Streams," *New Hampshire Archeologist* 11 (1962): 5–8; Gene Daniell and Jon Burroughs, comps. and eds., *Appalachian Mountain Club White Mountain Guide*, 26th ed. (Boston: Appalachian Mountain Club, 1998) and its six accompanying guide maps; Daniel Doan and Ruth Doan MacDougall, *50 More Hikes in New Hampshire: Day Hikes and Backpacking Trips from Mount Monadnock to Mount Magalloway*, 4th ed. (Woodstock, VT: Backcountry Publications, 1998); Robert A. Douglas-Lithgow, *Dictionary of American-Indian Place and Proper Names in New England, with Many Interpretations, etc.* (Salem, MA: Salem Press, 1909); John Farmer and Jacob B. Moore, *Gazetteer of the State of New-Hampshire* (Concord, NH: Jacob B. Moore, 1823); John C. Huden, *Indian Place Names of New England* (New York: Museum of the American Indian, Heye Foundation, 1962); Robert Julyan and Mary Julyan, *Place Names of the White Mountains*, rev. ed. (Hanover, NH: University Press of New England, 1993); *New Hampshire Atlas and Gazetteer* (Yarmouth, ME: DeLorme, 1999); the 1998–99 official *New Hampshire Highway Map*; Chandler E. Potter, *The History of Manchester...* (Manchester, NH: C. E. Potter, 1856; Salem, MA: USA Higginson, 1995), 26–28, 32–33; and Mary A. Proctor, *The Indians of the Winnipesaukee and Pemigewasset Valleys* (Franklin, NH: Towne and Robie, 1931), 61–64.

Abenaki (Abenaqui, Abeniki, Abnaki, Wabanakee, Wobanaki) **Brook** (crosses Mt. Clinton Rd., near Mt. Eisenhower in the White Mountains) and **Ravine**; also **Abeniki Mountain** and **Lake** (in the Dixville Notch area): "white land"; "land where the sun first bathes the earth in light"; "dawn land." There was also an old Indian trail by that name. The Abenaki Indians belonged to the Algonquian Confederacy centering in Maine; they also lived in the White Mountains area of Carroll County, NH. Parts of New Hampshire's Grafton County were occupied by the Ossipee and Pigwacket, who were affiliated with the Sokoki of the Abenaki tribe.

Abocadneticook (Baker River): "the place of the stream opening out of the mountains"; "stream narrowed by mountains."

Acteon Ridge (in the Waterville Valley region, running from Bald Knob to Jennings Peak): named after the last chief of the Pemigewasset.

Agiochook *see* **Kodaak Wadjo**

Ahquedaukenash (Aguadakgan, Ahquedaukee, Aquadoctan, Aquedoctan, Aquedohcan, Aquidaukenash, Aquidny) (the Weirs): "stopping place or dams"; "a landing place"; "the weirs." There was also an old Indian trail and an Indian village by that name at Weirs Beach.

Algonquin Brook and **Trail** (near Black Mountain in the Sandwich Range Wilderness in the White Mountains).

*Alton Bay *see* **Quannippi, Winninanebiskek**

*Amherst *see* **Souhegan**

Ammaroscoggin *see* **Androscoggin**

*Ammonoosuc** (Amanuseag, Amenonoosuc, Ammoosuc, Omanosek) **Lake** (in the White Mountains at the north end of Crawford Notch State Park), **River** and its various branches, **Ravine Trail** (near Mt. Washington, connecting the Cog Railway base station with the Lakes of the Clouds), and **Upper Ammonoosuc Trail** (in lower Berlin township): "at the narrow fishing river"; "small narrow fishing place"; "fish place." There was also an old Indian trail by that name.

*Amoskeag** (Amokeag, Amuskeag, Naimkeak, Namaoskeag, Namaske, Namaskeag, Namaskik, Naumkeag) (the area by the falls in Manchester): "fishing place"; "place of the fish." Amoskeag's long history of human occupation spans about 8,000 years.

*Androscoggin** (Namasekgoaggon; formerly Ammaroscoggin, Ameriscoggin) **River** (in the Mahoosuc Range area) and **Androscoggin Wayside Park** (near Errol): "to the fish spearing place"; "fish-curing place." There was also an old Indian trail by that name.

Annahooksett *see* **Hooksett**

Aroosabaug Lake (Mirror Lake near the town by the same double name): "bright pond." There was also an old Indian village near Mirror Lake.

*Ashuelot** (Ashaeolock, Ashwillet, Jossawilok, Namasawilok) **Pond** (near the town of Washington), **River**, **River Park** (near Keene), **town**, and **Wildlife Sanctuary** (by Ashuelot Pond): "to the good fishing place"; "wild rushing river"; "collection of many waters"; "to the place of the beautiful mountains"; "to the mountain"; "place between." There were also an old Indian trail and an Indian village by that name near Swanzey. Keene was formerly known as **Upper Ashuelot**; Swanzey as **Lower Ashuelot**.

Askutegnik River (Sugar River, near Claremont): "at the end of the river fork."

Asquam Ridge Trail (near North Woodstock; leads to Mt. Moosilauke's summit). *See also* **Squam**.

Asquamchumauke (Asquam Chumauke, Asquam Chommeock, Asquamchumaukee, Msquamchumaki) **River** (Baker

River): "salmon spawning place"; "water of the mountain place." There was also an old Indian trail by that name.

Asqueanunckon (Asqueanunckton) **Brook** "rapid stream which extends as far as mountain."

Assaguam Brook (crosses Mt. Clinton Rd. near Bretton Woods in the White Mountains).

Aswaguscawadic Stream (tributary of Lake Winnipesaukee): "compelled to drag canoe through [shallow grassy] stream."

Atie ompsk a ooe di Mountain (Moat Mountain): "dogs at rocks eating meat"; "wild animals resembling dogs among the rocks."

*****Attitash Mountain, Big** (also called West Moat Mountain) and **Little** (both in the White Mountains near North Conway): if from Narragansett, "blueberries"; if from Natick or perhaps Pennacook, "huckleberries" or "whortleberries."

Awassokik (Awassosaukee) **River** and **Pond** (Bearcamp River and Pond in Carroll County): "at the abode of the bear."

Awososwi Menahan (Awasaswi Menahan, Awososwi M'naan) **Island** (Bear Island on Lake Winnipesaukee): "bear island."

*****Baboosic** (Babboosic, Babboosuck, Baboosuc, Baboosuck, Baboosuk, Papoosuck) **Brook** (near Merrimack), **Lake** and **Little Babookic Lake** (both in Amherst): "sluggish current"; "middle brook"; "brook between"; "place of the child"; if from the Abenaki word *babeskw*, it means "leach or bloodsucker."

*****Baker River** see **Abocadneticook, Asquamchumauke**

Bear Island see **Awososwi Menahan**

*****Bearcamp River and Pond** see **Awassokik**

*****Beaver Brook** see **Gaentake**

*****Beaver Lake** see **Shoneeto**

*****Bedford** see **Souhegan**

*****Bellamy River** see **Magalloway**

Blue Mountain see **Waternomee**

*****Boscawen** see **Contoocook**

Cabassauk see **Merrimack**

Cabbo Lake (in Rockingham County): "sturgeon."

*****Canobie Lake** and **town** (both in Rockingham County): "abundant water."

Caribou (once called Calabo) **Mountain** and **Caribou Speckled Wilderness Area** (in the Speckled Mountain region): "the pawer"; "pawing animal."

Chateguay see **Kchitegu**

Chebeague (Chebeaque) **Village** (in Strafford County): "almost separated."

Chemung (Chemunek) **State Forest** (near Meredith Center) and a former Indian village near Farmington: if from Deleware, "big horn"; if from Natick, "a canoe" or "a canoe place."

Chenayok (Kchinayok) (Moultonborough Neck): "great point"; "principal neck of land." There was an old Indian village at Moultonborough Neck and an old Indian trail, also called the **Sobagwa Trail**, by that name.

*****Chickwolnepy Mountain** and **Stream** (near Milan): "frog pond." See also **Narmargungowack River**.

Chippewa Trail (near Center Haverhill): "Chippewa" is the same as "Ojibwa" or "Ojibway," the name of the North American Indians of Michigan, Wisconsin, Minnesota, and North Dakota. The word *ojibway* comes from Algonquian and means "to roast until puckered"—from the puckered seam on their moccasins.

Chochichok Falls (on Cocheco River in Dover): "at the rapid current"; "at the place of fast water"; "great falls"; perhaps "big kettle."

*****Chocorua Lake, Mountain, River,** and **town** (all in the White Mountains between Albany and West Ossipee): named after the legendary local chief who lived in the 1700s.

*Cocheco (Cochecha, Cochchechoe, Kokchikook, Quocheco) **River** and **town**: "at the place of the great pine trees"; "the river of shaking banks"; "falls and great falls"; "place of the rapid current." There was an old Indian trail and an old Indian village by that name. Cocheco was also the former name of Dover. The original Indian name for Cocheco (Dover) was Kecheachy.

Cochichawauke: "the place of the great cascade."

*Cohas (Cohass, Cohoos, Cowass, Koiss) **Brook**, **Little Cohas Brook** and **South Branch** (all in southeast Manchester), and **Cohoos Pond** (near Marlow): "small pine trees"; "white pine place." There were several Indian villages in the Cohas Brook area.

Cohasset (Goffs Falls): "place of the pines."

*Concord *see* **Penacook**

*Connecticut (Counitegou, Guonitogou, Kwiniteguh, Quannitegok, Quonektacut) **Lakes**, **Lakes State Forest**, **River**, and **River State Forest**: "at the place of the long river"; "long tidal river"; "the long river that meets the tide." There was also an old Indian trail by that name.

*Contoocook (Konwantegok, Pakunteku) **Island Park** (by Penacook), **Lake** (near Jaffrey), **River**, **State Forest** (by Henniker), and **town**: "the pine river from the place of many little falls"; "the river of fields"; "river that winds among little hills"; "nut trees river"; "small plantation at river." There was also an old Indian trail by that name. Contoocook was the former name of Boscawen. Both (different) towns now exist.

*Conway *see* **Kchitegu, Pequawket**

*Coos (Coosuc, Coosuck, Coosuk, Cosuk, Cowasuck) **County**, **Junction** (a town), and **Coosauk Fall** (in the Mt. Washing-

ton southern ridges): "small pine trees"; "place of white pines." One variant is Kojoss: "pine mountains." There was an old Indian Coos Trail, sometimes called the Penacook Trail, as well as an Indian village (Cowasuck) on the Lower Ammonoosuc River.

Cowissewaschook (Coowissewasseck, Cowesawaskoög, Keesaukee) **Mountain** (Mt. Kearsarge, between Warner and Wilmot Flat): "notched and pointed mountain of pines"; "high place"; "village of the Cowasuck." *See also* **Kearsarge**.

Cromwell's Falls *see* **Nesenkeag**

Cusumpe *see* **Kusumpe**

*Dover *see* **Cocheco**

*Dover Point *see* **Winnichahannet**

Eel Brook *see* **Nesenkeag**

Ellacoya State Park (by Lake Shore Park, a town on Lake Winnipesaukee's southern shore): named after the daughter of Ahanton in the legend "Kona and Ellacoya." (Ahanton was Kona's enemy, and Kona was Ellacoya's Indian lover.)

Ellis River (in the Mt. Washington southern ridges): name of unknown origin (perhaps originally spelled Elise or Elis), said to have been associated with a legend about an Indian maiden.

Escumbuit (Ascumboit, Ascumbuit, Mescambioutt) **Island** (in Island Pond near Hampstead): named after a Pigwacket chief; "at the watching place."

*Exeter *see* **Squamscott**

Gaentake (Beaver Brook in Rockingham County by Londonderry): "red river."

Garvins Falls *see* **Penacook**

*Goffs Falls *see* **Cohasset**

*Gonic (Msquamanaguanagonek, Squamanagonec, Squamanagonic) **Hill** and **town**, and **West Gonic**: "at the narrow salmon spearing place"; "salmon spearing place." There was an old Indian trail called Squamanagonic, as well as an old

Indian village by that name at the falls on Cocheco River in Rochester.

*Great East Lake *see* **Newichewanimak**

*Hampton *see* **Winnecowett**

Hick's Hill *see* **Mahomet**

*Hollis *see* **Nissitisett**

*Hooksett** (Annahooksett, Chehockset, Hooksek, Onnahookset, Onnaockset, Wonnehockset) (a **town**), **South Hooksett**, and **Hooksett** or **Annahooksett Falls** (in Suncook): "the place of the beautiful forest hill"; "the place of the beautiful forest."

Hoosac Hill (near Kensington): "stone place"(?); or perhaps from the Natick word *nahoosic*, "a pinnacle."

*Indian Head *see* **Pemigewasset**

*Island Pond *see* **Winigegwok**

*Israel River *see* **Sigwooganock, Singrawac, Soucook**

Jebucto (in Strafford County): named after an Indian who lived in Chebeague in the latter part of the seventeenth century.

*Kanasatka** (Kanosasaki) **Lake** (near Center Harbor): "place of the willows."

*Kancamagus Brook, Highway, Mountain**, and **Pass** (in the White Mountains near Waterville Valley): named after a nephew of Wonalancet and grandson of Passaconaway, possibly meaning "plenty of small fish."

Kaskaashadi *see* **Merrimack**

K'chi Pontegok Falls (in Strafford County, near Somersworth) and **K'chi Ponteguh** (Kchipontegu) **Falls** (in Cheshire County, at Walpole, opposite Bellows Falls, VT): "at the great falls"; "place of the great river falls."

Kchitegu (Chateguay): Indian name for Conway, formerly an old Indian village. *See also* **Pequawket**.

Kearsarge Brook, Mt. (also called Mt. Cowissewaschook, located between Warner

and Wilmot Flat), **Mt. Kearsarge North** (sometimes called Mt. Pequawket, in the White Mountains between Conway and Jackson), **Mt. Kearsarge State Forest** (by Mt. Kearsarge), and **town**: "pointed or peaked mountain"; "sharp-pointed mountain place"; "high place"; "land that is harsh, rough, difficult"; "the proud, selfish." The preceding meanings are derived from Abenaki words. In Algonquian, the word *kearsarge* has been said to mean: "born of the hill that first shakes hand with the morning light." *See also* **Cowissewaschook, Pequawket.**

Kecheachy *see* **Cocheco**

*Keene *see* **Ashuelot**

Keewayden (town near Mirror Lake).

Kenduskeag Trail (by Gorham, near the summit of Mt. Moriah, and a part of the Appalachian Trail): "a pleasant walk."

Kineo Mountain (in the Moosilauke region, in the angle formed by the Pemigewasset and Baker rivers, above Stinson Lake): "a sharp peak." There is also a Mt. Kineo in Maine.

Kinicum (Kinnicum) **Pond** (in Candia township): if from Pennacook, it may mean "the long one"; if from Natick, "a mixture" (i.e., of various substances with tobacco).

Koategwa (Koategw) **River** (Pine River): "pine river."

Kodaak Wadjo (Mt. Washington): "the top is so hidden"; "summit of the highest mountain." Mt. Washington was also called **Agiochook**, or **Agiocochook**, meaning "the place of the Great Spirit"; "the place of the Concealed One." The demon who allegedly dwelt on its highest peak was called *Maji Neowaska* (Bad Spirit). The Algonquian Indians called the mountain **Waumbik**, or "white rocks." *See also* **Waumbek**.

*Kolelemook** (Kolelimook, Kowalamak) **Lake** (by West Springfield): "lake of the pine trees, shallow in places"; "shining pond."

Kuncanowet (Kuncenowet) **Hills** (in Dunbarton and Goffstown townships) and **Town Forest** (in Dunbarton and Weare townships): "bear-mountain place"; "near the long sharp places [ridge of hills]."

*****Kusumpe** (Cusumpe, Kussompskauk) **Pond** (near Center Sandwich): "chocked-up pond"; possibly also "large rocks."

*****Lamprey River** *see* **Piscassic**

*****Litchfield** *see* **Naticook**

*****Magalloway** (Magallo, Magallibuaki) **Mountain, Mountain Trail,** and **River** (in northern NH): "place of the caribou"; "the shoveler" (referring to the caribou's pawing of the ground with hooves in winter for food). The northeast branch of the Bellamy River was called **Magallo River** ("caribou river").

Mahomet (Maharimutt, Mahermit, Moharimet, Moharmet, Moharmot, Mohermitis) **Hill** (Hick's Hill in Madbury) and **Planting Ground** or **Plantation** (near the Lamprey River in Durham): named after a seventeenth-century Indian chief; said to mean "lavish, wonderful" and also "a soothsayer, he whom others distrust."

Mahoosuc Arm, Mountain, Notch, Range, and **Trail** (in the Mahoosuc Range area near Gorham): if from Abenaki, it means "abode of hungry animals"; if from Natick, "pinnacle, mountain peak."

Mallego Brook (by Barrington) and **Plains** (in Dover township): "deep, ravine-like."

*****Mascoma** (Maskamok) **Lake** (by the **town** of Mascoma), **River,** and **State Forest** (near Canaan Center): if from Abenaki, it means "salmon fishing," "much grass," or "red rocks"; if from Natick, perhaps "big plantation," "big beach," or "grassy swamp." The word has also been translated as "at the place of the great woods or trees" and "place of the bear." There was also an old Indian trail by that name.

Mashamee River (in Grafton County): perhaps "big fish" or "place between."

Masheshattuck Hill (in Hillsborough County): "big wooded mountain."

*****Massabesic** (Mass-sebisek) **Lake, Little Massabesic Lake** (in Manchester and Auburn township), and **town:** "at the great lake"; "the place of much water"; "lake that bends in the middle"; "near the great brook." There were also an old Indian trail and several Indian villages by that name in the Lake Massabesic area.

Massapaug Pond (by Kingston): "large pond." An old Indian village was located there.

*****Massasecum Lake** (near Bradford): "great narrow lake"; also said to be named after a Pennacook warrior, meaning perhaps "tall slender, erect." One variant is **Massaguigum:** "great duck lake."

Menunquatucke Brook (in Belknap County): "strong flowing stream."

*****Merrimack** (Malamake, Merramacke, Merrimaege, Moloumak, Monnomake, Monomack, Mouromak) **County, River, River State Forest** (near Boscawen), and **town:** "deep waters"; "place of swift water"; "place of strong current"; "the river of swift and broken waters." There was also an old Indian trail by that name, as well as an Indian trading post so named in the town of Merrimack. Cabassauk ("place of the sturgeon") and Kaskaashadi ("place of broken water") were early names of the Merrimack River, and Moniack ("place of the islands") was the name for its mouth.

Metallak (Metalak, Metallacks, Metallic, Mettallack) **Island** (on Lake Umbagog) and **Mount Metalak** (near Millsfield): named after the last Cowasuck chief, who died in 1847. His grave is located on North Hill in Stewartstown.

*****Minnewawa** (Miniwawa) **Brook** (near Malborough): "berries among the poplars"; "many waters."

*Mirror Lake *see* **Aroosabaug**

Misaden (Misadene) (the White Mountains in Coos and Grafton counties): "great high mountain"; "great mountains." There was also an old Indian trail by that name.

*Moat Mountain *see* **Atie ompsk a ooe di**

*Moat Mountain, West *see* **Attitash**

*Mohawk River** and its **West Branch** (in Coos County): named after the Mohawk, a tribe of Iroquois Indians who lived predominantly in the Mohawk Valley of New York and raided New Hampshire periodically. By their enemies they were called *Maquas* ("Man-Eaters," also translated as "cowards," "cannibals," "hungry animals," and "wolves").

*Mollidgewock** (Mollywooket, Molnichwock) **Brook** (below Umbagog Lake), **Mollockett Brook** (near Berlin), and **Molly Ocket** (in the Carter-Baldface ranges): "at the deep place"; named after Molly Ocket, a Pigwacket (Arrosaguntacook?) woman whose Christian name was Mary Agatha. Around 1774 Molly moved to the Bethel, Maine, area and went by the name of Mollyockett. She died in 1816. Bethel residents still celebrate an annual Mollyockett Day in her memory. In Maine, there is a Mollidgewock Pond (below Umbagog Lake) and Molly Lockett Cave near Fryeburg.

Molls Rock (near the outlet of Umbagog Lake): named after "Molly Molasses," the nickname given by Metallak (see above) to his second wife.

*Monadnock** (Monadenok, Monadnaeg, Monadoc) **Mountain, Reservation, State Park** (all in the Jaffrey and Dublin townships), **Park** (in Claremont), and **Little Monadnock Mountain** (near Troy). **Pack Monadnock Mountain** and **North Pack Monadnock Mountain** are located near Peterborough: "to the place of the bare high mountain"; "place of the

unexcelled mountain"; "at the silver mountain." The name has also been translated as "at the mountain which sticks up like an island" and "at the most prominent island" (a reference to the peaks surrounded by land worn down by erosion).

Moniack *see* **Merrimack**

*Monomonac** (Monomonock, Wonomenok, Wonomonock) **Lake** (near Rindge): "island place"; "at the very deep place"; "watch or lookout place."

Montinicus Island (off the shore of Rockingham County): "little island far off, separated from the mainland."

*Moosilauke** (Moosilaukee, Moswilaki) **Brook, Mountain** and its **South Peak** (all near North Woodstock), and **Pond** (in lower Campton township): "bald place"; "at the place of the ferns"; "very good moose place"; "good moose place along the brook"; "at the smooth place" (i.e., on the summit).

Mootinoo Island (off the Isles of Shoals): "far off island."

Moultonborough Neck *see* **Chenayok**

Moz Mushkeg (in Grafton County near Piermont): "moose meadow."

Munt Hill (near Hampton Falls): named after an Indian who lived near there; sometimes translated as "a basket."

Musabek (in Grafton County): "moose head rock."

Muscatanupus *see* **Potanipo**

Muscatuapus (in Merrimack County): "large pickerel."

Musquash Brook, Pond (both in lower Hudson township), and **Swamp** (in Londonderry): "reddish-brown animal"; "muskrat."

Namkecke River (in Rockingham County): "fishing place."

Nanamocomuck Peak (on Mt. Passaconaway): unofficial or local name of a subpeak in honor of Nanamocomuck, Passaconaway's eldest son.

Narmargungowack River (flowing from Success, a township, toward Paulsburgh, now Milan township, and into the Androscoggin River); probably Chickwolnepy Stream.

Narragansett: from the Algonquian, "on a small cape." This was the former name of the territory comprising Amherst, Goffstown, and Bedford, named so because it contained Narragansett Grant towns, i.e., towns given to soldiers from the Narragansett War (1675).

Nasbaug (Milton, N.H., in Strafford County): "three ponds."

*Nashua** (Nashaway, Nashuok, Niswaog, Niswaok) **River** (also called by the Indians **Watague** or **Wataqua**, which means "pickerel") and **town** (also called Watanic): "place of two [rivers]"; "river with the pebbly bottom"; "beautiful stream with a pebbly bottom"; "place where water runs over stones"; "river in the middle"; "place or land between"; "between the rivers." *See also* **Watanic**.

Natanis Brook (in Cheshire County): from Abenaki, meaning "little Nathan."

*Naticook** (Naacook, Natacook, Naticot, Natukko, Natticott) **Brook** and **Lake** (both in South Merrimack township): "cleared land"; "at the place where the river flows downward." This was the former name of Litchfield.

Nesenkeag Brook and **Little Nesenkeag Brook** (Eel Brook in Litchfield): "they come here two-by-two"; "point between two streams." The name **Nesenkeag Falls** was changed to Cromwell's Falls.

*New Boston *see* **Piscataquog**

*Newfound Lake *see* **Passaquaney**

Newichewanimak (Newichwanamak, Newichwanimak) **Lake** (Great East Lake near Wakefield): "place of extended rapids, at the fork."

Newichewannock (Nechawonack, Nechewannick, Newichwannock, Newijwanok, Nichiquiwanick) **River** (Salmon Falls River): "to many little falls in the long distance"; "where rapids extend a considerable distance, at the fork"; "at the fork or confluence of two rivers." There was also an old Indian trail by that name.

Nichmug River (in Grafton County): "fishing place at the fork."

Nikisipik (near Franklin): "fork in the stream."

Nipmuck: "freshwater place"; "freshwater fishing place." There was also an old Indian village by that name near Richmond.

Nippo Brook, Hill, and **Pond** (all near Barrington).

Nissitisett (Nisitisit, Nissitisitt, Nissitissett, Missitisset) **River** (between South Brookline and West Hollis): "two brooks"; "between brooks." This was also the former name of Hollis.

No-ottut (in Merrimack County): "far away place."

*Nubanusit Brook** (in Harrisville township near Eastview) and **Lake** (in Nelson and Hancock townships).

Nullie Kunjewa Brook (in Coos County): "fishing place downstream."

Ogontz Lake (near Lyman): supposedly named after an Indian chief.

*Oliverian Brook *see* **Umpammonoosuc Brook**

*Opechee Bay, Bay State Forest,** and **Park** (near Laconia): "robin."

Oquasskikonaquan (Quascacanaquen, Quascacunquen) (the local name for Lake Sunapee at Newbury): "region of the long trout"; "slender trout at the end of the field"; "the long ridge"; "the long bank"; "entirely full of water." There was an Indian village by that name in Newbury.

Ordanakis (Ordonakis) (former Indian village in Lyme): perhaps meaning "at the place of small dwellings."

*Osceola Brook and **West Branch, Mountain** and its **East Peak** and **West Peak**, and **Mt. Osceola Trail** (all in the White Mountains near Waterville Valley, just south of Kancamagus Highway): "black drink," a ceremonial potion. Osceola was the name of a leader of the Seminole Indians in the Florida Everglades.

*Ossipee (Awoss-sebi, Ossiopee) **Lake, Mountains, River, town, Valley, Lake Natural Area**, and towns called **Ossipee Lake Shores** and **West Ossipee**: "the river on the other side"; "beyond the water." One variant is Joss-sebi: "mountain river." There were also an old Indian trail, an old Indian village and fort (both near Ossipee Lake), and an Indian trading post (near Effingham Falls) with the same name.

*Ottarnic (Otternick) **Pond** (near Hudson): "at the dwellings."

Ottauquechee Falls *see* **Waterquechee**

*Oyster River *see* **Shankhasset**

*Pack Monadnock *see* **Monadnock**

Pakwakek *see* **Pequawket**

Pannaway Salt Marshes (near the tidal creeks in Rockingham County): "where [rising tide] water spreads out."

Pantook Reservoir (in Coos County): "falls in the river."

Pasakasock (in Rockingham County): "place of division or of branching."

*Passaconaway Cutoff, Mountain, town, and **Trail** (all in the White Mountains): named after the famous chief of the Pennacook, Papisseconewa, whose name means "child of the bear," "papoose bear," or "bear cub."

Passaquaney (Pasaguaney, Pasqueney, Passaguanik) **Lake** (Newfound Lake, near Hebron): "landing place at the sandbar

on the fork of the river." There was an old Indian village by that name near Bristol.

*Paugus Bay, Bay State Forest (both between Weirs Beach and Laconia), **Brook, Mountain, Pass**, and a town called **Paugus Mill** (all in Albany township): "small pond"; named after the Pigwacket chief who led the Abenaki forces at the battle of Lovewell's Pond during which a number of Indians and whites, including Lovewell and Paugus, were killed.

*Pawtuckaway (Pettukaway) **Lake, Mountains, River**, and **State Park**, and **Mt. Pawtuckaway** (all near Nottingham): "place on the hill"; or perhaps "falls in river" or "clear, open, shallow river." *See also* **Penecoog**.

Peboamauk Fall and **Loop** (near Gorham): "winter's home"; "wintry place."

Pekketegw *see* **Piscataqua**

*Pembroke *see* **Suncook**

*Pemigewasset (Pemachewasset, Pemishquawasset, Pemshiwasset, Penijossek) **Lake** (near New Hampton), **Mountain** (Indian Head) and **Trail** (both in western Lincoln township), **River** and its seven branches, **Wilderness** and **Wilderness Trail** (both in Franconia township): "swift current"; "rapids"; "bear's grease river." There was an old Indian trail by that name and an old Indian village with the same name near Plymouth.

Pemmoquittaquomut (Pemmemittequonitt) **Pond** (near Hudson): "the place at two ponds joined by a strait"; "at the place of two ponds joined by a straight stream or ditch."

*Penacook (Pannukog, Penagooge, Pennacook, Pennicook) **Lake** (above Concord) and **town**: "at the crooked place"; "the crooked river"; "at the falling bank"; "at the bottom of the hill or highland"; "downhill"; "at the foothills." There was an old Indian village as well as an Indian trading post by that name. The old

Indian Coos Trail was sometimes called the **Penacook Trail.** There was also a **First Path Penacook Trail,** which led through Auburn, crossing Griffin Brook (formerly called **Penacook River** and by other names) where the present-day Hooksett Rd. crosses it today. The Concord area was once called Penacook (changed to Rumford by the English colonists), and Garvins Falls (in Concord) were called **Lower Penacook Falls.**

Penecoog Ridge (the Pawtuckaway Range in Merrimack County): "foothills"; "sloping land."

*Pennichuck (Penechunek, Penikchiok, Pennachuck) **Brook** and **Pond** (both between Hollis and South Merrimack): "at the rapids"; "at the place of the great rapids."

Pentucket (Pentegek) **Trail:** "at the place of the river rapids." There was an old Indian trail by that name as well.

*Pequawket (Pegwacket, Pegwakik, Pequaket, Pequawkett, Pigwacket) **Brook, Pond, Upper Pequawket Pond** (all near Conway), **town,** and **Pakwakek** (near Pickpocket Falls by Exeter): "crooked place"; "broken land"; "clear valley lands bordering a crooked stream." Pequawket was an early name for Conway (*see also* **Kchitegu**); another Indian village called Pequawket was located at what is now Fryeburg, ME. Mt. Kearsarge North was formerly Mt. Pequawket and is still referred to by that name.

Pine River *see* **Koategwa

*Piscassic (Pascassick, Piscasset, Pisgaissek, Pisscassick) **Ice Pond** (near Newfields) and **River** (called Lamprey River by Epping): "to the place of the little dark river."

*Piscataqua (Piscataquack, Piscatua, Pisgategwa) **River** (in Portsmouth; also called Pekketegw, or "branched river") and **town:** "the river, it is dark"; "dark or gloomy river"; "place where there is a pool"; "divided river"; "place where the river divides." Piscataqua was the Indian name of Portsmouth; its former English name was Strabery Banke.

*Piscataquog (Pisgateguok) **Mountain** (near Lyndeborough), **River** and its **Middle Branch** and **South Branch, River Park** (all in Goffstown), **North Branch** of the river and **State Forest** (both near Weare): "at the place of the dark river"; "village beside the pool"; "where the river divides"; "at the river branch." There was also an old Indian trail and an Indian settlement by that name. This was also a former name of West Manchester, abbreviated to "Squog," and of New Boston.

Pisgah Brook, Mountain, Mountain Range, Reservoir, and **State Park** (all in the Chesterfield and Hinsdale townships), **Mt. Pisgah** and **Mt. Pisgah Brook** (in Auburn between Little Massabesic Lake and North Chester): if Abenaki, this means "dark"; if Mahican, "muddy."

Pisgatoek River (former Indian village in Somersworth): "at the place of the river branch."

Plausawa Hill (by North Pembroke): named after an Indian killed near there in 1753, meaning perhaps "wild pigeon" or "short yell." Plausawa was involved in the kidnapping of two black slaves from Canterbury.

Ponemah Bog and **town** (near East Milford): from Chippewa, meaning "the blessed hereafter" or "place of rest."

Pontook (Pontoocook) **Reservoir** (in Dummer township): "falls in the river." The falls are located on the Androscoggin River above Berlin.

Portsmouth *see* **Piscataqua

*Potanipo (Pontanopa, Tanipus) **Hill** and **Lake** (both near Brookline): "cold pond" One variant is **Muscatanupus:** "small red tortoise."

*Powwow (Pow Wow, Powaw, Powow) Pond, River, River State Forest, and town (near East Kingston): "Indian sorcerer or medicine man"; also "ceremony"; "gathering."

Putchaug Brook (in Cheshire County): "a turning place"; "division place."

Quamphegan Falls (in Strafford County near Somersworth): "dip net."

Quannippi (Alton Bay): "long water"; "long lake." There was an old Indian trail and an Indian village at Alton Bay with that name.

Quinibaak (Quinnibaug) Lake (in Cheshire County near Stoddard): "at the long pond."

Quoquinnapasskessanahnog (Quoquinna-keesapassananagnog, Quoquinnapasskee-sanahnog, Quoqunnapassackessanahhoy) Brook and meadows (in Amherst and Mt. Vernon): "at the place of the long falls in many hills and meadows"; "where the panther hunts for small birds"; "where the broad-tailed hawk hunts for small birds."

Rattlesnake Island see Sisikwa Menahan

*Rock Rimmon (in West Manchester's Rimmon Park) and Rock Rimmon Hill (near Sandown): named after Chocorua's youngest daughter said, in legend, to have leaped off Rock Rimmon to her death.

*Rust Pond see Winnebosekek

Sabbatus Heights (town near Loudon Center): an Abenaki rendition of St. Jean Baptiste. There were several Abenaki Indians so called; one named Sabbatis was involved in the kidnapping of two black slaves from Canterbury and was killed there in 1753.

Sachem Peak (near the Sandwich Range Wilderness, south of Waterville Valley) and Village (near Hanover): "chief"; named after the chiefs of Indian nations, who were also called sagamores.

*Saco (Sokook) Lake (in the White Mountains at the north end of Crawford Notch State Park), River and its East Branch and Rocky Branch: "at the southern place"; "flowing out"; "outlet."

Sagamore Creek and Hill (below Portsmouth): "chief"; named after the chiefs of Indian nations, who were also called sachems.

Sagumskuffe (probably a variation of Sagoniskusse) (in Coos County): "place of the small hard rocks"; "difficult passage because of rocks."

Sahegenet Falls Recreation Area (near Ashland).

*Salmon Falls River see Newichewannock, Seminenal

Scatuate (near Dover): "slack water"; "ebb tide."

Schohomogomoc Hill (in Strafford County near Rochester): "lake with fire markings near it."

Schoodac (Schodac) Brook (near Warner): "trout place."

Sebossenek (Sebasenek) Trail (near Greenfield): "to the place of the stony brook."

Seminenal River (Salmon Falls River): "pebbles"; "coarse gravel."

Senikok: a former Indian village near Gilmanton Ironworks.

Shankhasset (Shankhassick, Shawunkhassik) River (Oyster River): "winding [river], more or less sandy"; "river of the wild goose"; "at the hidden outlet of a stream."

Shoneeto (Beaver Lake by Derry): perhaps "big outlet" or "rocky place."

Sigwooganock (Siwooganock, Sonooga-wanock, Wniganok) River (Israel River): "to the south"; "to the southern portage."

Singrawac River (Israel River): "springtime place."

Sisikwa Menahan Island (on Lake Winnipesaukee in Belknap County): "rattlesnake island."

*Skatutakee Lake and Mountain (near Harrisville).

Skookumchuck (Skookum Chuck) **Trail** (from Franconia Notch to the north ridge of Mt. Lafayette in the White Mountains) and **Brook**: if from Abenaki, possibly means "snake brook or place"; if from the Chinook Indian dialect of the Pacific Northwest, it means "dashing water" or "rapids."

Sobagwa Trail: "Ocean"; a former Indian trail also called the **Chenayok Trail**.

Sokoki Trail (former Indian trail) and **Sokokis Brook** (near Mt. Washington Cog Railway).

*__Soucook__ (Sawcook, Sowcook) **River** (between Concord and Pembroke) and **River State Forest** (near Loudon): "rocky place." There was an old Indian village as well as an Indian trading post in **Sowcook**, near Litchfield. Soucook River was once also the name of the Israel River in Coos County.

*__Souhegan__ (Sowanigan, Suheganock) **River**: "jutting or difficult portage"; "the river of unstable banks"; "worn-out land"; "watching place"; "still-water fishing." Souhegan West was the former name of Amherst. Souhegan East was the former name of Bedford. There was also an old Indian trail by that name. **Sawhegan Falls** (former name) were located in Coos County.

Sowniganock (in Lancaster township in Coos County): "to the south-going [trail]."

Squakheag (former Indian village and a fort near Hinsdale): "watching place"; or possibly "black swamp-earth"; "forearm"; "quaking bogs"; "red rocks"; "tears."

*__Squam__ (Asquam, Msquamnebis) **Lake** and **Little Squam Lake** (both near Holderness) and **Mountain** (above Squam Lake): "salmon place"; "salmon lake." The **Squam Mountain Range** begins at Sandwich Notch and runs toward Holderness.

Squamanagonic *see* **Gonic**

*__Squamscott__ (Swamscot, Msquamskook, M'squamscook) **River** (in the Exeter area) and **Squamscot Bog** (near Weare): "at the salmon place"; "the abode of the salmon"; "place at the end of the rocks"; "red rocks." Squamscott, an old Indian village, was the former name of Exeter, and Exeter River was formerly called Squamscott River.

*__Squantum__ (town near Jaffrey): "angry god"; but if the correct spelling is **Squontam**, the translation is "door" or "gateway."

Squog *see* **Piscataquog**

*__Strawbery Bank__ (Strabery Banke) *see* **Piscataqua**

*__Sugar River__ *see* **Askutegnik**

*__Sunapee__ (Sennippi) **Harbor, Lake, Little Sunapee Lake, Mountain** and its **North Peak** and **South Peak, town, Bald Sunapee Peak**, a town called **Mt. Sunapee**, and **Mt. Sunapee State Park** (all located along the Sullivan and Merrimack counties border): "stony water"; "rocky pond." One variant is **Sennippi wobagilmak**: "stony waters of the wild goose." There was also an old Indian trail by that name. The local name for Lake Sunapee at Newbury was **Oquasskikonaquan**.

*__Suncook__ (Senkek, Senkook, Suncoog) **Lower** and **Upper Lake** (between Gilmanton Ironworks and Center Barnstead), **River** and **Little Suncook River**, and **town**: "stony [water] place"; "stone river"; "place of the goose." This was the old name of Pembroke. Both (different) towns now exist. There was also an old Indian trail by that name.

*__Swanzey__ *see* **Ashuelot**

Tanipus *see* **Potanipo**

*__Tecumseh Mountain__ and **Brook** (in the White Mountains near Waterville Valley): "I cross somebody's path"; named after a chief of the Shawnee Indians, also called Meteor and Crouching Panther.

Tekebisek (Ticopeesok) (old village near Cold River in Cheshire County): "at the place of the cold water spring."

Tioga Brook, Hill (both near Elmwood), and **River**: "at the river forks."

T'makwa Sibo (in Cheshire County): "beaver brook."

*****Umbagog** (Unbagoog, Wambighe, Wombagwog) **Lake** and **State Park**, and **Lake Umbagog National Wildlife Refuge** (all near Errol): "white clear lake"; "big lake"; "clear lake"; "clear water."

Umpammonoosuc Brook (Oliverian Brook in Grafton County): "at the bare [treeless] extended deep outlet."

*****Uncanoonuc** (Uncanoonucks, Uncanoonucs) **Lake** and **Mountains** (**North Peak** and **South Peak**) (in Goffstown): "maiden's breasts."

Wabademsolduwak Wajowuk (White Mountains): "the white mountains."

*****Wachipauka** (Wachipauke) **Pond** and **Trail** (both near Glencliff): "mountain pond."

Wakondah Pond (near Center Harbor).

Wamsutta Trail (near Mt. Washington in the Great Gulf Wilderness): named after the first of six successive husbands of Weetamoo, a queen of the Wampanoag tribe. Wamsutta was the brother of Metacomen, better known as King Philip. *See also* **Weetamoo**.

Wankewan Lake (in Belknap County): "on the crooked route."

Wanosha Mountain (near Woodstock, east of Mt. Tecumseh).

*****Wantastiquet** (Wantastquet, Wantestiquet) **Mountain** (by Chesterfield): "at the end of the river."

*****Washington, Mt.** *see* **Kodaak Wadjo**

Washucke (Washuck, Wajok) **River** (in Rockingham County near Newmarket): "place on the hill"; "at the hilly place." There was also an Indian village by that

name at Wadley's Falls on the Lamprey River in Lee.

Watague River *see* **Nashua**

Watanic (Watananock) (Nashua, where the Nashua River flows into the Merrimack): a corruption of Askwategnik; "at the end of the river fork"; "climbing place"; "end of the mountain." There was an old Indian village and an Indian trading post at Watanic. *See also* **Nashua**.

Watannanuck Hill (in Hillsborough County): "the place where we climb."

Waternomee Falls (by Warren) and **Mountain** (known formerly as Blue Mountain, in Woodstock township near Lost River): "a place to climb." There is a Blue Mountain in lower Columbia township and another one in Albany township; Mt. Blue lies just north of Mt. Moosilaukee.

Waterquechee (Ottauquechee) **Falls** (in Sullivan County): "swift mountain stream"; "cattails, rushes, near a swift current."

Wattanumon Brook (in Merrimack County): named after a Pennacook chief who died in 1712 on the Baker River.

Waukeena Lake (near Danbury).

*****Waukewan Lake** (near Meredith).

*****Waumbek** (Wombek) **Mountain** (near Jefferson) and **Junction** (near Whitefield): "to the white place"; "place of the white rock." Variants include **Waumbekket, Waumbekketmethna, Wawobadenik**: "snowy mountains"; "the white mountains"; "at the place of the white mountains." There was also an old Indian trail by that name. *See also* **Kodaak Wadjo**.

Wawbeek (town in Tuftonboro township near Melvin Village).

Weekasoak Brook (in Rockingham County): "place of small dwelling."

*****Weetamoo** (Weetamoe) **Mountain** (near Campton), **Rock, Trail**, and **Falls** (on Mt. Chocorua), and Six Husbands Trail and **Wetamoo Cascade** (along the Wamsutta Trail): named after a queen of the Wampanoag tribe of eastern Rhode Island and southern Massachusetts who had six husbands (some say at different times). Weetamoo is the heroine in John Greenleaf Whittier's poem "The Bridal of Pennacook." She drowned while fleeing a militia on August 6, 1676, six days before her famous brother-in-law, Metacomen (King Philip), was killed. They were both decapitated and their heads were impaled on poles for public display. *See also* **Wamsutta**.

*Weirs *see* **Ahquedaukenash**

West Manchester *see* **Piscataquog**

*White Mountains *see* **Misaden, Wabademsolduwak Wajowuk, Waumbek**

*Wickwas** (Wequash, Wickwas, Wicwas; also called Wigwam) **Lake** (near Meredith Center): "head of the bay"; "a swan"; named after a chief of the Pequot ("destroyers") who died at Saybrook, CT, in 1642.

Winigegwok (Winegegwok, Wnegigwak) (Island Pond near Stoddard): "place of the otter"; "abode of otters."

Winnebosekek (Winnebassakek) (Rust Pond, south of Wolfeboro): "at the place where the water flows out of the pond"; "portage at the outlet."

Winnecowett (Winnacowett, Winnacunet Winnecumek, Winnecumet, Winnecunnet, Winnicoek, Winnicumek, Winnicumet) (former name of Hampton): "beautiful place of the pines"; "place of pleasant pines."

*Winnepocket** (Winnepauket, Winnipocket, Winnibaakek) **Lake** (near Webster): "to the place where the water flows out of the pond"; "at the portage from the pond."

Winnichahannet (Wecohamet, Wecohannet, Winachahanat, Winnichahanat,

Winnikchihanek) (Dover Point): "at the place surrounded by the great waters flowing out"; "current flows around this place."

Winniconic (town near Stratham).

*Winnicut** (Winnecott, Winnicott) **Mills** (a town) and **River**: "at the place in the pines where the water flows in"; "where water flows out"; "at the portage"; "pleasant tidal river." An old Indian village called Winnicut stood where the river winds by Greenland.

Winninanebiskek (Alton Bay): "at the narrow place where the water flows out of the lake"; "the land around the lake." There was an old Indian trail by that name which began at the outlet of Lake Winnipesaukee.

*Winnipesaukee** (Winnebisaki, Winnepesaukee, Winnepiseogee, Wiwininebesaki) **Lake, River,** and **town**: "the lake in the vicinity of which there are other lakes and ponds"; "a lakes region"; "the beautiful water of the high place"; "the smile of the Great Spirit"; "the lake of smiling waters"; "land around the lakes"; "land at outlets around here." There was also an old Indian trail by that name.

*Winnisquam** (Minnesquam, Winnimsquam) **Lake** (near Laconia) and **town**: "around here there are salmon"; "salmon fishing at lake outlet"; "where the salmon waters flow out"; "salmon lake"; "beautiful water."

Winniweta Falls and **Trail** (in western Jackson township).

*Winona Lake** and **town**: if from the Chippewa, it means "firstborn daughter." It could also be an Abenaki term.

Wisconemuck Pond (in Hillsborough County): perhaps "place of walnut trees" or "pottery-making place."

Wniganok *see* **Sigwooganock**

Wobanadenek Trail: "to the place of the high white mountains."

*__Wonalancet Mountain, River__, and **town** (all in the White Mountains): named after a child of Passaconaway; translated as "breathing pleasantly" and also as "governor."

Wonomonock *see* **Monomonac**

Bibliography

Adams, Lincoln H. "A Brief History of the New Hampshire Indians." Manchester City Library, New Hampshire Room files, 1975.

_____. "A Cremation Burial Site on Rattlesnake Island, Lake Winnipesaukee, West Alton, New Hampshire." *New Hampshire Archeological Society, Miscellaneous Papers* 3 (1968): 7–10.

Agogino, George A. "The Paleo-Indian Chronology." *New Hampshire Archeologist* 13 (1964): 1–5.

"Archeological Survey of Litchfield, New Hampshire." Report on file at New Hampshire Division of Historical Resources, 1988.

Aubéry, Joseph. *Abnaki Dictionary.* Manuscript in the archives of Nicolet College, Quebec, and Maine Historical Library, Portland. Copied in 1891 by the Rev. Michael Charles O'Brien.

Bayly, Steven L. "Myth, History and Archeology in the White Mountains." *New Hampshire Archeologist* 37, no. 1 (1997): 59–69.

Belknap, Jeremy. *The History of New Hampshire.* 1st vol. 1784, 2d vol. 1791, 3d vol. 1792. Dover, NH: O. Crosby and J. Varney, 1812; New York: Sources of Science, 1970.

_____. *Belknap's New Hampshire: An Account of the State in 1792,* ed. G. T. Lord. Hampton, NH: Peter E. Randall, 1973.

Bennett, M. K. "The Food Economy of the New England Indians 1605–1675." *Journal of Political Economy* 63, no. 5 (1955): 369–97.

Bent, Allen H. *A Bibliography of the White Mountains.* Boston: Houghton Mifflin, 1911. Reprint edited by E. J. Hanrahan. Somersworth, NH: New Hampshire Publishing, 1971.

Bolian, Charles E. "Weirs Beach: A Preliminary Report of the 1976 Excavations." *New Hampshire Archeologist* 19 (1976–77): 47–55.

Bouras, Edward F., and Paul M. Bock. "Recent Paleoindian Discovery: The First People in the White Mountain Region of New Hampshire." *New Hampshire Archeologist* 37, no. 1 (1997): 48–58.

Bourque, B. "Aboriginal Settlements and Subsistence of the Maine Coast." *Man in the Northeast* 6 (1973): 3–20.

Bouton, Nathaniel. *The History of Concord from Its First Grant in 1725, to the Organization of the City Government in 1853, with a History of the Ancient Penacooks.* Concord, NH: B. W. Sanborn, 1856.

_____, ed. *Collections of the New Hampshire Historical Society Containing Province Records and Court Papers from 1680–1692: Notices of Provincial Councilors, and Other Articles Relative to the Early History of the State.* Vol. 8. Concord: McFarland and Jenks, 1866. See the articles by Edward Ballard: "Character of the Penacooks" (428–45), "Indian Modes of Applying Names" (446–50), and "Indian Names" (451–52).

_____, ed. *Provincial Papers of New Hampshire.* Vols. 1–3. Concord, N.H.: George E. Jenks, 1867.

Bowles, Ella Shannon. *New Hampshire: Its History, Settlement and Provincial Periods.* Concord: New Hampshire State Board of Education, 1938.

Boyd, Pliny Steele. *Up and Down the Merrimac: A Vacation Trip.* Boston: Lothrop, 1879.

Bradley, James W. *Origins and Ancestors: Investigating New England's Paleo-Indians.* Andover, MA: Robert S. Peabody Museum of Archaeology, 1998.

Bragdon, Kathleen J. *Native People of Southern New England, 1500–1650.* Norman: University of Oklahoma Press, 1996.

Briggs, L. Cabot. "Prehistoric Indian Skeletons from New Hampshire." *Man in the Northeast* 1 (1971): 51–53.

Brown, Percy S. "The Indian Fort at Lochmere,

N.H." *New Hampshire Archeologist* 3 (1952): 1–8.

_____. "Indian Names in New Hampshire." *New Hampshire Archeologist* 7 (1954): 11–21.

Bunker, Victoria. "The Eddy Site." Field notes on file at Phillips Exeter Academy, 1986.

_____. "New Hampshire's Prehistoric Settlement and Chronology." *New Hampshire Archeologist* 33–34, no. 1 (1994): 20–28.

_____. "The Place Between: Archeology at the Mine Falls Park Site, Nashua, New Hampshire." *New Hampshire Archeologist* 36, no. 1 (1996): 38–64.

_____. "Two Woodland Components in Litchfield, New Hampshire." *New Hampshire Archeologist* 29, no. 1 (1988): 1–47.

Burrage, Henry S. *Early English and French Voyages 1534–1608*. New York: Scribner's, 1906.

Burt, Frank H. "The Nomenclature of the White Mountains." *Appalachia* (December 1915): 359–90 and (June 1915): 261–68.

Burtt, J. Frederick. "Methods of Fishing Used by the Indians on the Merrimack River." *New Hampshire Archeologist* 2 (1951): 2–5.

_____. "Religion of the North American Indians." *New Hampshire Archeologist* 17 (1972): 15–21.

Calloway, Colin G. *Dawnland Encounters: Indians and Europeans in Northern New England*. Hanover, NH: University Press of New England, 1991.

_____. "Green Mountain Diaspora: Indian Population Movements in Vermont, c. 1600–1800." *Vermont History* 54, no. 4 (Fall 1986): 197–228.

_____. *Western Abenakis of Vermont, 1600–1800*. Norman: University of Oklahoma Press, 1990.

_____. "Wonalancet and Kancamagus: Indian Strategy and Leadership on the New Hampshire Frontier." *Historical New Hampshire* 43 (Winter 1988): 264–90.

Carlson, Catherine. "Report on the Faunal Remains from the 1967–1969 Excavations at the Smyth Site (NH38-4)." *New Hampshire Archeologist* 23 (1982): 91–102.

Carson, Janine A. "Indians of New Hampshire." *New Hampshire Archeologist* 6 (1956): 10–16.

Carter, George Calvin. *The Indian History of New Hampshire*. Manchester, NH: n.p., 1948.

_____. "Indian Names in New Hampshire." May 12, 1968. Manchester City Library, New Hampshire Room files.

_____. *Passaconaway: The Greatest of the New England Indians*. Manchester, NH: Granite State Press, 1947.

Ceci, L. "Maize Cultivation in Coastal New York: The Archaeological, Agronomical, and Documentary Evidence." *North American Archaeologist* 1, no. 1 (1979): 45–74.

Champlain, Samuel de. *The Voyages and Explorations of Samuel de Champlain (1604–1616)*. Trans. Annie Nettleton Bourne. Ed. Edward Gaylord Bourne. New York: Barnes, 1906.

_____. *Voyages of Samuel de Champlain, 1604–1618*. Ed. W. L. Grant. New York: Scribner's, 1907.

Cheswell, Wentworth. "Note on Indian Remains Found in New Market, N.H." Massachusetts Historical Society, Belknap Papers, 1790.

Coffin, F. Parkman. "Indian Names on the Piscataqua River, Great Bay, and Its Tributary Streams." *New Hampshire Archeologist* 11 (1962): 5–8.

Cogley, Richard. *John Eliot's Mission to the Indians Before King Philip's War*. Cambridge, MA: Harvard University Press, 1999.

Colby, Solon B. "Atkinson's Fort: 1746–47." *New Hampshire Archeologist* 4 (1950s?): 3–7.

_____. *Colby's Indian History: Antiquities of the New Hampshire Indians and Their Neighbors*. Center Conway, NH: Walkers Pond Press, 1975.

_____. "The Mystery Stone of Merideth." *New Hampshire Archeological Society, Miscellaneous Papers* 1 (1968): 15–17.

_____. "A New Hampshire Effigy Pipe." *New Hampshire Archeologist* 16 (1971): 19.

_____. "Samoset and Squanto." *New Hampshire Archeological Society, Miscellaneous Papers* 1 (1962): 15–17.

Cook, Sherburne F. *The Indian Population of New England in the Seventeenth Century*. Berkeley: University of California Publications in Anthropology, 1976.

_____. "The Significance of Disease in the Extinction of the New England Indians." *Human Biology* 45, no. 3 (1973): 485–508.

Coolidge, Austin J., and J. B. Mansfield. *History and Description of New England: New Hampshire*. Boston: Austin J. Coolidge, 1860.

Crosby, Alfred W., Jr. *The Columbian Exchange*. Westport, CT: Greenwood, 1972.

Curran, Mary Lou. "New Hampshire Paleo-Indian Research and the Whipple Site." *New Hampshire Archeologist* 33–34, no. 1 (1994): 29–52.

_____. "The Whipple Site and Paleo-Indian Tool Assemblage Variation: A Comparison of Intrasite Structuring." *Archaeology of Eastern North America* 12 (1984): 5–24.

Daniell, Gene, and Jon Burroughs, comps. and eds. *Appalachian Mountain Club White Mountain Guide.* 26th ed. Boston: Appalachian Mountain Club, 1998.

Day, Gordon M. "Henry Tufts as a Source on the Eighteenth Century Abenakis." *Ethnohistory* 21, no. 3 (Summer 1974): 189–97.

_____. "The Name Contoocook." *New Hampshire Archeological Society, Miscellaneous Papers* 1 (1962): 18–22.

_____. "The Problem of Openengos." *Studies in Linguistics* 23 (1973): 31–37.

_____. *Western Abenaki Dictionary.* 2 vols. Hull, Quebec: Canadian Museum of Civilization, 1994–95.

DeCorse, Chris R. "Analysis of Feature 6 at the Marshall Pottery Site." *New Hampshire Archeologist* 20 (1978–79): 31–48.

_____. "A Report on the Smith Farm Site: Brentwood, N.H." *New Hampshire Archeologist* 22, no. 1 (1981): 1–7.

Dethlefsen, Edwin S., L. Cabot Briggs, and Leo P. Biese. "The Clement Site: Analysis of Skeletal Material." *Man in the Northeast* 13 (1977): 86–90.

_____, and Nancy Demyttenaere. "The Clement Site: Features and Artifacts." *Man in the Northeast* 13 (1977): 90–96.

Dincauze, Dena Ferran. "An Archaic Sequence for Southern New England." *American Antiquity* 36, no. 2 (April 1971): 194–98.

_____. "The Late Archaic Period in Southern New England." *Arctic Anthropology* 12 (1975): 23–34.

_____. "The Neville Site: 8,000 Years at Amoskeag." *New Hampshire Archeologist* 18 (1975): 2–4.

_____. *The Neville Site: 8,000 Years at Amoskeag, Manchester, New Hampshire.* Cambridge, MA: Harvard University Peabody Museum Monographs, 1976.

Doan, Daniel, and Ruth Doan MacDougall. *50 More Hikes in New Hampshire: Day Hikes and Backpacking Trips from Mount Monadnock to Mount Magalloway.* 4th ed. Woodstock, VT: Backcountry Publications, 1998.

Dobyns, Henry F. *Native American Historical Demography.* Bloomington: Indiana University Press, 1976.

Dollar, Clyde D. "The High Plains Smallpox Epidemic of 1837–38." *Western Historical Quarterly* 8, no. 1 (1976): 15–38.

Douglas-Lithgow, Robert A. *Dictionary of American-Indian Place and Proper Names in New England, with Many Interpretations, etc.* Salem, MA: Salem Press, 1909.

Drake, Samuel G. *Biography and History of the Indians of North America, from Its First Discovery to the Present Time; Comprising Details in the Lives of All the Most Distinguished Chiefs and Counsellors, Exploits of Warriors, and the Celebrated Speeches of Their Orators; also a History of Their Wars, Massacres and Depredations, as well as the Wrongs ... which the Europeans and Their Descendants Have Done to Them; with an Account of Their Antiquities, Manners and Customs, Religion and Laws; likewise Exhibiting an Analysis of the Most Distinguished, as well as Absurd Authors, Who Have Written upon the Great Question of the First Peopling of America.* 11th ed. Boston: Benjamin B. Mussey, 1851; Ann Arbor, MI: UMI Books on Demand, 1993.

Duggan, Colleen B. "Dugout Canoes of New Hampshire." *New Hampshire Archeologist* 37, no. 1 (1997): 40–47.

Dupre, Mary Bentley. "Preliminary Report of First Fort, Boscawen, N.H. (NH31–34)." *New Hampshire Archeologist* 26, no. 1 (1985): 117–25.

_____. "Searching for New Hampshire Redware Potters." *Historical New Hampshire* 40, nos. 1–2 (1985): 47–60.

Eastman, David. "Archeological Dig." *New Hampshire Magazine* (October 1974): 1–4.

Eastman, Herbert W., comp. *Semi-Centennial of the City of Manchester, New Hampshire: September 6, 7, 8, 9, 1896.* Manchester, NH: John B. Clarke, 1897.

Eliot, John. *The Indian Grammar Begun.* Cambridge, MA: Marmaduke Johnson, 1666.

Ewing, Robert, and Charles Bolian. "Argillite Workshops in Tamworth, New Hampshire." *New Hampshire Archeologist* 32, no. 1 (1991): 87–95.

Farmer, John, and Jacob B. Moore. *Gazetteer of the State of New-Hampshire.* Concord, NH: Jacob B. Moore, 1823.

Feldman, Mark. *The Mystery Hill Story.* North Salem, NH: Mystery Hill Press, 1977.

Finch, Eugene D. "The Alexander Site: NH39-2." *New Hampshire Archeologist* 11 (1962): 1–5.

_____. "Cartagena Island." *New Hampshire Archeologist* 12 (1963): 1–5.

_____. "The Great Bay Site." *New Hampshire Archeologist* 15 (1969): 1–13.

_____. "The Litchfield Site: A Preliminary Report." *New Hampshire Archeologist* 16 (1971): 1–15.

_____. "The Stanley Site, NH47-18." *New Hampshire Archeologist* 14 (1967): 13–16.

Fletcher, Alice C. *Indian Games and Dances with Native Songs.* Boston: C. C. Birchard, 1915.

Foster, Donald W. "The Stanley Site Revisited." *New Hampshire Archeologist* 23 (1982): 37–63.

_____, Victoria B. Kenyon, and George P. Nicholas II. "Ancient Lifeways at the Smyth Site, NH 38-4." *New Hampshire Archeologist* 22, no. 2 (1981): 1–91.

Funk, Robert E. "Early Man in the Northeast and the Late–Glacial Environment." *Man in the Northeast* 4 (1972): 7–39.

Gahan, Laurence K. "Methods of Translating Indian Place Names." *Bulletin of the Massachusetts Archeological Society* 21, nos. 3–4 (1960): 46–47.

Gallup, Ronald W. *Algonquian New Hampshire and Its Pre-Historic Woodland People.* N.p.: n.p., 1980.

Garvin, James L. "'The Ceramic Evidence' and the Historian." *Historical New Hampshire* 40, nos. 1–2 (1985): 1–8.

Gengras, Justine B. "Radiocarbon Dates for Archeological Sites in New Hampshire." *New Hampshire Archeologist* 36, no. 1 (1996): 8–15.

_____, and Victoria Bunker. "Rescue Archeology at the Lodge Site, NH31-6-6." *New Hampshire Archeologist* 38, no. 1 (1998): 1–33.

Glidden, Charles H. "The Legend of Wonalansett." *New England Magazine* (August 1893): 797–804.

Goodby, Robert G. "Native American Ceramics from the Rock's Road Site, Seabrook, New Hampshire." *New Hampshire Archeologist* 35, no. 1 (1995): 46–60.

Gookin, Daniel. *Historical Collections of the Indians of New England, of Their Several Nations, Numbers, Customs, Manners, Religion, and Government, before the English Planted There.* 1792. N.p.: Towtaid, 1970.

Gordon, Myron, and Philip M. Marston. "Early Fishing Along the Merrimack." *New England Naturalist* 8 (September 1940): 1–10.

Gore, Effie K., and Eva A. Speare, comps. *New Hampshire Folk Tales.* Plymouth, NH: New Hampshire Federation of Women's Clubs, 1932.

Gorges, Sir Ferdinando. *Sir Ferdinando Gorges and His Province of Maine. Including the Brief Relation, the Brief Narration, His Defence, the Charter Granted to Him, His Will, and His Letters.* Boston: Prince Society, 1890.

Gramly, Richard Michael. "Prehistoric Industry at the Mt. Jasper Mine, Northern New Hampshire." *Man in the Northeast* 20 (1980): 1–23.

_____, and Stephen L. Cox. "A Prehistoric Quarry-Workshop at Mt. Jasper, Berlin, N.H." *Man in the Northeast* 11 (1976): 71–74.

_____, and Kerry W. F. Rutledge. "Molls Rock: A Multi-Component Site in Northern New Hampshire (with an Appendix on Faunal Remains by Dr. Arthur E. Spiess)." *Man in the Northeast* 24 (1982): 121–34.

Grumet, Robert S. *Historic Contact: Indian People and Colonists in Today's Northeastern United States in the Sixteenth through Eighteenth Centuries.* Norman: University of Oklahoma Press, 1995.

Hammond, Isaac W., ed. *State Papers, 1725–1800.* Vol. 18. Manchester, NH: John B. Clarke, 1890.

Harrington, Faith. "Archeological Testing at the Original Location of Fort No. 4, Charlestown, N.H. (NH34-4)." *New Hampshire Archeologist* 26, no. 1 (1985): 127–34.

_____. "The Broad Brook Site (NH41-17), Pisgah State Park, New Hampshire." *New Hampshire Archeologist* 25, no. 1 (1984): 12–30.

_____. "Sea Tenure in Seventeenth-Century New Hampshire: Native Americans and Englishmen in the Sphere of Coastal Resources." *Historical New Hampshire* 40, nos. 1–2 (1985): 18–33.

_____, and Victoria B. Kenyon. "New Hampshire Coastal Sites Survey, Summer 1986." *New Hampshire Archeologist* 28, no. 1 (1987): 52–62.

Hecker, Howard M. "Jasper Flakes and Jack's Reef Points at Adams Point: Speculations on Interregional Exchange in Late Middle Woodland Times in Coastal New Hampshire." *New Hampshire Archeologist* 35, no. 1 (1995): 61–83.

_____. "Preliminary Physical Anthropological Report on the 650-Year-Old Skeleton from Seabrook, New Hampshire." *Man in the Northeast* 21 (1981): 37–60.

Hencken, Hugh O'Neill. "The 'Irish Monastery' at North Salem, New Hampshire." *New England Quarterly* 12, no. 3 (1939): 429–42.

Hodge, Frederick W., ed. *Handbook of the American Indians North of Mexico.* Bureau of Ethnology, Bulletin 30. Washington, DC: Government Printing Office, vol. 1 1907; vol. 2 1910. New York: Rowman and Littlefield, 1975.

Holmes, Paul E. "The Harvey Mitchell Site (NH46-12), Newton Junction, N.H." *New Hampshire Archeologist* 23 (1982): 64–90.

_____. "The Noyse Rock Shelter: A Final

Report." *New Hampshire Archeologist* 17 (1972): 7–12.

Hoornbeek, Billee. *The Archaeological Survey of the Lakes Region of New Hampshire.* Durham: Archaeological Research Services, University of New Hampshire, 1979.

_____. "An Investigation into the Cause or Causes of the Epidemic which Decimated the Indian Population of New England, 1616–1619." *New Hampshire Archeologist* 19 (1976–77): 35–46.

Howe, Dennis E. "The Beaver Meadow Brook Site: Prehistory on the West Bank at Sewall's Falls, Concord, New Hampshire." *New Hampshire Archeologist* 29, no. 1 (1988): 49–107.

Hubbard, William. *The History of the Indian Wars in New England from the First Settlement to the Termination of the War with King Philip, in 1677, from the Original Work by the Rev. William Hubbard. Carefully Revised, and Accompanied with an Historical Preface, Life and Pedigree of the Author and Extensive Notes by Samuel G. Drake.* 1677. 2 vols. Bowie, MD: Heritage, 1990.

Huden, John C. *Indian Place Names of New England.* New York: Museum of the American Indian, Heye Foundation, 1962.

Hume, James D. "Geological Factors Important to Archeological Interpretations in the Merrimack Valley, N.H." *New Hampshire Archeologist* 28, no. 1 (1987): 1–17.

Hume, Patricia W. "The Maurice Yeaton Farm Site (NH38-60)." *New Hampshire Archeologist* 32, no. 1 (1991): 96–105.

_____, and Donald Foster. "A Guide to New Hampshire Sites and Collections." *New Hampshire Archeologist* 33–34, no. 1 (1994): 114–26.

_____, and Paul E. Holmes. "Two Sites on Little River: The Plaistow Dump Site (NH46-34) and the BROX/Falloway Site (NH46-35)." *New Hampshire Archeologist* 38, no. 1 (1998): 34–51.

Humphrey, Richard V., ed. *The Mystery Hill Source Book, 1907–1945: A Collection of All the Known Published Accounts of Mystery Hill at North Salem, N.H., between 1907 and 1945.* Salem, NH: Teaparty Books, 1979.

Hunt, Elmer Munson. *New Hampshire Town Names and Whence They Came.* Peterborough, NH: Noone House, 1970.

_____. "The Origin of Some New Hampshire Mountain Names." *Historical New Hampshire* (April 1955): 1–28.

Jennings, Francis. *The Invasion of America: Indians, Colonialism and the Cant of Conquest.* New York: Norton, 1976.

Johnson, Frederick. "The Indians of New Hampshire." *Appalachia* 6–7 (1940): 3–14.

Josselyn, John. *An Account of Two Voyages to New-England: Made during the Years 1638, 1663.* Boston: William Veazie, 1865.

Julyan, Robert, and Mary Julyan. *Place Names of the White Mountains.* Rev. ed. Hanover, NH: University Press of New England, 1993.

Kenyon, Victoria B. "Chert and Crystal Quartz during the Late Archaic." *New Hampshire Archeologist* 23 (1982): 131–35.

_____. "The Lund Collection: Nashua, New Hampshire." *New Hampshire Archeologist* 26, no. 1 (1985): 71–79.

_____. "Middle Woodland Ceramic Patterning in the Merrimack River Valley." *Archaeology of Eastern North America* 14 (1986): 19–34.

_____. "Middle Woodland Pottery of the Central Merrimack Valley in New Hampshire." *New Hampshire Archeologist* 23 (1982): 103–18.

_____. "Prehistoric Archaeology in the Merrimack Valley." *Man in the Northeast* 25 (1983): 1–5.

_____. "Prehistoric Pottery of the Garvins Falls Site." *New Hampshire Archeologist* 26, no. 1 (1985): 43–60.

_____. "Prehistoric Pottery at the Smyth Site." *New Hampshire Archeologist* 22, no. 1 (1981): 31–48.

_____. "The Prehistoric Pottery of the Smyth Site." *Ceramic Analysis in the Northeast.* Ed. James B. Petersen. In ser. *Occasional Publications in Northeastern Anthropology* 9 (1985): 89–107.

_____. "Prehistoric Site Location in the Merrimack Valley of New Hampshire." *New Hampshire Archeologist* 25, no. 1 (1984): 55–65.

_____. "The Smolt Site: Seasonal Occupation in the Merrimack Valley." *New Hampshire Archeologist* 24 (1983): 1–61.

_____, and Donald W. Foster. "The Smyth Site (NH38-4): Research in Progress." *New Hampshire Archeologist* 21 (1980): 44–54.

Kilbourne, Frederick W. *Chronicles of the White Mountains.* Boston: Houghton Mifflin, 1916.

King, Thomas Starr. *The White Hills: Their Legends, Landscapes, and Poetry.* Boston: I. N. Andrews, 1859.

Knight, Maureen, Robert A. Low, and Sally A. Low. *Sokoki: New Hampshire Indians Remembered in Pictures.* Vol. 1. N.p.: n.p., 1983.

Laurent, E. Margaret. "Indian Music and Dance." *New Hampshire Archeological Society, Miscellaneous Papers* 2 (1963): 7–11.

Laurent, Joseph. *New Familiar Abenakis and English Dialogues, the First Ever Published on the Grammatical System.* Quebec: Léger Brousseau, 1884.

Laurent, Stephen. "The Diet that Makes the Red Man." *New Hampshire Archeologist* 9 (1959): 6–9.

_____. "New Hampshire's First Language." *New Hampshire Archeologist* 10 (1960): 5–6.

Leary, Daniel J. "The Osgood Farm Site." *New England Antiquities Research Association Journal* 19, no. 3 (1985): 41–58.

Leland, Charles G. *Algonquin Legends of New Hampshire.* Boston: Houghton Mifflin, 1898.

Lottero, Patricia A. *New Hampshire Indians: A Guide for Instruction.* Plymouth, NH: Institute for New Hampshire Studies, Plymouth State College, 1983.

Lyford, James, ed. *History of Concord, New Hampshire.* Concord, NH: Rumford, 1903.

Marshall, Harlan A. "Description and Manner of Construction of Indian Relics Found in the Manchester, New Hampshire, Area." Manuscript, 1941. Manchester Historic Association files.

_____. "Description of Ancient Indian Village Sites Situated on Little Massabesic Brook, Auburn, New Hampshire." Manuscript, 1944. Manchester City Library, New Hampshire Room files.

_____. "Indian Stone Pots and Decorated Clay Pot Fragments Found in and Adjacent to Manchester, N.H." Manuscript, 1941. Manchester City Library, New Hampshire Room files.

_____. "John Eliot: Apostle, Friend and Adviser of the Indians of Central New England." Manuscript, n.d. (1940s?). Manchester Historic Association.

_____. "The Manners, Customs and Some Historical Facts about the Indians of Northern New England." Manuscript, n.d. (1940s?). Manchester Historic Association files and Manchester City Library, New Hampshire Room files.

_____. "Some Ancient Indian Village Sites Adjacent to Manchester, New Hampshire." *American Antiquity* 7, no. 4 (April 1942): 359–63.

Masta, Henry Lorne. *Abenaki Indian Legends, Grammar and Place-Names.* Victoriaville, Québec: La Voix des Bois Francs, 1932.

Mather, Cotton. *Diary of Cotton Mather, 1681–1724.* Boston: Collections of the Massachusetts Historical Society, 1911–12.

Maurault, Joseph Pierre Anselme. *Histoire des Abenakis depuis 1605 jusqu' a nos jours.* Sorel, Quebec: n.p., 1866.

Maymon, Jeffrey, and Charles Bolian. "The Wadleigh Falls Site: An Early and Middle Archaic Period Site in Southeastern New Hampshire." *Occasional Publications in Maine Archaeology* 9 (1992): 117–34.

McClintock, John N. *History of New Hampshire.* Boston: B. B. Russell, 1889.

McNeill, William H. *Plagues and Peoples.* New York: Anchor, 1976.

Merrill, Georgia Drew. *History of Carroll County.* 1889. Somersworth, NH: New Hampshire Publishing, 1917.

Moore, William E. *Contributions to the History of Derryfield, New Hampshire: Indians and Early Settlements.* Pt. 4. 1897. A paper read before the Manchester Historic Association. *Manchester Historic Association Collections.* 2, pt. 2, ch. 8 (1900–1901): 75–87.

Moorehead, Warren King. *The Merrimack Archaeological Survey.* Salem, MA: Peabody Museum, 1931.

Morton, Thomas. *New English Canaan; or New Canaan Containing an Abstract of New England. Composed in Three Bookes. The First Setting Forth the Originall of the Natives, Their Manners and Customes. Together With Their Tractable Nature and Love Towards the English. II. The Natural Indowments of the Countrie, and What Staple Commodities it Yeeldeth. III. What People are Planted There, Their Prosperity, What Remarkable Accidents Have Happened Since the First Planting of It; Together with Their Tenents and Practice of Their Church.* 1632. Washington, DC: P. Force, 1838. Reprinted as *New English Canaan: or, New Canaan.* New York: Arno, 1972.

[Mourt's Relation.] *The Journal of the Pilgrims at Plymouth, in New England in 1620: Reprint from the Original Volume. With Historical and Local Illustrations of Provinces, Principles, and Persons: By George B. Cheever, D. D.* New York: J. Wiley, 1848. Reprinted as *A Journal of the Pilgrims at Plymouth; Mourt's Relation, a Relation or Journal of the English Plantation Settled at Plymouth in New England, by Certain English Adventurers Both Merchants and Others. Edited From the Original Printing of 1622.* New York: Corinth, 1963.

Mudge, John T. B. *The White Mountains: Names, Places, and Legends.* Etna, NH: Durand, 1992.

New Hampshire Atlas and Gazetteer. Yarmouth, ME: DeLorme, 1999.

Nicholas, George Peter, II. "The Cohas Brook

Site (NH45-24), Manchester, New Hampshire: A Preliminary Report." *New Hampshire Archeologist* 20 (1978–79): 1–30.

———. "Late Pleistocene–Early Holocene Occupation of New Hampshire Glacial Lakes: Paleoindian Settlement, Subsistence, and Environment." *New Hampshire Archeologist* 21 (1980): 55–65.

———. "Meadow Pond (NH49-1): Changing Site-Landform Associations at a Multiple Component Site." *New Hampshire Archeologist* 25, no. 1 (1984): 31–54.

Ohl, Andrea. "The Dennis Farm Site: Late and Final Woodland Utilization of an Upland Location on the Connecticut River Drainage." *New Hampshire Archeologist* 32, no. 1 (1991): 26–72.

Penhallow, Samuel. *History of the Wars of New-England, with the Eastern Indians. Or, a Narrative of Their Continued Perfidy and Cruelty, From the 10th of August, 1703, to the Peace, 1713. and Renewed 13th of July, 1713. And from the 25th of July, 1722, to their Submission 15th December, 1725. Which Was Ratified August 5th 1726.* 1726. New York: Kraus Reprint, 1969.

Piotrowski, Thaddeus. *History of the American Indians in the Manchester, N.H., Area.* Manchester, NH: n.p., 1977.

Piper, Doris D. *Stories of Old New Hampshire.* Orford, NH: Equity, 1963.

Piper, Winthrop W. "Place-Names of New Hampshire: Physical Features from Origin to 1857." M.A. thesis, Columbia University, 1949.

Poor, Harry W. "Ossipee Ramblings along Old Indian Trails." *New Hampshire Archeological Society, Miscellaneous Papers* 1 (1962): 9–15.

Poore, B. P., and F. P. Eaton. *Sketches of the Life and Public Services of Frederick Smyth of New Hampshire.* Manchester, NH: John B. Clarke, 1885.

Pope, Laura. "Wadleigh Falls Island NH39-1: A Preliminary Site Report." *New Hampshire Archeologist* 22, no. 1 (1981): 8–15.

Potter, Chandler E. *The History of Manchester, Formerly Derryfield, in New Hampshire, Including That of Ancient Amoskeag, or the Middle Merrimack Valley; Together with the Address, Poem, and Other Proceedings, of the Centennial Celebration, of the Incorporation of Derryfield: At Manchester, October 22, 1851.* Manchester, NH: C. E. Potter, 1856. Reprinted as *History of Manchester, NH, Formerly Derryfield, in New Hampshire, Including That of Ancient Amoskeag, or the Middle Merri-*

mack Valley. Salem, MA: USA Higginson, 1995.

Potter, Jane S. "Early Contact Period Activity on a Great Thoroughfare: The Connor Site (27-CO-34)." *New Hampshire Archeologist* 38, no. 1 (1998): 52–66.

———. "New Hampshire's Landscape and Environment." *New Hampshire Archeologist* 33–34, no. 1 (1994): 9–19.

———. "Phase II Intensive Archeological Survey, Nashua Project." Report on file at the New Hampshire Division of Historical Resources.

———, and Patricia Hume. "The Jim Dodge Site (NH37-12)." *New Hampshire Archeologist* 28, no. 1 (1987): 63–70.

Price, Chester B. *Historic Indian Trails.* Rye Beach, NH: New Hampshire Archeological Society, 1989. As an article: "Historic Indian Trails of New Hampshire." *New Hampshire Archeologist* 8 (1958): 2–13, reprinted in 14 (1967): 1–12.

———. "Historic Indian Trails of New Hampshire." A map originally printed by the New Hampshire Archeological Society in 1967. Reprinted in 1974.

———. "Peace Monuments of the Indians." *New Hampshire Archeologist* 6 (1956): 9–10.

Pring, Martin. *A Voyage Set Out from the Citie of Bristoll with a Small Ship and a Barke for the Discoverie of the North Part of Virginia ... 1603.* New York: Scribner's, 1906.

Proctor, Mary A. *The Indians of the Winnipesaukee and Pemigewasset Valleys.* Franklin, NH: Towne and Robie, 1931.

Purchas, Samuel. *The Description of the Countrey of Mawooshen, discovered by the English in the Yeere 1602 ... and etc.* 1625. In *Hakluytus Posthumus, or Purchas His Pilgrimes.* Glasgow: J. MacLehose and Sons, 1905–7; London: Henry Fetherstone, 1625.

Putnam, Frederick W. "Description of a Carved Stone Representing a Cetacean, Found at Seabrook, N.H." *Essex Institute Bulletin* 5 (1873): 111–14.

Quinn, David B. *England and the Discovery of America.* New York: Knopf, 1974.

Rasles, Sébastian. *A Dictionary of the Abnaki Language in North America.* 1724. Cambridge: E. W. Metcalf, 1832. Ed. John Pickering, in ser. *American Academy of Arts and Sciences, Memoirs,* n.s., 1 (1832): 375–565.

Robinson, Brian S. *The Nelson Island and Seabrook Marsh Sites: Late Archaic, Marine-Oriented People on the Central New England*

Coast. In ser. *Occasional Publications in North-eastern Anthropology* 9 (1985).

_____. "Seabrook Tidal Marsh Site: A Preliminary Report." *New Hampshire Archeologist* 19 (1976–77): 1–7.

_____, and Charles Bolian. "A Preliminary Report on the Rocks Road Site (Seabrook Station): Late Archaic to Contact Period Occupation in Seabrook, New Hampshire." *New Hampshire Archeologist* 28, no. 1 (1987): 19–51.

Robinson, J. Dennis. "Digging Up New Hampshire's Past." *New Hampshire Profiles* (June 1975): 22–25.

Rothovius, Andrew E. "The New Thing at Mystery Hill Is 4,000 Years Old." *Yankee* 39, no. 9 (1975): 102–9, 162–64.

Russell, Howard. *Indian New England Before the Mayflower.* Hanover, NH: University Press of New England, 1980.

Salwen, B. "Post-Glacial Environments and Cultural Change in the Hudson River Basin." *Man in the Northeast* 10 (1975): 43–70.

Sanborn, Edwin D. *History of New Hampshire from Its First Discovery to the Year 1830.* Manchester, NH: John B. Clarke, 1875.

Sargent, Howard R. *Archeological Salvage at the Weirs, Laconia, New Hampshire.* New Hampshire Water Supply and Pollution Control Commission, 1980.

_____. "Artifacts from Plymouth, N.H." *New Hampshire Archeologist* 2 (1951): 5–7.

_____. "The Clement Site: Field Investigation." *Man in the Northeast* 13 (1977): 79–86.

_____. "Hearth from Kezar Lake, Sutton, N.H." *New Hampshire Archeologist* 2 (1951): 1–2.

_____. "The Pickpocket Falls Site." *New Hampshire Archeologist* 9 (1959): 2–6.

_____. "A Preliminary Archeological Reconnaissance in the Winnipesaukee River Basin: Part I." Copy on file at the New Hampshire State Historic Preservation Office.

_____. "Preservation History: The Archeological Record." *New Hampshire Archeologist* 18 (1975): 18–23.

_____. "Radiocarbon Dates and Their Bearing on New Hampshire Archeology." *New Hampshire Archeologist* 7 (1954): 1–10.

_____. "Report from New Hampshire." *Man in the Northeast* 3 (1972): 58–59.

_____. "Report on the Smyth Site." *Manchester Historic Association Bulletin* 3, no. 6 (1968): 1–5.

_____. "A Summary of the Archeology of New Hampshire." *Map of Indians of New Hampshire.* Detroit: Hearne, 1973.

_____. "Two Sites on Baker River." *New Hampshire Archeologist* 6 (1956): 6–9.

_____. "An Ulu from George's Mills, New Hampshire." *New Hampshire Archeologist* 1, no. 1 (1950): 7.

_____, and Francois G. Ledoux. "Two Fluted Points from New England." *Man in the Northeast* 5 (1973): 67–68.

Schoolcraft, Henry R. *Indian Tribes of the United States.* Philadelphia: Lippincott, 1860.

Sherman, Steve. "The First Settlement." *New Hampshire Profiles* 35, no. 8 (1986): 66–68, 70.

Silver, Linnea, and Walter T. Silver. "Cook's Cabin Site." *New Hampshire Profiles* 24, no. 12 (1975): 36–37.

Silver, Walter T. "The Indian 'Fort' at Lochmere." *Historical New Hampshire* 17 (1962): 49–60.

Simmons, William. *Spirit of New England Indians.* Hanover, NH: University Press of New England, 1986.

Simpson, Scott W. "Human Skeletal Remains from Concord, New Hampshire." *New Hampshire Archeologist* 25, no. 1 (1984): 66–73.

_____. "The Ossipee Cranium: A Preliminary Analysis." *Man in the Northeast* 24 (1982): 147–50.

Skinas, David C. "The Wadleigh Falls Site (NH39-1): A Preliminary Report of the 1980 Excavations." *New Hampshire Archeologist* 22, no. 1 (1981): 16–30.

Smith, Carlyle S. *The Archeology of Coastal New York.* New York: Anthropological Papers of the American Museum of Natural History, 1950.

Smith, John. *A Description of New England; or, The Observations and Discoveries of Captain John Smith (Admiral of That Country) In the North of America, in the Year of Our Lord 1614; With the Success of Sixe Ships, That Went the Next Year, 1615; and the Accidents Befell Him Among the French Men of Warre: With the Proofe of the Present Benefit This Countrey Affoords; Whither This Present Yeare, 1616, Eight Voluntary Ships are Gone to Make Further Tryall.* 1616. Washington, DC: P. Force, 1837; Rochester, NY: G. P. Humphrey, 1898.

_____. *General History of Virginia, New England and the Summer Isles. Sixthe Booke: The General Historie of New England.* 1624. Boston: Massachusetts Historical Society, 1833.

Snow, Dean R. *The Archaeology of New England.* New York: Academic Press, 1980.

Speare, Eva A. *Indians of New Hampshire.* Littleton, NH: Courier, 1965.

Speck, Frank. *Penobscot Man: The Life of a Forest Tribe in Maine.* New York: Octagon Books, 1940; Philadelphia: University of Pennsylvania Press, 1976.

Spiess, Arthur E., Mary Lou Curran, and John R. Grimes. "Caribou (*Rangifer Tarandus L.*) Bones from New England Paleoindian Sites." *North American Archaeologist* 6, no. 2 (1984–85): 145–59.

Squires, James Duane. *The Story of New Hampshire.* Princeton, NJ: Van Nostrand, 1964.

Starbuck, David R. "A Bibliography of New Hampshire Archeology." *New Hampshire Archeologist* 28, no. 1 (1987): 77–94.

_____. "Excavations at Sewall's Falls (NH31-30) in Concord, N.H." *New Hampshire Archeologist* 23 (1982): 1–36.

_____. "Further Excavations at Sewall's Falls (NH31-30)." *New Hampshire Archeologist* 25, no. 1 (1984): 1–11.

_____. "The Garvins Falls Site (NH37-1): The 1982 Excavations." *New Hampshire Archeologist* 26, no. 1 (1985): 19–42.

_____. "Historical Archeology in New Hampshire." *New Hampshire Archeologist* 33–34, no. 1 (1994): 81–96.

_____. *A Middle Archaic Site: Belmont, New Hampshire.* New Hampshire Department of Public Works and Highways, 1982.

_____. "Post-Glacial Environments and Culture Change in the Hudson River Basin." *Man in the Northeast* 13 (1977): 96–99.

_____. "Survey and Excavation along the Upper Merrimack River in New Hampshire." *Man in the Northeast* 25 (1983): 25–41.

_____. "Three Seasons of Site Survey and Excavation at Sewall's Falls (NH31-30)." *New Hampshire Archeologist* 26, no. 1 (1985): 87–102.

_____, and Charles Bolian, eds. *Early and Middle Archaic Cultures in the Northeast.* In ser. *Occasional Publications in Northeastern Anthropology* 7 (1980).

_____, and Mary Bentley Dupre. "The Hazeltine Pottery Site, Concord, N.H. (NH37-8)." *New Hampshire Archeologist* 26, no. 1 (1985): 135–45.

Stark, William. *Centennial Poem ... Read at the One Hundredth Anniversary of Manchester, N.H., Oct. 22, 1851.* Manchester, NH: Office of Notes and Queries, 1906.

Stewart-Smith, David. "The Indians of the Merrimack Valley: An Introduction." *Bulletin of the Massachusetts Archaelogical Society* 60, no. 2 (Fall 1999): 57–63.

_____. "The New England Settlers and the New England Indians." Baccalaureate study, Vermont College of Norwich University, April 1990.

_____. "The Pennacook Indians and the New England Frontier, circa 1604–1733." Ph.D. diss., Union Institute, Cincinnati, OH. Ann Arbor, MI: UMI Dissertation Services, 1999. Author no. 9908552.

_____. "The Pennacook: Lands and Relations, an Ethnography." *New Hampshire Archeologist* 33–34, no. 1 (1994): 66–80.

Stone, Robert E. "Megalithic Mystery Hill." *Northeast Historical Archaeology* 1, no. 1 (1971): 22–23.

_____. "A New England Megalithic Culture." *New Hampshire Archeological Society, Miscellaneous Papers* 3 (1968): 1–5.

_____. "Preliminary Survey: North Salem Rock Shelter." *New Hampshire Archeological Society, Miscellaneous Papers* 1 (1962): 22–34.

_____. "They're Solving the Riddle of Mystery Hill." *New Hampshire Profiles* 20, no. 5 (1971): 22–27.

_____, and Osborn Stone. "Further Progress: Excavation of a Strange Well at Mystery Hill, N. Salem, N.H." *New Hampshire Archeologist* 12 (1963): 6–8.

Strauss, Alan E. "Argillite Blade Cache Found near Sewall's Falls (NH31-30)." *New Hampshire Archeologist* 26, no. 1 (1985): 81–86.

Swanton, John R. *The Indian Tribes of North America.* Smithsonian Institution. Bureau of American Ethnology. Bulletin 145. Washington, DC: Government Printing Office, 1953.

Switzer, David C. "Archeology under New Hampshire Waters: The Present and the Future." *Historical New Hampshire* 40, nos. 1–2 (1985): 34–46.

Sylvester, Herbert M. *Indian Wars of New England.* 3 vols. Boston: Clarke, 1910.

Tapley, D. J. "A Remarkable Indian Relic." *American Naturalist* 6 (1872): 696–701.

Thomas, Peter A. *In the Maelstrom of Change: The Indian River Trade and Cultural Process in the Middle Connecticut River Valley, 1635–1665.* New York: Garland, 1990.

_____. "Squakheag Ethnohistory: A Preliminary Study of Culture Conflict on the Seventeenth-Century Frontier." *Man in the Northeast* 5 (1973): 27–36.

Thornton, Russell. *American Indian Holocaust and Survival: American Indian Population since*

1942. Norman: University of Oklahoma Press, 1987.

Trigger, Bruce, vol. ed., William G. Sturtevant, gen. ed. *Handbook of the North American Indians*. Vol. 15: *Northeast*. Washington, DC: Smithsonian Institution, 1978.

Wallace, Cyrus Washington. "Amoskeag in Early Pioneer Days." *Manchester Historic Association Collections* 4 (1908–10): 159–67.

Wardwell, J. B. "Description of an Indian Relic." *Essex Institute Bulletin* 6 (1874): 145–46.

Watson, Harry L. "Indians and Indian Relics of the Merrimack Valley." Talk given at the Manchester Institute on April 8, 1927. Manchester Historic Association files.

White, William, and Eugene D. Finch. "Further Surface Finds at NH40-1." *New Hampshire Archeologist* 18 (1975): 9–17.

_____. "Surface Finds at NH40-1." *New Hampshire Archeologist* 9 (1959): 9–12.

Wickham, Shawne K. "Give Us Passaconaway's Bones, New Hampshire Indians Ask of France." *New Hampshire Sunday News* (October 17, 1993).

Wilbur, C. Keith. *The New England Indians*. Old Saybrook, CT: Globe Pequot Press, 1996.

Wilcomb, Edgar Harlan. *Ancient Acquadoctan, the Weirs: Stories of a Century of Indian Warfare in New Hampshire: Lake Winnipesaukee Reminders of the Early Days*. Worcester, MA: 1923.

Willey, George Franklyn. *Willey's Semi-Centennial Book of Manchester, 1846–1896, and Manchester ed. of the Book of Nutfield. Historic Sketches of That Part of New Hampshire Comprised Within the Limits of the Old Tyng Township, Nutfield, Harrytown, Derryfield, and Manchester, From the Earliest Settlements to the Present Time*. Manchester, NH: George F. Willey, 1896.

Williams, H. U. "The Epidemic of the Indians in New England 1616–20, with Remarks on Native American Infections." *Johns Hopkins Hospital Bulletin* (November 1909): 340–49.

Willoughby, Charles C. *Antiquities of the New England Indians*. Cambridge, MA: Peabody Museum, Harvard University, 1935.

Winship, George Parker. *Sailors' Narratives of Voyages Along the New England Coast, 1524–1624*. Boston: Houghton Mifflin, 1905.

Winter, Eugene. "The Garvins Falls Site (NH37-1): The 1963–1970 Excavations." *New Hampshire Archeologist* 26, no. 1 (1985): 1–18.

_____. "The Smyth Site at Amoskeag Falls: A Preliminary Report." *New Hampshire Archeologist* 18 (1975): 5–8.

Winthrop, John. *Journal of the Transactions and Occurences in the Settlement of Massachusetts and the Other New England Colonies*. Reprinted as *Winthrop's Journal: "History of New England" 1630–1649*. Ed. James Kendall Hosmer. New York: Scribner's, 1908; New York: Barnes and Noble, 1959.

Wood, William. *New England's Prospect*. 1634. Ed. Alden Vaughan. Amherst: University of Massachusetts Press, 1993.

Young, Alexander, ed. *Chronicles of the First Planters of the Colony of Massachusetts Bay, from 1623 to 1636*. Boston: Charles C. Little and James Brown, 1846.

Index